The Heart Sūtra Explained: Indian and Tibetan Commentaries

SUNY Series in Buddhist Studies

Kenneth Inada, Editor

The Heart Sūtra Explained: Indian and Tibetan Commentaries

Donald S. Lopez, Jr.

State University of New York Press

Published by
State University of New York Press, Albany

Printed in the United States of America

For information, address State University of New York
Press, State University Plaza, Albany, N.Y., 12246

Library of Congress Cataloging in Publication Data

Lopez, Jr., Donald S., 1952-
The Heart Sutra explained.

(SUNY series in Buddhist studies)
Bibliography: p. 215
Includes index.
1. Tripiṭaka. Sūtrapiṭaka. Prajñāpāramitā. Hṛdaya
—Criticism, interpretation, etc. I. Title. II. Series.
BQ1967.L67 1987 294.3'85 87-6479
ISBN 0-88706-589-9
ISBN 9-88706-590-2 (pbk.)

10 9 8 7 6 5 4 3 2 1

Contents

To J.M.S.

Acknowledgements

Among the various causes and conditions that conjoined to allow me to undertake and complete this study, there are several that deserve special mention. In January 1982, Yeshe Thupten, a distinguished Tibetan monk and scholar, came to Middlebury College where he taught a Winter Term course on the *Heart Sūtra*. In preparation for translating for him, I made a preliminary translation of the first of the Tibetan commentaries that appears in this study, that of bsTan-dar-lha-ram-pa. Yeshe Thupten also provided me with a detailed oral commentary on this text during his stay in Vermont. In 1983, I received a summer stipend from the National Endowment for the Humanities to begin this study. During the tenure of the award, I translated four Tibetan commentaries on the *Heart Sūtra*, two of which are included here. I received a research leave from Middlebury College for the spring semester of 1986, during which I made a study of the extant Indian commentaries and completed the first draft of the manuscript.

I wish to express my thanks to the National Endowment for the Humanities and to Middlebury College for providing me with the time and financial assistance to complete this study. In addition to Yeshe Thupten, I would like to express my gratitude to Jeffrey Hopkins of the University of Virginia for his aid in unravelling some of the more intractable Tibetan passages and to David Eckel of Harvard University for many useful queries and suggestions on the Indian commentaries. Geshe Thupten Gyatso of the Tibetan Buddhist Learning Center in Washington, New Jersey provided insightful comments on the tantric commentary on the *Heart Sūtra* translated in Chapter 7. Thanks are also due to Richard Martin, proprietor of the Tibetan collection of the Alderman Library at the University of Virginia, for supplying xerographic versions of the sūtras and *śāstras* to the frozen hinterlands of Vermont.

Introduction

The *Heart Sūtra* is perhaps the most famous Buddhist scripture.[1] Its cryptic delineation of the meaning of emptiness and its radical economy of expression have exercised a fascination over the minds of Buddhist thinkers in India, China, Japan, Korea, Tibet, and Central Asia. Over seventy manuscripts of the sūtra were unearthed at Tun-huang. The *Heart Sūtra* has evoked commentaries from many of the pivotal figures in the history of Buddhist thought, including Kamalaśīla, Atīśa, Fa-tsang, K'uei-chi, Kūkai, and Hakuin Zenji.

The *Heart Sūtra* exists in two versions, the more extensive adding a prologue and epilogue to the briefer form. But even in its extensive version, the *Heart Sūtra* is the shortest of the major Buddhist sūtras, and this brevity accounts in part for its great popularity. The players are few and formidable: Śākyamuni Buddha, Avalokiteśvara, and Śāriputra, with Prajñāpāramitā, the mother of the Buddhas, silently present. As with so many sūtras, the structure is one of question and answer, but here only one question is asked, "How does one practice the perfection of wisdom?" Avalokiteśvara's answer, given first in one sentence and then expanded, contains references to all the major categories of Buddhist philosophy, proclaiming that they do not exist. Ingrained in his answer are the two most famous lines of this most famous of sūtras. The first is the potent and problematic declaration, "Form is emptiness; emptiness is form." The other is the mantra that culminates Avalokiteśvara's instruction, *"gate gate pāragate pārasaṃgate bodhi svāhā".* These two lines are considered at length in the chapters that follow.

The meaning of the *Heart Sūtra* has always seemed elusive to its readers, as is evident from widely divergent doctrines discovered in it by commentators. Speaking of some of the Chinese and Japanese commentaries, Edward Conze observed that "they tell us more what the text meant to them within their own culture than what the Indian original intended to convey."[2] It was Conze's view that this original meaning could be discovered in the seven Indian commentaries that remain extant in Tibetan translation (or at least six of them; he disapproved of Vimalamitra's commentary).[3] It has been noted, however, that, "A text always has several epochs and reading must resign itself to that fact,"[4] so that the endeavor to determine "what the Indian original intended to convey" must always remain futile. Nevertheless, it is the Indian commentaries on the *Heart Sūtra* that concern us here.

One purpose of this study is to attempt to discern how the *Heart Sūtra* was variously understood during the Pāla Dynasty, which ruled Bengal from c. 750-1155 and Bihar from c. 750 until the Muslim invasions of 1199. It was during this period that Buddhist thought in India effectively came to an end. All of the seven extant Indian commentaries appear to have been composed during this period, the earliest probably being that of Kamalaśīla (c. 740-795) and the latest that of Mahājana (11th cent.). If Conze's dating of the *Heart Sūtra* at 350 C.E. is accepted, then these commentaries were written some five centuries after the sūtra. During these centuries the major Mahāyāna *śāstras* appeared that shaped the character of late Indian Buddhist thought: the works of Asaṅga and Vasubandhu, of Dignāga and Dharmakīrti, of Maitreyanātha, of Bhāvaviveka and Candrakīrti. This half-millennium also saw the rise of tantric Buddhism. The Indian commentators were writing in an epoch quite different from that of the author of the sūtra. Nonetheless, it was a time in which the *Prajñāpāramitā* sūtras continued to enjoy great popularity, as attested by the account of the reign of Pāla King Dharmapāla by the Tibetan historian Tāranātha:

> Upon ascending the throne, the king invited the teachers of the Prajñāpāramitā. . . . The king built some fifty centers for the doctrine, of which thirty-five were centers for the study of the Prajñāpāramitā. . . . From the time of this king, the Prajñāpāramitā was propagated widely.[5]

The authors of the commentaries were scholars who knew the Mahāyāna sūtras and śāstras and, therefore, were well-versed in Mādhyamika and Yogācāra philosophy, in the Hīnayāna and Mahāyāna *abhidharma*, in the delineations of meditative praxis that appear in works like the *Śrāvakabhūmi*, in the *tathāgatagarbha* doctrines, in the elaborate delineations of the Hīnayāna and Mahāyāna paths as set forth in the *Abhisamayālaṃkāra* and its commentaries, and in tantric thought. These are the contexts they bring to their understanding of the *Heart Sūtra* and which they project onto it.

The Place of the Heart Sūtra in the Prajñāpāramitā Literature

Edward Conze distinguished four periods in the development of the Prajñāpāramitā literature: (1) the elaboration of the basic text (ca. 100 B.C. to 100 C.E.), (2) the expansion of the text (ca. 100 C.E. to 300 C.E.), (3) the restatement of the doctrine in short sūtras and verse summaries (ca. 300-500), and (4) the period of tantric influence.[6] Conze placed the composition of the *Heart Sūtra* in the third period, at about 350 C.E., although others would date it two centuries earlier.[7] The "basic text" to which Conze refers is the *Perfection of Wisdom in 8000 Lines* (*Aṣṭasāhasrikāprajñāpāramitāsūtra*), the oldest portions of which are generally considered to be among the earliest wisdom scriptures of the various movements in Indian Buddhism that came to be known as the Mahāyāna.[8] One view is that from this prototype there grew, through a process of interpolation, duplication, and iteration, the longer versions of the Prajñāpāramitā, such as those in 18,000, 25,000, and 100,000 lines. This was followed by a period of contraction and distillation, of which the *Heart Sūtra* and the *Diamond Sūtra* are the best examples, although it is in the *Prajñāpāramitā sarvatathāgatamātā ekākṣarā* (*The Perfection of Wisdom in One Letter, the Mother of All Tathāgatas*, that letter being *a*) that the process of contraction seems to have reached its logical conclusion.

Traditional accounts of the rise of the Mahāyāna do not, of course, follow this chronology. All the Prajñāpāramitā sūtras were considered the word of the Buddha (*buddhavacana*), either being actually spoken by Śākyamuni or the speaker being directly empowered by him (as is the case with the *Heart Sūtra*). Thus, the prologues of the sūtras report that the Prajñāpāramitā sūtras were set forth by the Buddha on Vulture Peak in what the gods in the *8000* declared to be the second turning of the wheel of the doctrine,[9] reinterpreting and superseding that delivered at the deer park in Sarnath. (The teaching of the second wheel was later held to be provisional by the Yogācārically inclined authors of the seventh chapter of the *Saṃdhinirmocanasūtra*, in which the third turning of the wheel is described.)[10] According to the Tibetan historian Bu-ston, the Prajñāpāramitā sūtras in 100,000, 25,000, 18,000, 10,000, and 8,000 lines were all spoken simultaneously by the Buddha.[11]

The authors of the Prajñāpāramitā sūtras were sensitive to the charges made by the various Hīnayāna schools that these new sūtras were fabrications because no reference was made to them in the early councils in which the teachings of the Buddha were compiled. In response, it was claimed that the new sūtras had been taught by the Buddha to a select group of disciples, their content being, at that time, inappropriate to a general audience. The sūtras were then placed into the hands of various deities and *nāgas* for safekeeping until the world was ready for their teaching. To prove that this was the Buddha's intention, prophecies were written into the new sūtras, such as that in the *Laṅkāvatāra*, where the Buddha proclaimed that four centuries after his passage into nirvāṇa, a monk named Nāgārjuna would reestablish the Mahāyāna.[12] And indeed, according to the traditional biographies of Nāgārjuna, he went to the land of nāgas from whence he retrieved the *100,000*.

The Structure of the Sūtra

The *Heart Sūtra* exists in two basic versions, a shorter and a longer, with the shorter beginning with Avalokiteśvara contemplating the meaning of the profound perfection of wisdom and ending with the mantra and the longer adding a prologue, in which the Buddha enters into *samādhi*, and an epilogue, in which he rises from the samādhi and praises Avalokiteśvara. In that it is a distillation of the Prajñāpāramitā, there is little new in the *Heart Sūtra*; Conze has traced much of the shorter version to the sūtras in 8,000, 25,000, and 100,000 lines,[13] including the famous declaration that, "Form is emptiness; emptiness is form"; the negations, "in emptiness, there is no form, no feeling . . . no non-attainment"; and the epithets of the mantra.

The *Heart Sūtra*, however, cannot be considered simply as a pastiche. Its significance derives from the manner in which its components are woven together, as well as from what it retains, what it adds, and what it deletes from the formulae of the longer sūtras. These elements are most easily identified by briefly surveying the progression of the text (the longer version), a process repeated in far greater detail in the chapters that follow.

The prologue of the sūtra has two parts, a prologue common to other Prajñāpāramitā sūtras and a prologue unique to the *Heart Sūtra*. The former begins with the standard formula, "Thus did I hear at one time," and goes on to identify the site of the sūtra, Vulture Peak, and the audience, a great assembly of monks and of Bodhisattvas. The mention of Bodhisattvas in the audience provides some evidence of the lateness of the sūtra in relation to the longer texts, such as the *8000*, where the audience is composed of 1,250 monks, with no reference to

Bodhisattvas. It is in the unique prologue that the leading characters of the sūtra are introduced: Śākyamuni Buddha, Avalokiteśvara, and Śāriputra. The Buddha does not speak in the prologue, but enters into the samādhi called "perception of the profound." The Buddha says nothing until the epilogue, but rather silently empowers Śāriputra to ask and Avalokiteśvara to answer, illustrating a view of the Buddha characteristic of much of the Mahāyāna, a view classically portrayed in the *Lotus Sūtra:* the Buddha is no longer simply the teacher but is transformed into the principle of enlightenment, a silent, eternal, numinous presence, the *dharmakāya.*

Even in the earlier Prajñāpāramitā sūtras, much of the exposition is done not by the Buddha, but by the Elder Subhuti. But Subhuti is absent here, replaced by Avalokiteśvara, the Bodhisattva of compassion. The *Heart Sūtra* is the only major Prajñāpāramitā text in which Avalokiteśvara appears.[14] His presence is another indication of the relatively late date of the sūtra, suggesting that the sūtra was written at a time when the cult of the Bodhisattva of compassion, textually associated with the twenty-fourth chapter of the *Lotus Sūtra* and with the Pure Land sūtras, had become well-established. That Avalokiteśvara expounds the Perfection of Wisdom, rather than Subhuti, suggests also that by the time of the sūtra, the fissures between the movements calling themselves the Mahāyāna and more conservative elements had developed to the point that it was no longer deemed appropriate that the new wisdom be proclaimed by a *śrāvaka*, a Hīnayāna disciple of the Buddha, but could be spoken only from the mouth of a celestial Bodhisattva.

The presence of Avalokiteśvara is also significant for thematic reasons. The *Heart Sūtra* is renowned as the essence of the longer sūtras; one of the commentators remarks that there is not a single doctrine that occurs in the *100,000* that is not contained in this short sūtra. Yet there is no reference whatsoever to the other major theme of the Prajñāpāramitā, the compassion and skillful methods of the Bodhisattva. Atīśa, at the outset of his commentary on the *Heart Sūtra*, categorizes the Prajñāpāramitā sūtras into two types, those that teach the essence of the doctrine and those that teach the realizations (*abhisamaya*) whereby Bodhisattvas proceed to enlightenment. The *Heart Sūtra* teaches the first and the longer sūtras expound the second.[15] The *Heart Sūtra* does not set forth the path; it says that there is no path. This apparent omission is mitigated by the simple presence of Avalokiteśvara in the text: the wisdom essential for the achievement of Buddhahood is proclaimed by a Bodhisattva who has traversed the long path, a Bodhisattva who is said to be the embodiment of compassion.

A common element of the longer sūtras absent from the *Heart Sūtra* is the polemic against the Hīnayāna disciples of the Buddha, inferior to the Bodhisattvas both in their wisdom and in their aspiration to enlightenment. This condescension is implied by the presence of Śāriputra, renowned in the Hīnayāna schools as the wisest of the Buddha's disciples, but who here is uninformed and perplexed, asking Avalokiteśvara how to practice the perfection of wisdom. This is a role that he plays in many of the Prajñāpāramitā sūtras as well as in the *Lotus* and the *Vimalakīrti.*

The body of the sūtra between the prologue and the epilogue is made of two parts: Avalokiteśvara's short answer to Śāriputra's query and his long answer, the latter of which comprises the "form is emptiness" statement, the series of negations, and the mantra. "Form is emptiness; emptiness is form. Emptiness is not other than form; form is not other than emptiness," is at once the most celebrated and problematic passage in the text. Here, in a statement startling in economy, the sūtra addresses the perennial problem of the relation of appearance and reality, the ultimate and the conventional. In the section of negations, Avalokiteśvara goes through the major categories of Buddhist philosophy—the five aggregates, the chain of dependent origin, the four truths—and seems to deny the existence of them all.

Before the rather stock epilogue, in which the Buddha rises from meditation to praise Avalokiteśvara's teaching, there occurs the mantra, further evidence of the relative lateness of the sūtra's composition. With the possible exception of *oṃ maṇi padme hūṃ*, this is the most famous and oft-recited of Buddhist mantras, a mantra that occurs not in a tantric text, but in a sūtra. Further, this is not a mantra composed of "unintelligible syllables"; it seems to say, "Gone, gone, gone beyond, gone completely beyond, enlightenment." The commentators treatment of the mantra is particularly interesting; for some it summarizes the entire sūtra, setting forth the entire path to Buddhahood in five words.

The Indian Commentators

The longest commentary on the sūtra is that of Vimalamitra; it fills some thirty-three folio sides in the Peking edition of the Tibetan *tripiṭaka.* According to traditional biographies, Vimalamitra was born in western India, probably in the eighth century, and studied at

Bodhgāyā. He was a disciple of the tantric master Buddhaguhya. He is also said to have studied *atiyoga* under the *mahāsiddha* Śrīsiṃha in China. He was invited to bSam-yas monastery in Tibet during the reign of King Khri-srong-lde-btsan, where he lectured on the sūtras and tantras and aided in the translation of texts from Sanskrit to Tibetan, wearing the garb of a tantric *yogin* rather than monastic robes. He is said to have remained in Tibet for thirteen years before returning to China. He was the pivotal figure in the establishment of the Great Completion (*rDzogs-chen*) lineage in Tibet. According to the indices of the Peking edition of the Tibetan tripiṭaka, Vimalamitra is credited with the authorship of over twenty works, nineteen of which are tantric commentaries. In addition to his *Heart Sūtra* commentary, he wrote a brief text on refuge and two important texts on meditation, one dealing with sudden non-conceptual meditation (the *Sakṛtprāveśika-nirvikalpabhāvanārtha*)[16] and the other dealing with the gradual approach (the *Kramaprāveśikabhāvanārtha*). He was also involved in the translation of many texts, most notably the *Heart Sūtra*.[17]

The *Heart Sūtra* commentary is the only sūtra commentary credited to Vimalamitra. It is the longest and the most erudite of the seven, displaying an extensive knowledge of Buddhist literature, as well as considerable acquaintance with a wide range of philosophical positions and categories. It is replete with quotations from sūtras such as the *Lalitavistara*, the *Daśabhūmika*, the *Saṃdhinirmocana*, and the *Samādhirāja*; tantras such as the *Vairocanābhisambodhi;* and śāstras such as Nāgārjuna's *Ratnāvalī*, Maitreyanātha's *Abhisamayālaṃkāra*, and Dharmakīrti's *Pramāṇavārttika*. It is methodical in style, dealing with each word of the sūtra in turn, but with numerous excursuses into related topics, often accompanied by lists.[18] Although the work of one of the most influential Indian tantric yogins to visit Tibet, the author appears careful to provide what he considered an orthodox interpretation of the sūtra, with few references to the Vajrayāna, except when discussing the mantra. The commentary has something of the tone of a lecture in which Vimalamitra used the *Heart Sūtra* as an occasion to expound on a wide range of topics for an audience perhaps not as well-versed in Buddhist thought as he. This impression is confirmed by the colophon, which states that Vimalamitra explained the *Heart Sūtra* to an audience of monks at the temple of Tshangs-pa'i-'byung-gnas. The commentary was thus composed in Tibet and was translated by Vimalamitra himself with the aid of Tibetan scholars.

The second commentary is that of Jñānamitra, about whom nothing is known. There is only one other work of his extant in the canon, a commentary on the *Prajñāpāramitānayaśatapañcāśatkā*. Because he is not mentioned in the traditional histories nor named as the translator of any work, it is unlikely that he went to Tibet. His work is of moderate length compared to the others, filling fourteen folio sides. His work is precisely structured, dividing the sūtra under seven headings and dealing with each in sequence. His commentary is clear and straightforward, at times pedestrian. He points out, for example, that the title is provided at the beginning of the sūtra because, otherwise, one would not know which sūtra it was. In his discussion of the "form is emptiness" line, he evinces an affinity for the Yogācāra.

Considerably more idiosyncratic is the commentary of Vajrapāṇi, who flourished in the eleventh century. According to the *Blue Annals*, he was a disciple of Maitripa and a master of the tantric practice of *mahāmudrā*. Although he seems to have spent most of his life in Nepal, he travelled to Tibet, where he taught *mahāmudrā* and bestowed numerous initiations. The *Blue Annals* reports in some detail seven miracles he is said to have performed.[19] He is credited with the composition of seven works and was involved in the translation of some twenty-nine more. His *Heart Sūtra* commentary, which is twenty-one folio sides in length, is his only non-tantric work listed in the canon.[20] Nonetheless, it has a distinctively tantric flavor. His commentary is the least methodical of the seven, passing over some major sections, such as the "form is emptiness" line rather cursorily while pausing to give long commentaries on a single phrase, such as the statement that Bodhisattvas have passed beyond all error. His discussion of the mantra is the most extensive of the seven. Although certainly scholarly, his work has the texture of that of a meditation master, describing the *Heart Sūtra* in terms of his own practice and experience. He speaks repeatedly of the glories of the experience of being without mindfulness (*tran pa med pa*) and contrasts the perspectives of those who have and have not encountered the primordial mind (*sems dngas ma*). The colophon reports the circumstances of its composition. Some Tibetan translators had come to visit Vajrapāṇi in Lalitapura (Patan) in Nepal and requested that he teach them the *dharma*. On the day that he was to begin, the Tibetans recited a sūtra. Vajrapāṇi asked them which sūtra it was and they identified it as the *Heart Sūtra*, causing Vajrapāṇi to declare that the Buddha's prophecy that the *Heart Sūtra* would go to Tibet had come true. He then asked the Tibetans whether they had received instructions on the meaning of the sūtra and, learning that they had not, provided his commentary.[21]

Praśāstrasena's commentary, also of moderate length (twenty-two folio sides) was the commentary that Conze described as "a straightforward, admirable and exemplary attempt actually to illuminate the text."[22] Nothing is known about the author. This is the only work of his extant. It is similar to that of Jñānamitra, clear and straightforward, although somewhat more informative on a number of points. It is the work of a distinguished savant, displaying, primarily through allusion rather than direct reference, a sophisticated knowledge of Buddhist literature and philosophy, with a special acquaintance with the *Akṣayamatinirdeśa*, which he cites repeatedly. The author displays considerable knowledge of both Mādhyamika and Yogācāra and does not hesitate to mix the two in the interpretation of a single passage, providing evidence of the eclectic nature at least of his own thought, and perhaps that of Pāla Buddhism. Because of its clarity and completeness, it is the first that one would read; perhaps that is why Conze translated part of it.

The briefest commentary was composed by the most famous of the seven authors, the *paṇḍita* Kamalaśīla (c. 740-795), a leading thinker of the Yogācāra-Svātantrika branch of Mādhyamika. The foremost student of Śāntarakṣita, his most important philosophical works include the *Madhyamakāloka* and his commentary on his teacher's *Tattvasaṃgraha.* His most influential writings were his three texts, each entitled *Bhāvanākrama*, which he is said to have composed at the request of King Khri-srong-lde-btsan after having come to Tibet to debate the Northern Ch'an Ho-shang Mo-ho-yen in what has come to be known as the Council of Lhasa.[23] His commentary on the *Heart Sūtra*, only five folio sides in length, is concerned primarily with aligning the content of the sūtra with the five paths of the Bodhisattva, and makes no attempt to deal fully with the subject matter of the sūtra.

Whereas Kamalaśīla's work is probably the earliest of the seven texts, that of Atīśa (c. 982-1054) is among the latest. The great Bengali scholar went to Tibet in 1042, where he collaborated with Tibetan translators such as Rin-chen-bzang-po in the translation of many of the major Mādhyamika treatises. Because of his translation work and his own writing and teaching, Atīśa is the key figure in the latter propagation (*phyi dar*) of the Buddhist dharma in the snowy land of Tibet. His most famous work is his *Bodhipathapradīpa* with its autocommentary,[24] which became the model for the Tibetan *lam rim* genre. Like that work, Atiśa's *Heart Sūtra* commentary was composed in Tibet. The second shortest of the seven (ten folio sides in length), it is actually a subcommentary on Vimalamitra's work. He does not go through the sūtra word by word, but rather clarifies and expands upon certain points made by Vimalamitra, such as the relationship between the eight profundities and the three doors of liberation. In addition, Atiśa, like Kamalaśīla, is concerned with demonstrating the correspondence between the sections of the sūtra and the five paths, with Atīśa providing more detail.

The final and probably latest commentary is that of Mahājana, about whom very little is known. This is his only work extant; he is listed as translator of nine works, indicating that he visited Tibet, probably in the eleventh century.[25] His commentary is nineteen folio sides in length and is similar to the works of Jñānamitra and Praśāstrasena in its deliberate progress through the sūtra. It is distinguished from the others by the strong influence of Yogācāra, which is evident from the start when Mahājana quotes a long prophecy about Asaṅga from the *Mañjuśrīmūlatantra.* He also interprets the "form is emptiness" line in terms of the Yogācāra doctrine of the three natures (*trisvabhāva*). The other distinguishing feature of Mahājana's commentary is his attempt to explain the sūtra in terms of many of the categories of the path developed in the Hīnayāna and Mahāyāna *abhidharma* and in the *Abhisamayālaṃkāra.*

There are, then, commentators both celebrated and unknown, tantric *siddhas*, and scholastic exegetes. The wide variety of commentators demonstrates the importance of the *Heart Sūtra* for the period. Those authors for whom only one or two texts are extant wrote on the *Heart Sūtra*; those pivotal thinkers of the age, such as Vimalamitra, Kamalaśīla, and Atīśa, who wrote so many other works, wrote also on the *Heart Sūtra*; those tantric masters whose corpus is almost exclusively devoted to the Vajrayāna wrote also on the *Heart Sūtra.*

Hence the *Heart Sūtra* was important to these Pāla Dynasty scholars. The reasons for its importance are less evident. In attempting to discern the concerns that contributed to the importance of the text for these thinkers, two factors, one of absence, the other of presence, may be germane. First, the dearth of extant commentaries on the sūtra during the five centuries following its composition is striking, as is the strong link between the authors of the seven extant commentaries and Tibet: five of the seven went to Tibet and at least three of the commentaries seem to have been written there.

The absence of Indian commentaries from an earlier period could simply be ascribed to the loss of the śāstras to the familiar elements of monsoon water and Muslim fire; it could be speculated that many early *Heart Sūtra* commentaries are simply no longer in existence. There are, however, no references to the *Heart Sūtra* in the standard Indian compendia of Mahāyāna sūtras, Nāgārjuna's *Sūtrasamuccaya* and Śāntideva's *Śikṣāsamuccaya;* nor is it cited by Candrakīrti in the *Prasannapadā* or the *Madhyamakāvatārabhāṣya.* Hsuan-tsang

(602-664) translated the text from Sanskrit into Chinese and reported in the records of his journey to the west a legend about Bhāvaviveka (c. 500-570?), that the Svātantrika master recited the *Heart Sūtra dhāraṇī* (*hsin-to-lo-ni*) for three years in order to meet with Avalokiteśvara.[26] Thus, there appears little evidence for the circulation of the *Heart Sūtra* as an independent text in India prior to the sixth century.

How, then, is the sudden interest in the text by the Pāla commentators accounted for? Here, their connection with Tibet should be considered. For Indian paṇḍitas in Tibet, the *Heart Sūtra* provided a perfect vehicle for the exposition of Buddhist doctrine. It was short and could be easily memorized by their students; it contained references to the basic categories of Buddhist doctrine and hence had mnemonic value; it was ambiguous enough for them to interpret in accordance with their own particular doctrinal dispositions; and it contained a mantra, appealing to the Tibetans' attraction to the Vajrayāna. It is possible that even at the time of Vimalamitra and Atīśa, the *Heart Sūtra* was current in Tibet, translated from the Chinese rather than the Sanskrit.

This is not to suggest that all seven of the Indian commentators had the same interest in the text. Vimalamitra apparently used the text as lecture notes for an audience of Tibetan monks and nobles, introducing them to a wide spectrum of Buddhist theory and praxis. Vajrapāṇi used the sūtra to convey the experience of the non-dual reality to a group of Tibetan translators. The motivations of Kamalaśīla, Atīśa, and Mahājana were, perhaps, more programmatic. All three used the *Heart Sūtra*, so potent in its apophasis, to delineate the structure of the path, using the heart of *prajñā* to expound *upāya*. The gradual path to enlightenment was, of course, championed in the eighth century by Kamalaśīla in his *Bhāvanākrama* versus the Ch'an position of Ho-shang-mo-ho-yen. In the second propagation of the doctrine during the eleventh century, Atīśa and Mahājana, through their emphases on the methodical and progressive practice of the path in their *Heart Sūtra* commentaries, may have been seeking to counter the then current antinomian character of Tibetan tantric Buddhism.[27]

But what of the commentators who seem not to have journeyed to Tibet, Praśāstrasena and Jñānamitra? No historical information about them is available from which to concoct a motivation for commenting on the *Heart Sūtra*. To them may be ascribed only the wish to expound the meaning of the perfection of wisdom as it was understood by them during the final synthesis of Buddhist thought in India. Again, the shape, depth, and density of the sūtra made it a perfect, seemingly bottomless vessel into which the myriad streams of Buddhist thought in Pāla India could be poured and preserved.

The Tibetan Commentators

To discern how the sūtra was understood a millenium after the Pāla commentators by scholars of one of the schools of Tibetan Buddhism, the *dGe-lugs-pa*, two Tibetan commentaries have been translated here, presumably the kind of texts to which Conze alluded when he spoke in his memoirs of Tibetan commentaries on the *Heart Sūtra* as "a vast untended field waiting for younger scholars to cultivate it."[28] They are considered briefly here.

Both commentaries are works of dGe-lugs-pa polymaths who flourished in the late eighteenth and early nineteenth centuries. The first commentary is by the Mongolian monk bsTan-dar-lha-ram-pa (pronounced "Den-dar-hla-ram-ba") of A-lags-sha, a disciple of kLong-grol-bla-ma.[29] He was born in 1758 and the last work for which a date is known was written in 1839, indicating that he lived over eighty years. His collected writings contain works on a wide range of topics. He wrote commentaries on Dignāga's *Ālambanaparīkṣā*, Dharmakīrti's *Saṃtānāntarasiddhi*, and works on logic, grammar, monastic discipline, and mind training (*blo sbyong*), as well as a Tibetan-Mongolian dictionary.

His *Heart Sūtra* commentary, subtitled, "Jewel Light Illuminating the Meaning," begins with a discussion of the assertions of the four major Buddhist philosophical schools concerning the ontological status of the Buddha's words. He then considers where and when the Perfection of Wisdom sūtras were taught, and follows with a brief history of the sūtras in India and Tibet. He then comments on the sūtra sentence by sentence, drawing primarily on Vimalamitra, Praśāstrasena, and Mahājana, usually without attribution. Displaying a typically dGe-lugs interest in logic and reasoning, he discusses how to prove that the self does not exist and takes up the technical problem of whether something that does not exist, such as the self, can serve as the subject of a syllogism, a question that he considers in greater detail in his work on the reasoning of the one and the many (*gCig du brel gyi rnam bzhag*). His commentary provides a useful composite of the Indian commentaries filtered through the light of Tsong-kha-pa's thought.

The other Tibetan commentary included here is that of dKon-mchog-bstan-pa'i-sgron-me, the incarnate lama of Gung-thang, the name by which he is better known.[30] Gung-thang (1762-1823), from the Amdo region of Tibet, was the disciple of the second 'Jam-dbyangs-bzhad-pa, dKon-mchog-'jigs-med-dbang-po. Among his best-known works are a study of the four truths, commentaries on Tsong-kha-pa's work on the *ālayavijñāna* and his *Legs bshad snying po*, and a brief text on the three doors of liberation.

According to the colophon, his commentary on the *Heart Sūtra* mantra, subtitled, "Illuminating the Hidden Meaning," was dictated to a student in the noon breaks during a meditation retreat in the winter of 1816. It is the work of a brilliant scholar setting forth the central topics of the Mahāyāna path within the context of the words of the mantra. In the work, he quotes from most of the important Indian Mahāyāna śāstras, producing a work that is synthetic yet creative, technically sophisticated yet evocative. He injects meaning into the mantra in a manner that rarely seems forced. In the course of the work, Gung-thang follows Vimalamitra and Atīśa most closely, adding constructively especially to Atīśa in providing a rationale for his division of the sūtra according to the five paths and explaining what Atīśa might have meant when he said that the entire sūtra can be included in the words of the mantra. Gung-thang also provides a penetrating analysis of the implications of the presence of a mantra in a sūtra.

A complete study of the Indian commentaries would include an annotated translation of all seven. This will be the subject of a separate volume. In the chapters that follow, the *Heart Sūtra* is considered line by line through selections from the exegeses of the Pāla Dynasty paṇḍitas. In choosing among the seven commentators on a particular passage or term, I have attempted to provide a digest of representative readings, deciding what is representative based on a comparison of the seven. When all are in general agreement on meaning of a particular point, I have chosen the commentary that is the most clear and concise. When a single commentator has pursued a point that the others pass over, I have noted his reading. When the commentators differ on the meaning of a key passage, I have provided each of their views. As a result, this digest is bound by the structure of the sūtra, with the consequence that the commentators' occasional digressions from that structure have been left for a future study. To provide the reader with some of the philosophical context which the Pāla writers often take for granted, I have provided discussions of certain categories and doctrines, relying as much as possible on texts that could have been available to them.

It is hoped that readers of this study will gain some sense of the richness and fluidity of Buddhist philosophy in northeastern India during the Pāla period, where Yogācāra, Mādhyamika, *tathāgathagarbha*, and tantra appear to have been mixed and synthesized into a fertile soil that yielded the final fruit of Buddhist thought in India.

Part I

Indian Commentaries

Chapter 1

The Sūtra

The Sūtra on the Heart of the Transcendent and Victorious Perfection of Wisdom[1]

Thus did I hear at one time. The Transcendent Victor was sitting on Vulture Mountain in Rājagṛha together with a great assembly of monks and a great assembly of Bodhisattvas. At that time the Transcendent Victor was absorbed in a samādhi on the enumerations of phenomena called "perception of the profound." Also at that time, the Bodhisattva, the Mahāsattva, the Superior Avalokiteśvara was contemplating the meaning of the profound perfection of wisdom and he saw that those five aggregates also are empty of inherent existence. Then, by the power of the Buddha, the venerable Śāriputra said this to the Bodhisattva, the Mahāsattva, the Superior Avalokiteśvara, "How should a son of good lineage train who wishes to practice the profound perfection of wisdom?"

The Bodhisattva, the Mahāsattva, the Superior Avalokiteśvara said this to the venerable Śāriputra: "Śāriputra, a son of good lineage or a daughter of good lineage who wishes to practice the profound perfection of wisdom should view [things] in this way: They should correctly view those five aggregates also as empty of inherent existence. Form is emptiness; emptiness is form. Emptiness is not other than form; form is not other than emptiness. In the same way, feeling, discrimination, compositional factors, and consciousnesses are empty. Śāriputra, in that way, all phenomena are empty, that is, without characteristic, unproduced, unceased, stainless, not stainless, undiminished, unfilled. Therefore, Śāriputra, in emptiness, there is no form, no feeling, no discrimination, no compositional factors, no consciousness, no eye, no ear, no nose, no tongue, no body, no mind, no form, no sound, no odor, no taste, no object of touch, no phenomenon. There is no eye constituent, no mental constituent, up to and including no mental consciousness constituent. There is no ignorance, no extinction of ignorance, up to and including no aging and death and no extinction of aging and death. Similarly, there are no sufferings, no origins, no cessations, no paths, no exalted wisdom, no attainment, and also no non-attainment.

Therefore, Śāriputra, because Bodhisattvas have no attainment, they depend on and abide in the perfection of wisdom; because their minds are without obstructions, they are without fear. Having completely passed beyond all error they go to the completion of nirvāṇa. All the Buddhas who abide in the three times have been fully awakened into unsurpassed, perfect, complete enlightenment through relying on the perfection of wisdom.

Therefore, the mantra of the perfection of wisdom is the mantra of great knowledge, the unsurpassed mantra, the mantra equal to the unequalled, the mantra that thoroughly pacifies all suffering. Because it is not false, it should be known to be true. The mantra of the perfection of wisdom is stated:

tadyathā oṃ gate gate pāragate pārasaṃgate bodhi svāhā

Śāriputra, Bodhisattva Mahāsattvas should train in the profound perfection of wisdom in that way.

Then the Transcendent Victor rose from that samādhi and said to the Bodhisattva, the Mahāsattva, the Superior Avalokiteśvara, "Well done. Well done, well done, child of good lineage, it is just so. Child of good lineage, it is like that; the profound perfection of wisdom should be practiced just as you have taught it. Even the Tathāgatas admire this." The Transcendent Victor having so spoken, the venerable Śāriputra, the Bodhisattva, the Mahāsattva, the Superior Avalokiteśvara, and all those surrounding and those of the world, the gods, humans, demigods, and *gandharvas* were filled with admiration and praised the words of the Transcendent Victor.

Chapter 2

The Title

The Sūtra on the Heart of the Transcendent and Victorious Perfection of Wisdom

The Sanskrit term often translated as "perfection of wisdom" is *prajñāpāramitā*. *Jñā* means consciousness, knowledge, or understanding and *pra* is an intensifier; hence, *prajñā* is wisdom. According to the *Heart Sūtra* commentator Praśāstrasena, there are three kinds of understanding (*jñā*): the mundane, the supramundane, and the unsurpassed. Mundane understanding is corrupted with the belief that the impermanent is permanent, the impure is pure, the miserable is pleasurable, and that the selfless is self.[1] Supramundane understanding is that of the Hīnayāna disciples of the Buddha, who realize that persons are selfless, that conditioned phenomena are impermanent and miserable, and that nirvāṇa is peaceful. The unsurpassed understanding is that of the Tathāgatas, realizing that persons and phenomena are selfless and understanding signlessness, wishlessness, and emptiness (discussed in Chapter 5). Wisdom (*prajñā*) is this unsurpassed understanding.[2]

The term *pāramitā*, commonly translated as "perfection," has two etymologies. The first derives it from the word *parama*, meaning "highest," "most distant," and hence, "chief," "primary," "most excellent." Hence, the substantive can be rendered "excellence" or "perfection". This reading is supported by the *Madhyāntavibhāga* (V. 4), where the twelve excellences (*parama*) are associated with the ten perfections (*pāramitā*).[3] The *Heart Sūtra* commentator Vimalamitra supports this understanding of the term when he writes, "That of which there is nothing superior in the world is said to be excellent (*parama*); the excellence of wisdom is the perfection of wisdom.[4]

A more creative yet widely reported etymology divides *pāramitā* into *pāra*[5] and *mita*, with *pāra* meaning "beyond," "the further bank, shore, or boundary," and *mita*, meaning "that which has arrived," or *ita* meaning "that which goes." *Pāramitā*, then, means "that which has gone beyond," "that which goes beyond," or "transcendent." This reading is reflected in the Tibetan translation *pha rol tu phyin pa*, ("gone to the other side") and is supported by such renowned figures as Asaṅga, Vasubandhu, and Candrakīrti, as well as the *Heart Sūtra* commentators Jñānamitra, Praśāstrasena, and Vajrapāṇi. There is a range of opinion, however, as to what it is that has passed beyond and what constitutes the further shore. Asaṅga says in the *Mahāyāna-saṃgraha* that the perfections go beyond in the sense that they surpass all the roots of virtue of worldly beings, śrāvakas, and *pratyekabuddhas.*[6] Vasubandhu says in commenting on *Abhidharmakośa* IV.112b that the perfections have gone beyond to their respective accomplishment (*sampad*).[7] Candrakīrti, in the first chapter of his *Madhyamakāvatāra*, defines the "beyond" as the shore or port of the ocean of *saṃsāra* and identifies it with Buddhahood, which has the nature of having abandoned all of the afflictive obstructions (*kleśāvaraṇa*) and the obstructions to omniscience (*jñeyāvaraṇa*). The renowned six perfections of giving, ethics, patience, effort, concentration, and wisdom that are practiced on the Bodhisattva path receive the name "gone beyond" because when they are performed with a dedication to enlightenment, it is certain that they will go beyond to Buddhahood.[8] Haribhadra identifies the omniscient wisdom of a Buddha, which results from hearing, thinking, and meditation as the beyond and defines wisdom as the thorough discrimination of phenomena.[9] Vajrapāṇi says that "gone beyond" means having passed beyond being an object of the mind, by which he presumably means ordinary consciousness.[10] The readings of Praśāstrasena and Jñānamitra are translated later in the chapter.[11]

The relationship between *prajñā* and *pāramitā* is not explicitly addressed by the *Heart Sūtra* commentators, although it can be inferred that it is wisdom which has gone to the further shore of nirvāṇa, or it is wisdom by which the ocean of saṃsāra is traversed to arrive at the far shore. The Tibetan translation of *prajñāpāramitā* puts *prajñā* in the genitive case which, in this instance, according to an oral commentary, can be read in either an instrumental or appositional sense. Thus *prajñāpāramitā* could be read as either, "the wisdom which goes beyond or by which one goes beyond" or as "the state of having gone beyond, which is wisdom."[12] Praśāstrasena writes:

> This understanding (*jñā*) refers to the highest understanding. Superior (*ārya*) [(an adjective often affixed to the titles of Mahāyāna sūtras)] means that with this understanding, one is far separated from sorrow and suffering. *Pra* [means] the wisdom that is supreme among the

mundane and supramundane, that is the highest, hence, *prajñā*. Regarding "gone beyond" (*pāramitā*), the sufferings of birth and death are this side, nirvāṇa is the far side. Sentient beings who are driven by the desires of saṃsāra are [caught] in the middle. This wisdom acts as a raft and ship, delivering them to the shore of nirvāṇa.[13]

Dignāga proclaims that the actual perfection of wisdom is possessed only by a Buddha; indeed, that wisdom is the Buddha. It is the omniscience referred to as the knowledge of all aspects (*sarvākārajñāna*), the illusion-like, non-dual wisdom of a Buddha, thoroughly discerning phenomena. He explains, however, that texts and paths can also be designated with the name, "perfection of wisdom." Dignāga says in his *Prajñāpāramitāpiṇḍārtha*, 1 (*Summarized Meaning of the Perfection of Wisdom*):

The perfection of wisdom is the non-dual wisdom;
It is the Tathāgata.
That term [is used] for texts and paths
Because they have that object [as their] goal.[14]

Based on this statement, Tibetan commentators have delineated several varieties of the perfection of wisdom, one that is actual, or literal, and two that are designated with the term, or metaphoric. The actual perfection of wisdom is a Buddha's final exalted knowledge of all aspects (*sarvākārajñāna*), the Mahāyāna path of no more learning (*aśaikṣamārga*), sometimes called the fruitional perfection wisdom. It is the final wisdom, directly realizing all the modes and varieties of phenomena in a single instant.[15] The fruitional perfection of wisdom has gone beyond in the sense that it is the fulfillment of its causes, the practices of hearing, thinking, and meditating that occurred on the path. It exists only in the continuum of a Buddha, is non-dual, and is illusion-like in that it itself is empty of true existence.[16]

According to Dignāga's commentator, Triratnadāsa, the omniscience of a Buddha is a primary perfection of wisdom whereas the Perfection of Wisdom sūtras and the Bodhisattva paths are secondary perfections of wisdom; it is not the case that these are not actual perfections of wisdom.[17] Calling texts and paths "perfections of wisdom" is a case of designating a cause with the name of its effect in that the sūtras set forth the perfection of wisdom and the practice of the path brings it about. Those who wish to achieve the fruitional perfection of wisdom must listen to and contemplate the textual perfections of wisdom and must practice the path perfections of wisdom.[18]

Dignāga's view, that the main meaning of the perfection of wisdom is the knowledge of all aspects possessed only by a Buddha, is not shared by all. For example, Ratnākaraśānti asserted that the first two Bodhisattva paths are causes of the perfection of wisdom, Buddhahood is the fruition of the perfection of wisdom, and the Bodhisattva's final moment of wisdom before becoming a Buddha is the actual perfection of wisdom.[19] There are numerous statements in the sūtras and śāstras that use the term "perfection of wisdom" in the context of the path, such as the sūtra passage:

> How could millions of blind men, with no one to lead them
> And not knowing the path, arrive at the city?
> In the same way, without wisdom, the five blind perfections,
> Having no leader, cannot touch enlightenment.[20]

The *Saṃdhinirmocana* speaks of three perfections, all of which occur on the Bodhisattva path.[21] As noted above, the *Madhyāntavibhāga* (V. 4) connects the perfections (*pāramitā*) with the twelve excellences (*parama*) that occur on the Bodhisattva path.[22]

Hence, it seems useful to understand the term translated here as "perfection of wisdom" both as the wisdom, possessed only by a Buddha, which has gone beyond all forms of saṃsāra and as the wisdom that goes beyond, which occurs on the path to enlightenment. It is the wisdom directly realizing emptiness that has gone or is going to the final state of Buddhahood. The prajñāpāramitā is thus the wisdom gone to the further shore, the wisdom that goes to the further shore, the transcendent wisdom, the perfection of wisdom.

The first word in the Sanskrit title of the *Heart Sūtra* is *bhagavatī*, the feminine form of the word *bhagavat*. It is a common epithet of the Buddha, often translated as "lord" or "blessed one"; here it describes the perfection of wisdom. The many meanings of *bhaga* in Sanskrit literature, in addition to being a name for the sun and the moon, include "fortune," "happiness," "prosperity," "welfare," "dignity," "majesty," "excellence," and "beauty." *Vat* is a suffix denoting possession.

Buddhist commentators, both of the Hīnayāna and Mahāyāna schools have provided elaborate etymologies of *bhagavat*,[2] some of which occur in the discussions of *bhagavatī* in the Indian commentaries on the *Heart Sūtra*.

The Indian commentators construe *bhaga* in two ways, one implying destruction, the other implying fortune.

The perfection of wisdom destroys the two obstructions, the afflictive obstructions (*kleśāvaraṇa*) and the obstructions to omniscience (*jñeyāvaraṇa*).[24] Although there is considerable disagreement among the Mahāyāna schools as to what constitutes the two obstructions and how they are abandoned,[25] there is general consensus that the afflictive obstructions include the afflictions (*kleṣa*) such as desire, hatred, and ignorance, and prevent the attainment of liberation from rebirth. The afflictive obstructions are abandoned by śrāvakas and pratyekabuddhas on the Hīnayāna path. The obstructions to omniscience are more subtle predispositions and latencies that prevent the attainment of the omniscience of a Buddha. They are not abandoned by *arhats* but are overcome by Bodhisattvas over the course of the ten stages (*bhūmi*), with the afflictive obstructions being abandoned along the way.[26]

In addition to destroying the two obstructions, the Pāla commentators say that the perfection of wisdom destroys the Māras, which are commonly enumerated as four: The Māra of the aggregates (*skandhamāra*), the Māra of the afflictions (*kleśamāra*), the Māra of death (*maraṇamāra*), and the Māra who is the son of a god (*devaputramāra*).[27] The four Māras are alluded to in many of the major Sanskrit śāstras, including the *Mahāprajñāpāramitāśāstra*,[28] Vasubandhu's *Abhidharmakośabhāṣya*,[29] Candrakīrti's *Prasannapadā*,[30] Maitreya's *Uttaratantra*,[31] Prajñākaramati's commentary to the *Bodhicaryāvatāra*,[32] and Asaṅga's *Śrāvakabhūmi*.[33] Tibetan expositions of the four Māras draw heavily on Asaṅga and appear most commonly in commentaries and monastic textbooks on the fourth chapter of Maitreyanātha's *Abhisamayālaṃkāra*, specifically at line IV.62a, where "overcoming enemies" (*śātravāṇām-atikramaḥ*) is listed as the first of the ten aspects of the Buddha's skillful methods (*upāyakauśalam*).[34]

Asaṅga says in the *Śrāvakabhūmi:*

> The Māra of the aggregates is the five appropriated aggregates. The Māra of the afflictions is the afflictions that operate in the three realms. The Māra of death is that which causes the time of death for sentient beings among the types of sentient beings. The deity Māra is that which becomes the deity Īśvara born in the Desire Realm who comes in order to impede and distract those who are striving for virtue to transcend completely the aggregates, afflictions, and death.[35]

Based on this passage, Tibetan monastic textbooks describe the Māra of the aggregates as either the contaminated aggregates that arise in dependence on actions or that which is based on the predispositions of ignorance. It is of two varieties, the subtle and the coarse, with the former identified as the mental body that arises in dependence on the predispositions of ignorance and the latter identified as the five appropriated aggregates (*upādānaskandhāḥ*).

The Māra of the afflictions is described as the obstructions that prevent the achievement of liberation. It also has coarse and subtle forms. The subtle form is, for example, the seeds of the afflictive obstructions (*kleśāvaraṇa*). The coarse forms include the six root afflictions and the twenty secondary afflictions.[36]

The Māra of death is the factor that terminates the life faculty (*jīvitā-indriya*) against the individual's will. Its subtle form is the inconceivable transmigration whereby Bodhisattvas on the eighth, ninth, and tenth stages take birth in the world and the coarse form is the factor that, due to actions and afflictions, terminates the life faculty against one's will.

The deity (literally, "son of a deity" [*devaputra*]) Māra is described as god of the Desire Realm (*kāmadhātu*) who impedes the defeat of the other three Māras. An example of this deity is the lord of the Heaven of Controlling Others' Emanations (*paranirmitavaśavartina*), Nandikeśvara, who sees with his clairvoyance those disciples seeking liberation and omniscience and shoots them with his five arrows, the arrows of desire, hatred, obscuration, pride and jealousy, thereby distracting them from their quest. His arrows are flowers, leaving no wound.

The four Māras are delineated in terms of death: where one dies is the Māra of the aggregates, that by which one dies is the Māra of the afflictions, the entity of death is the Māra of death, and that which impedes the transcendence of those three is the deity Māra. All four are called *māra* (obstacle) because they prevent the attainment of nirvāṇa, the deathless state.[37]

The question of when the various Māras are destroyed over the course of the Hīnayāna and Mahāyāna paths receives considerable attention in the Tibetan commentaries on the *Abhisamayālaṃkāra*. The fourteenth century Tibetan scholar Tsong-kha-pa says in his *Legs bshad gser 'phreng* (*Golden Rosary*):

> The Māra of the afflictions does not exist from the eighth stage on. Regarding the Māra of death, death due to actions and afflictions does not occur from the first stage on, but the transmigration (*'chi 'pho ba*) of mind and body is not overcome until the attainment of Buddhahood. Therefore, the Māra of death and the Māra of the aggregates exist until the attainment of Buddhahood. Since the deity Māra impedes [the defeat] of the [other] three, it exists as long as those three continue to operate.[38]

According to Tsong-kha-pa's disciple, rGyal-tshab, on the

Hīnayāna path, the deity Māra is destroyed at the time of the path of seeing, because at that time the meditator possesses an actual antidote to doubts about abiding in refuge in the Three Jewels. The Māra of the afflictions is destroyed upon becoming an *arhat* because at that time the afflictive obstructions are utterly abandoned. When the meditator becomes an arhat who is both fully liberated from the afflictive obstructions and is a master of meditative absorption (*samāpatti, snyoms 'jug*),[39] the coarse Māra of death is destroyed because abandoned at that time is the experience of birth and death in terms of coarse exertion. The coarse Māra of the aggregates is destroyed upon attaining the remainderless nirvāṇa because the meditator has abandoned the contaminated aggregates that arise through the power of actions and afflictions.

For the Mahāyāna, the deity Māra is destroyed when the Bodhisattva exhibits the signs of irreversibility on the path of preparation (*prayogamārga*), because at that time the Bodhisattva attains the ability to perform special deeds of physical and verbal irreversibility, through having acquired the faith of belief in the Three Jewels. The coarse Māra of the afflictions is destroyed at the eighth stage because there the Bodhisattva has abandoned the afflictive obstructions. The Bodhisattva also destroys the coarse Māra of death at the eighth stage because he abandons the Māra of death who causes death through coarse exertion. It is also at the eighth stage that the Bodhisattva destroys the coarse Māra of the aggregates. The destruction of all coarse and subtle forms of the four Māras occurs upon the attainment of Buddhahood.[40]

The perfection of wisdom is thus a destroyer because it provides the means by which the coarse and subtle forms of the four Māras are destroyed.

The other meaning of *bhaga* emphasized in the etymology of *bhagavan* is "fortune." The *Heart Sūtra* commentator Śrīmahājana cites a verse listing the six fortunes with which a Buddha is endowed.

> The marvels of complete lordship,
> Of qualities, of fame, of glory,
> Of wisdom, and of effort,
> These six are called fortunes.[41]

Śrīmahājana sets forth the six fortunes in terms of the five wisdoms of a Buddha. He explains that lordship refers to the Buddha's abandonment of the two obstructions whereby he has gained mastery through destroying the four Māras. Quality (*dharma*) is the Buddha's natural virtue, such as the ten powers.[42] Both of the first two fortunes are the nature of the totally pure *dharmadhātu*, corresponding to the Buddha's wisdom of the sphere of reality (*dharmadhātujñāna*) which remains in eternal awareness of the Nature Body (*svabhāvikakāya*) of a Buddha, identified as the final reality, naturally pure and free of all defilements.[43] Fame refers to the qualities of the Buddha's Form Body (*rūpakāya*), the cause of his fame. This has the nature of the mirror-like wisdom (*ādarśajñāna*) which, without conceiving of self, constantly and blissfully observes all phenomena, both ultimate and conventional, exactly as they are. Glory is the wisdom of equality (*samatājñāna*) whereby the Buddha observes all sentient beings without distinction, equally with love and compassion. Śrīmahājana calls it the sky treasury of all phenomena. Wisdom is the wisdom of individual understanding (*pratyavekṣājñāna*), the direct realization of the general and specific qualities of all phenomena. Effort is earnest action, the wisdom of performing activities (*kṛtyānusthānajñāna*), which serves as the cause of the various emanations of the Buddha that appear in the world for the welfare of others.[44]

To draw yet further meaning from *bhagavan*, some commentators interpret *van* not merely as a suffix denoting possession, but relate it to the *van* of *nirvāṇa* and give it the meaning of "transcendent" or "supramundane." Jñānamitra says:

> *Van* [means] the unlocated nirvāṇa (*apratiṣṭhitanirvāṇa*). Since all minds, intellects, and consciousnesses are overturned by the meaning of this perfection of wisdom, that is, since it is free from all predispositions, it is transcendent.[45]

To gain some sense of how *bhagavan* was understood in late Indian Mahāyāna Buddhism, it is useful to see how the term was translated into Tibetan. It was often the case in the translation of Sanskrit words into Tibetan that more than one of the Sanskrit connotations was rendered into the Tibetan term. Thus, Buddha became *sangs rgyas*, meaning "awakened-spread," incorporating two meanings of *budh* as "awakening" and "opening." *Sattva* of *bodhisattva* became *sems dpa'*, meaning "mind-hero," taking note of the fact that among the many meanings of *sattva*, these two were significant in the translation of *bodhisattva*. *Bhagavan* became *bcom ldan 'das*, literally, "destruction-endowed-transcendent," indicating a preference for the reading of *"bhaga"* as "destruction" rather than "fortune" and reading *"van"* both as a suffix denoting possession and as related to *nirvāṇa*, as stated by Jñānamitra.[46] An oral commentary states that *bcom* means the destruction of the two obstructions and indicates the Buddha's marvelous abandonment; *ldan* means that the Buddha is endowed with the Wisdom Truth Body (*jñānadharmakāya*), the omniscient consciousness, and indicates the Buddha's marvelous realization; and *'das* means that the Buddha has passed beyond the extremes of mundane existence and solitary peace.[47]

The feminine ending *tī*, agreeing in gender with *prajñāpāramitā* connotes the feminine nature of the perfection of wisdom. As stated in the *Heart Sūtra* itself, all Buddhas arise from the practice of the perfection of wisdom. Therefore, it is called the mother of all the Buddhas.[48] The metaphor of the perfection of wisdom as mother is employed by Tsong-kha-pa in his differentiation of the three vehicles in the introduction to his *sNgags rim chen mo* (*Great Exposition of Secret Mantra*). As a Prāsaṅgika, he holds that śrāvakas, pratyekabuddhas, Bodhisattvas, and Buddhas all understand the same emptiness of inherent existence (*svabhāva*). Therefore, the vehicles are to be differentiated in terms of method (*upāya*) rather than wisdom (*prajñā*). The perfection of wisdom is the common mother of these four sons, but their fathers—method—are different. The four are known by different names because the father is the criterion for determining nationality or lineage.[49]

The Perfection of Wisdom sūtras are a vast literature comprising hundreds of texts. In Tibet, seventeen of the sūtras were known as the "mothers and sons",[50] but three were best known: the *Perfection of Wisdom in One Hundred Thousand Stanzas* (*Śatasāhasrikāprajñāpāramitāsūtra*), the *Perfection of Wisdom in 25,000 Stanzas* (*Pañcaviṃśatisāhasrikāprajñāpāramitāsūtra*) and the *Perfection of Wisdom in 8000 Stanzas* (*Aṣṭasāhasrikāprajñāpāramitāsūtra*). These were known respectively as the vast, intermediate, and brief mother sūtras. According to the Tibetan scholar and historian Bu-ston (1290-1364 C.E.), these three sūtras were spoken simultaneously by the Buddha because each sūtra involves the same interlocutors and each contains the same prophecy about the enlightenment of Gaṅgādevī.[51]

Five of the most important of the Mahāyāna sūtras were known in Tibet as the five "one hundred thousand." The *Perfection of Wisdom in One Hundred Thousand Stanzas* was known as the one hundred thousand of mind; the *Nirvāṇa Sūtra*, said to contain one hundred thousand testaments of the Buddha made prior to his entry into nirvāṇa, was called the hundred thousand of speech; the *Ratnakūṭa Sūtra*, with names of one hundred thousand Buddhas, was the hundred thousand of body; the *Avataṃsaka Sūtra*, with one hundred thousand prayers, was the hundred thousand of auspiciousness; and the

Laṅkāvatāra Sūtra, said to possess methods for subduing one hundred thousand demons, was called the one hundred thousand of activity. Each of these sūtras was regarded as having a condensed version, which the Tibetans called the five royal sūtras, because they were recited in the religious services of the early kings. The condensation of the *Perfection of Wisdom in One Hundred Thousand Stanzas* was the *Heart Sūtra*, called the sūtra of the view. The condensation of the *Nirvāṇa Sūtra* was the *Ātajñāna*, called the sūtra of deeds, while that of the *Ratnakūṭa Sūtra* was the *Vajravidāraṇī*, called the sūtra of ablution. The *Bhadracarīpraṇidhāna*, called the sūtra of prayers, was the condensation of the *Avataṃsaka Sūtra*, and the *Āpattideśanā*, the sūtra for the confession of sins, was said to be the condensation of the *Laṅkāvatāra Sūtra*.[52] There seems to have been something of a cult of the text surrounding the Perfection of Wisdom sūtras in Tibet during the period of the first propagation (*snga dar*) of the doctrine. Not only were the numbers of *ślokas* dutifully counted, but also the number of dots between syllables; the *Perfection of Wisdom in One Hundred Thousand Stanzas* purportedly has 4,100,000 dots.[53]

The word *hṛdaya* means both heart and essence. The *Heart Sūtra* is said to be the heart of the three mother sūtras. According to Indian physiology, the heart is where the consciousnesses that pervade the body gather. In the same way, all of the meanings of the vast, intermediate, and brief mother sūtras are gathered in this small sūtra.[54] It is the essence because there is no meaning contained in the *Perfection of Wisdom in One Hundred Thousand Stanzas* that is not contained in the *Heart Sūtra*. This point is made by the commentator Jñānamitra, whose exegesis of the title provides an appropriate summary to this chapter.

> "Heart of the Transcendent and Victorious Perfection of Wisdom" expresses the nature of the sūtra. Hence, it is called *Heart of the Transcendent and Victorious Perfection of Wisdom*. If it were not named at the outset, one would not know which sūtra it was. Therefore, the name is stated. However, this is not merely the designation of a name; there is nothing contained in any sūtra that is not in this *Heart of the Perfection of Wisdom*. Consequently, it is called the sūtra of sūtras.
>
> Regarding that [title], *bhagavan* means the destruction of Māras. Māras, such as the Māra of the aggregates, are not found when sought with this meaning of the perfection of wisdom and no Māras abide there. Thus, it destroys (*bhaga*). [*Bhaga*]*van* [means] endowed with the six fortunes. That is, because all the good qualities of knowledge arise from the blessings of the perfection of wisdom, it is endowed

(*van*). *Van* means the unlocated nirvāṇa. Because all minds, intellects, and consciousnesses are overturned by this meaning of the perfection of wisdom, that is, because it is free from all predispositions, it is transcendent (*van*). With regard to [the feminine ending] *tī*, all the Buddhas arise from practicing the meaning of the perfection of wisdom; they are given birth by the meaning of the perfection of wisdom. Therefore, because the perfection of wisdom acts as the mother of all the Buddhas, *tī* [is used].

Regarding *prajñā*, reality is known just as it is by the three wisdoms of hearing, thinking, and meditating. Therefore, it is called wisdom (*prajñā*). Regarding *pāramitā*, because wisdom does not see any phenomena whatsoever, it has passed beyond signs, the two extremes, and birth and death. Therefore, it is said to have gone beyond (*pāramitā*). Regarding *hṛdaya*, there is nothing supreme and profound in the *Perfection of Wisdom in One Hundred Thousand Stanzas* that is not contained in this small sūtra. Therefore, it is the essence (*hṛdaya*).[55]

Chapter 3
The Prologue

Thus did I hear at one time. The Transcendent Victor was sitting on Vulture Peak in Rājagṛha together with a great assembly of monks and a great assembly of Bodhisattvas. At that time the Transcendent Victor was absorbed in a samādhi on the enumerations of phenomena called "perception of the profound." Also at that time, the Bodhisattva, the Mahāsattva, the Superior Avalokiteśvara was contemplating the meaning of the profound perfection of wisdom and he saw that those five aggregates also are empty of inherent existence.

The commentator Praśāstrasena analyzes the *Heart Sūtra* in terms of five topics: the marvelous time, the marvelous teacher, the marvelous place, the marvelous audience, and the marvelous doctrine. The first four of these topics are identified in the prologue to the sūtra. The prologue has two parts, the common prologue and the unique prologue.

The Common Prologue

The common prologue is, "Thus did I hear at one time. The Transcendent Victor was sitting on Vulture Peak in Rājagṛha together with a great assembly of monks and a great assembly of Bodhisattvas." Such a formula, beginning with "Thus did I hear at one time," and going on to identify where the Buddha was when the sūtra was set forth and who was in the audience, is common to both the Hīnayāna and Mahāyāna sūtras.

"Thus did I hear at one time" (*evaṃ mayā śrutam ekasmin samaye*)[1] is the declaration at the beginning of a sūtra that attests to its authenticity as one heard directly from the Buddha on a particular occasion by the Buddha's personal attendant, Ānanda, who is traditionally regarded as the compiler (*saṃgītikartā*) of the sūtras. Atīśa cites Dignāga's explanation (in his *Prajñāpāramitāpiṇḍārtha* (3-4)) of the purpose of the compiler's declaration:

> In order to establish his validity, the compiler
> Explicitly indicates the teacher, the audience,
> The time, and the place
> As factors [causing] the faithful to enter [the teaching].
> Just as in the world,
> A speaker who was a witness and
> Who indicates the place and time
> Is known to be a valid speaker.[2]

The commentator Vajrapāṇi has high praise for the word *evaṃ* (thus), the word with which sūtras begin. Those four letters are the source of the 84,000 doctrines taught by the Buddha and are the basis of all marvels.[3] The meaning of the other words of the formula are less clear because, in the case of the Perfection of Wisdom sūtras, there is some controversy as to the identity of the "I" who heard them and to the meaning of "at one time."

The Mādhyamika philosopher Bhāvaviveka argues in his *Tarkajvālā* that Ānanda could not have been the compiler of the Perfection of Wisdom sūtras because their subject matter, particularly the doctrine of emptiness, was beyond the comprehension of Hīnayāna disciples such as Ānanda. He claims, then, that it was the Bodhisattvas Samantabhadra, Mañjuśrī, Maitreya, and Guhyādhipati (Vajrapāṇi) who compiled the Mahāyāna sūtras.[4] In his *Heart Sūtra* commentary, Jñānamitra says that Mañjuśrī heard and compiled all the Mahāyāna sūtras.[5]

The eighth century master Haribhadra, although agreeing that Ānanda was himself incapable of compiling the Perfection of Wisdom sūtras, contends that he nonetheless did compile them upon being empowered to do so by the blessings of the Buddha.[6] According to the commentator Praśāstrasena, "heard" simply means that it was heard directly and does not imply that the meaning was necessarily understood.[7]

These two positions provide insight into the dilemma of authority that confronted the Mahāyāna exegetes. They were compelled to establish that the Mahāyāna sūtras were authentic as the word of the Buddha (*buddhavacana*) in spite of the fact that the sūtras only began to appear some four centuries after the Teacher's death. In the fourth chapter of his *Tarkajvālā*, Bhāvaviveka summarizes the Hīnayāna argument that the Mahāyāna is not the word of the Buddha. The Mahāyāna sūtras were not included in either the original or subsequent compilations of the tripiṭaka; by teaching that the Tathāgata is permanent, the Mahāyāna contradicts the doctrine that all conditioned phenomena are impermanent; because the Mahāyāna teaches that the tathāgatagarbha is all-pervasive, it does not abandon the conception of self (*ātmagraha*); because the Mahāyāna teaches that the Buddha did not pass into nirvāṇa, it suggests that nirvāṇa is not peaceful; the Mahāyāna sūtras contain prophecies that the great śrāvakas will become Buddhas; the Mahāyāna belittles the arhats; the Mahāyāna praises Bodhisattvas above the Buddha; the Mahāyāna perverts the entire teaching by propounding that Śākyamuni was an emanation; the statement in the Mahāyāna sūtras that the Buddha was constantly in meditative equipoise (*samāhita*) is infeasible; by saying that great sins can be completely absolved, the Mahāyāna teaches that actions have no effects. "Therefore, the Buddha did not set forth the Mahāyāna; it was created by beings who were certainly demonic in order to deceive the obtuse and those of evil minds."[8]

Bhāvaviveka takes it as his task to counter these attacks, arguing that the basic doctrines of Buddhism, such as the four truths, the harmonies of enlightenment (*bodhipakṣa*), the paths, and the powers of the Buddha appear in the same terms in the Hīnayāna and Mahāyāna sūtras. Furthermore, there are contradictions even among the various versions of the Hīnayāna canon. Bhāvaviveka goes on the offensive, quoting Mahāyāna sūtras to indicate that this teaching was not intended for those of Hīnayāna ilk and provides examples of Mahāyāna sūtras in which there are no śrāvakas present in the audience. For example, to call into question the status of Ānanda as compiler of the Buddha's word, he cites the *Śiṃśapāvanasūtra*, "Ānanda, the doctrines that I have understood but have not taught to you are more numerous than the leaves in this grove of *śiṃśapā* trees."[9]

Bhāvaviveka argues for a radical discontinuity between the Hīnayāna and Mahāyāna canons, asserting that the reason the Hīnayāna schools have no evidence of the Buddha teaching the Mahāyāna sūtras is that those sūtras were intended solely for Bodhisattvas, not for śrāvakas and pratyekabuddhas; the Hīnayāna disciples were not even present when the sūtras were delivered. Haribhadra, while seeking also to maintain the primacy of the Mahāyāna, opts for a more accomodating position whereby the Mahāyāna sūtras, like the Hīnayāna sūtras, were all compiled by Ānanda, although as a śrāvaka he could only compile them through the benevolent empowerment of the Buddha.[10] Hence, for Haribhadra, the "I" of "Thus did I hear at one time" consistently refers to the same person in both the Hīnayāna and Mahāyāna sūtras.

Haribhadra provides a unique reading of "at one time", however.

Rather than only meaning "on one occasion", he states in his *Abhisamayālaṃkārāloka* that it also means "in one instant"; by the blessings of the Buddha, Ānanda heard the entire sūtra in one instant.[11] This is one example of the extraordinary pedagogical talents attributed to the Buddha in the Mahāyāna sūtras. For example, in the eighth chapter of the *Tathāgatācintyaguhyanirdeśasūtra* (*Sūtra on the Inconceivable Secrets of the Tathāgata*) Vajrapāṇi explains to the Bodhisattva Śāntamati that sentient beings not only perceive the words of the Buddha as issuing from his mouth, but also from his crown protrusion, the hair on his head, his forehead, his eyes, his ears, his shoulders, his hands, his fingers, his penis, his ankles, and the soles of his feet. Furthermore, although sentient beings abide throughout the three billion worlds, he teaches them all in their respective languages.[12] Yet Vajrapāṇi prefaces this catalogue of the secrets of the Buddha's speech by saying, "Śāntamati, from the night when the Tathāgata became a complete Buddha, manifesting unsurpassed perfect, complete enlightenment, until the night when he passed without remainder into final nirvāṇa, the Tathāgata did not speak even a single syllable, nor will he speak. Why? Śāntamati, the Tathāgata is constantly in absorption; the Tathāgata does not breathe."[13]

There is a wide range of opinion among Tibetan historians over the question of when during his lifetime the Buddha taught the Perfection of Wisdom sūtras. Some conclude that they were set forth in the month before the Buddha's death. Others hold that he taught the Perfection of Wisdom in the year after his enlightenment. Some say that the exposition of the sūtras continued over a period of thirty years. Others hold that the sūtras in 100,000, 25,000, 18,000, 10,000 and 8000 stanzas were expounded simultaneously.[14]

The marvelous place is the Vulture Peak, east of the city of Rājagṛha, the capital of Magadha. Vulture Peak (*gṛdhrakūṭaparvata*, literally "Mass of Vultures Peak"), one of the five mountains outside of Rājagṛha, is the site of the exposition of the Perfection of Wisdom sūtras by the Buddhas of the past, present, and future. Numerous explanations are provided as to how it acquired its name. For example, the *Heart Sūtra* commentator Praśāstrasena says that is shaped like a mass of vultures,[15] whereas Jñānamitra explains that flocks of vultures gather at its summit.[16] The teaching of the insubstantiality of all phenomena that occurred on Vulture Peak seems to have provided it with a special permanence. Vimalamitra says that the peak has become a *stūpa* and is utterly indestructible by the fire at the end of the aeon.[17] This quality is also ascribed to the vajra seat (*vajrāsana*) in Bodhgāyā where the Buddha achieved enlightenment. It is also said that this is the only mountain through which beings of the intermediate state (Sanskrit, *antarābhava*; Tibetan *bar do*) are unable to pass. Many Indian Buddhist schools posited the existence of an intermediate state that occurs between death and the next rebirth. In this state, beings are said to have subtle bodies which are youthful versions of the beings they will become. Among the abilities of such beings is that of passing unobstructedly through objects.[18]

Rājagṛha is the famous city of King Bimbisāra that was often frequented by the Buddha. Meaning "residence of the king," its name derived from a legend that it was built by a king after a previous palace in Kuśinagara had had to be abandoned because it was destroyed by fire.[19] Rājagṛha is considered the best place for laypeople while the Vulture Peak is the best place for those who have gone forth from the worldly life to become monks. Both locations are therefore mentioned as the marvelous place of the exposition of the sūtra.[20]

The marvelous retinue is the great assembly of monks and the great assembly of Bodhisattvas. The Sanskrit term *bhikṣu*, usually translated as monk, is derived from *bhikṣ*, a desiderative form of the verbal root *bhaj* (to apportion, to divide, to share), and comes to mean "one who wishes to be shared with." The Tibetan translation is *dge slong*, literally "virtue-request," maintaining the primary meaning of *bhikṣu* in the second component, which Śrīmahājana explains to mean that they seek the marvelous wealth of virtue from others;[21] an oral commentary explains that "virtue-request" means that they seek the virtue which is nirvāṇa or that they request merit that accords with the dharma.[22] The *Heart Sūtra* commentator Vimalamitra provides a fabricated etymology, apparently relating *bhikṣ* to *bhaj* to *bhanj*, "to shatter, to destroy." He wrote, "Because they destroy the afflictions (*kleśa*), they are monks (*bhikṣu*).[23]

The gathering of monks is called an assembly (*saṃgha*). Candrakīrti, in his *Triśaraṇasaptati* (*Seventy Stanzas on the Triple Refuge*), etymologizes *saṃgha* as that which is not separated by the Māras from the Buddha, from the excellent doctrine, and from friends who practice purity:

> Because they cannot be separated
> From the Buddha, Dharma, and Saṃgha
> By billions of Māras,
> It is clearly called *saṃgha*.[24]

The Tibetan translation of *saṃgha* is *dge 'dun*, literally, "virtue-aspiration" and is said to mean those who have the aspiration for the virtue of liberation.[25] An assembly (*saṃgha*) is defined as four or more monks. An assembly jewel (*saṃgharatna*) is a person who is a Superior (*ārya*), someone who has attained the path of seeing (*darśanamārga*) by either the Hīnayāna or Mahāyāna path.[26] The assembly of monks is called great because of its size and because of its greatness in such qualities as wisdom and the ability to create magical emanations.[27]

In the marvelous audience there was also a great assembly of Bodhisattvas. The Sanskrit term *bodhisattva* is compounded from two words, *bodhi* and *sattva. Bodhi* is derived from the verbal root *budh*, "to wake," so that *bodhi* means the state of being awake, that is, enlightenment. The second component of the term is more problematic. In his classic study, *The Bodhisattva Doctrine in Buddhist Sanskrit Literature*, Har Dayal lists seven possible interpretations of *sattva*,[28] three of which may be considered here. The first meaning of *sattva* is "sentient being," in which case the compound *bodhisattva* would be read as "a being seeking enlightenment." A second meaning of *sattva* is "mind" (*citta*) or "intention" (*abhipraya*), so that a Bodhisattva would be "one whose mind or intention is directed toward enlightenment." Thirdly, *sattva* has the sense of strength or courage, making the compound *bodhisattva* mean "one whose strength is directed toward enlightenment."

Again, to gain some sense of how the term was understood by late (circa eighth century) Mahāyāna scholars in India, it is helpful to consider the Tibetan translation of *bodhisattva*, which is *byang chub sems dpa'*. *Byang chub* is the translation of *bodhi*, enlightenment. *Sems* means "mind" or "intention" and *dpa'* can serve as a noun meaning "strength" or "courage" or as an adjective meaning "courageous" or "heroic." This suggests that the Indian and Tibetan translators who coined the term *byang chub sems dpa'* to translate *bodhisattva* were aware of both the second and third meanings of *sattva* mentioned earlier and felt that both should be incorporated into the Tibetan translation with the resulting meaning, "one who is heroic in his or her intention to achieve enlightenment."

Tibetan scholars later construed their own etymologies of *byang chub sems dpa'*, drawing meaning simply from the Tibetan terms without reference to the Sanskrit. The term *byang chub* is the Tibetan translation of *bodhi*. *Byang* means purified and *byang pa* means learned. *Chub* means accomplished. Because Bodhisattvas are seeking to purify all faults and attain all good qualities, they are purified and accomplished (*byang chub*). Or, because they have studied (*byang pa*) the two truths repeatedly and arrived at (*chub*) their meaning, they are accomplished in learning (*byang chub*). As mentioned, the Tibetan translation of *sattva* is *sems dpa'*, literally "mind-heroic." Bodhisattvas are called heroic contemplatives (*sems dpa'*) because they contemplate the welfare of transmigrators and annihilate demons and because they have endured hardship in repeatedly contemplating the two truths.[29]

A Bodhisattva is a person who has created the aspiration to enlightenment (*bodhicitta*), which is defined in a famous passage from the *Abhisamayālaṃkāra* (I.18a):

> The creation of the aspiration is the wish for
> Perfect and complete enlightenment for the sake of others.[30]

Bodhisattvas thus have two goals, the welfare of others and their own enlightenment. The liberation from suffering of all sentient beings is said to be their chief goal, while their own attainment of Buddhahood is the most effective means by which this goal may be achieved. The creation of the aspiration to enlightenment is highly praised in the Mahāyāna literature. The *Abhisamayālaṃkāra* (I.19-20) goes on to provide a list of twenty-two similes to illustrate its nature. It is like the earth because it is the basis of all auspicious qualities, it is like gold because it does not change until enlightenment, it is like the waxing moon because it increases all virtuous qualities, it is like fire because it burns and consumes the obstructions to the three kinds of omniscience, it is like a treasure because it satisfies all sentient beings, and so forth.[31] Śāntideva says of the aspiration to enlightenment (*Bodhicaryāvatāra* III.29):

> It is the supreme medicine that
> Quells the sickness of transmigrators.
> It is the tree where transmigrators rest,
> Wandering and fatigued on the road of mundane existence.[32]

This aspiration to enlightenment is said to be of two types: the wishful aspiration to enlightenment (*bodhipraṇidhicitta*) and the practical aspiration to enlightenment (*bodhiprasthānacitta*), which are compared to the wish to go someplace and actually setting out on the journey.[33] The wishful aspiration to enlightenment is the genuine desire to become a Buddha to benefit all sentient beings. The nature of that benefit is specified by Haribhadra in his version of the wishful aspiration, "Having become a complete and perfect Buddha, may I strive to teach the doctrines of the three vehicles for the welfare of others in accordance with [their] abilities."[34] He thus suggests that the greatest benefit that a Buddha can bestow and the ability that the Bodhisattva seeks over the long course of the path is that of teaching the doctrine effectively.

The practical mind of enlightenment begins with taking a formal vow to achieve Buddhahood for the sake of others,[35] after which the Bodhisattva begins the practices which will eventually fructify in the achievement of Buddhahood. Kamalaśīla, one of the *Heart Sūtra* commentators, identifies those practices in another of his works, the *Bhāvanākrama* (I). They are the four immeasurables, consisting of equanimity (*upekṣā*), love (*maitrī*), compassion (*karuṇā*), and joy (*mudita*); the four means of gathering students (*saṃgrahavastu*), consisting of giving gifts (*dāna*), speaking pleasantly (*priyavadita*), teaching others to fulfill their aims (*arthacarya*), and acting in accordance with one's own teaching (*samanārthatā*); and the six perfections (*pāramitā*), consisting of giving (*dāna*), ethics (*śīla*), patience (*kṣānti*), effort (*vīrya*), concentration (*dhyāna*), and the perfection of wisdom (*prajñāpāramitā*), the topic of the *Heart Sūtra*.

Kamalaśīla cites the *Sarvadharmasaṃgrahasūtra* to the effect that Bodhisattvas practice each of the six perfections for sixty aeons.[36] In the *Abhisamayālaṃkāra* (I.43), it is explained that Bodhisattvas practice six types of each of the six perfections. That is, they practice the giving of giving, the giving of ethics, the giving of patience, and so on, totalling thirty-six combinations.[37] The six perfections are, thus, what the Bodhisattva practices to fulfill the promise to achieve enlightenment for the sake of others. They are the Bodhisattva deeds (*bodhisattvacaryā*).

The assembly of Bodhisattvas is great because of three greatnesses: the Bodhisattvas' greatness of abandonment, greatness of realization, and their great intention, which makes them supreme among all sentient beings.[38] According to Vimalamitra, the statement in the prologue, "a great assembly of monks and a great assembly of Bodhisattvas", indicates a sequence of progressing importance, that Bodhisattvas are superior to monks and thus are mentioned last.[39] Monks in the Perfection of Wisdom sūtras are generally understood to be Hīnayāna disciples of the Buddha, śrāvakas and pratyekabuddhas. Except for this rather veiled judgment, the *Heart Sūtra*, perhaps owing to its brevity, does not engage in the kind of explicit deprecation of the Hīnayāna disciples that occurs so often in the longer sūtras. For example, in the *Perfection of Wisdom in 25,000 Stanzas*, the Buddha says to Śāriputra:

> A glow worm, being a mere insect, does not think that its light could illuminate the Continent of Jambudvīpa, or shine over it. Just so, the śrāvakas and pratyekabuddhas do not think, not even one of them,

that they should, after winning full enlightenment, lead all beings to nirvāṇa. But the sun, when it has risen, sheds its light over the whole of Jambudvīpa. Just so a Bodhisattva, after he has accomplished the practices that end in full enlightenment, leads countless beings to nirvāṇa.[40]

The Unique Prologue

The fifth section of the sūtra, the marvelous doctrine, begins with the unique prologue, that part of the prologue that is not found in other sūtras. It is:

At that time, the Transcendent Victor was absorbed in a samādhi on the enumerations of phenomena called "perception of the profound." Also at that time, the Bodhisattva, the Mahāsattva, the Superior Avalokiteśvara was contemplating the practice of the profound perfection of wisdom and saw that those five aggregates also are empty of inherent existence.

According to Vimalamitra, "at that time" refers to the moment when the roots of virtue of the members of the audience had ripened such that they were ready to hear the teaching.[41] Hundreds of samādhis are enumerated in the Mahāyāna sūtras, with samādhi being described as the state in which the mind is placed one-pointedly on a virtuous object.[42] The samādhi into which the Buddha enters at the opening of the *Heart Sūtra*, called "perception of the profound", receives considerable discussion from the commentators. According to Mahājana, the "profound" of the samādhi called "perception of the profound" is emptiness and is so called because it is difficult to understand; emptiness cannot be understood by Bodhisattvas who have recently entered the path.[43] It is not difficult to perceive the reflection of the sun or moon on the surface of a lake, but is difficult to perceive their reflections in space. In the same way, it is said that it is easy to perceive the conventional, but difficult to perceive the ultimate.[44] The term translated as "perception" (*avabhāsa*) has two senses here, meaning both perception or appearance and lustre, splendor, or light. If it is taken to mean "perception" or "appearance", it is the wisdom that understands something as profound as emptiness or the wisdom to which the profound appears. It also has the sense of light or illumination because the samādhi called profound light completely dispels the darkness of ignorance.[45] The enumerations of phenomena are the classical categories of Buddhist epistemology: the five aggregates (*skandha*), the twelve sources (*āyatana*), and the eighteen constituents (*dhātu*). These are discussed at length in Chapter 6. The word phenomenon (*dharma*) is derived from the root *dhṛ*, "to hold" or "to bear", and thus is defined as that which bears its own entity. Any object of knowledge is a phenomenon.

A Tibetan oral commentary places significance in the conjunction of the terms "perception of the profound" and "enumerations of phenomena", seeing in it an allusion to the omniscient consciousness of the Buddha capable of realizing directly and simultaneously all of the modes and varieties of phenomena, that is, both emptiness and the phenomena qualified by emptiness. All other beings are incapable of such simultaneous realization; if they directly realize emptiness, they cannot discern the phenomena qualified by emptiness; and if they perceive conventional truths, they cannot directly realize emptiness at that time. Only a Buddha, therefore, can remain directly aware of reality while acting in the world; he can perceive the profound emptiness while remaining in full awareness of all the enumerations of phenomena. That this ability is unique to a Buddha implies that when the sūtra says that Avalokiteśvara, a Bodhisattva, was viewing the aggregates and saw that they were empty, his vision was not direct, but inferential, because he was able to speak out of this vision, something that even a highly advanced Bodhisattva could not do in direct realization of emptiness.[46]

Because all the deeds of Buddhas and Bodhisattvas are for the sake of others, there must have been an altruistic purpose in the Buddha's entering into this samādhi. Vimalamitra explains that by entering samādhi, the Buddha caused the minds of everyone in the audience to ripen in such a way that the meaning of the samādhi was demonstrated to each of them.[47] According to Śrīmahājana, the Buddha only appeared to enter into samādhi; from the ultimate perspective, the Buddha constantly and uninterruptedly turns the wheel of dharma in ways that are appropriate.[48]

In commenting on the uncommon prologue, Praśāstrasena writes:

> "At that time" refers to being absorbed in samādhi at the time when the Transcendent Victor was staying in Rājagṛha. It might be asked in which samādhi he was absorbed when it says "samādhi." Therefore, it says "[perception] of the profound [in the] enumerations of phenomena." Regarding that, a phenomenon is that which bears its own specific and general characteristics (*lakṣaṇa*). The enumerations

> of those phenomena refer to the categories of phenomena, that is, the five aggregates, the constituents, and the sources. The profound means the emptiness of inherent existence (*svabhāva*) which is unproduced and unceased. When absorbed in meditative equipoise, the non-production and non-cessation of phenomena are realized. Therefore, the name of the samādhi is "perception of the profound [in the] enumerations of phenomena." "Perception" means realization. "Absorbed" is a word that means placing the mind continually and one-pointedly in samādhi.[49]

It is at the end of the prologue that the chief speaker of the sūtra is introduced, Avalokiteśvara. Avalokiteśvara is the most famous of the Mahāyāna Bodhisattvas and is said to be the embodiment of all of the compassion of all the Buddhas.[50] Despite his importance, his appearance in the Perfection of Wisdom sūtras is rare; the *Heart Sūtra* is the only major Perfection of Wisdom sūtra in which he appears. His name means "the capable one who looks down." Because he looks down on all sentient beings at all times and in all ways with great love and compassion, he is the one who looks down (*avalokita*). Because he has achieved the power to dispel the sufferings of sentient beings, he is the capable one (*īśvara*).

He is a Bodhisattva and a *mahāsattva*. This term, often used in concord with "Bodhisattva", means "one who has a great mind."[51] The *Prajñāpāramitāsañcayagāthā* says:

> Those who abide in the supreme Mahāyāna of the Conqueror
> [Have] great giving, great awareness, and great power.
> They wear the great armor and have tamed the deceiving demons.
> Therefore, they are called Mahāsattvas.[52]

Haribhadra explains the term in his *Abhisamayālaṃkārāloka:*

> He first achieves the greatness of mind seeking to become the supreme among all sentient beings, because he has set out with that aim in mind, and then he causes sentient beings who wish to achieve the supreme state to do so, through teaching them the doctrine and by other means. . . . A Bodhisattva having a great *sattva* or mind, is called a *mahāsattva*.[53]

Such a description seems to add little to prior descriptions of the Bodhisattva. Why then are both Bodhisattva and Mahāsattva used? Haribhadra has an answer:

> Bodhisattvas are those whose *sattva*, or intentions, are directed toward the fulfillment of their own welfare, namely, the enlightenment which is non-attachment to all phenomena. It may be argued that even śrāvakas can be so. Thus, the word *mahāsattva* is added. Those whose minds are directed towards the fulfillment of the great welfare of others are called Mahāsattvas. An objection might be raised that such a Mahāsattva can be found elsewhere, as in the case of a good non-Buddhist. Thus, the word *bodhisattva* is added.[54]

Praśāstrasena says that Avalokiteśvara is a Bodhisattva because of establishing himself in highest enlightenment and a Mahāsattva because of placing all sentient beings in the unlocated nirvāṇa.[55] According to Vimalamitra, the greatness of the Mahāsattva is due to the greatness of his perfection and his abiding on a great ground (*bhūmi*).[56] Śrīmahājana states that a Mahāsattva is a Bodhisattva who will not turn back on the path to Buddhahood.[57]

The word "Superior" (*ārya*), used here to describe Avalokiteśvara, ordinarily refers to a person who has directly realized selflessness and achieved the path of seeing on the Hīnayāna or Mahāyāna path, referring to how such vision places one above the level of common beings (*pṛthagjana*). In the *Heart Sūtra* commentaries, it is given a more exalted meaning: Avalokiteśvara is said to be a Superior because he has risen above and left behind the two obstructions. The commentators do not consider the implication that this would mean that Avalokiteśvara is a Buddha. According to the Tibetan oral tradition, Avalokiteśvara is a Bodhisattva of the tenth stage (*bhūmi*).[58]

Commenting on the last line of the prologue, "Also at that time, the Bodhisattva, the Mahāsattva, the Superior Avalokiteśvara was contemplating the practice of the profound perfection of wisdom and saw that these five aggregates also are empty of inherent existence," Praśāstrasena writes:

> "Also at that time" refers to the fact that at the very time at which the Transcendent Victor was absorbed on Vulture Peak, Avalokiteśvara was viewing the emptiness of inherent existence of the five aggregates. [In the term "Bodhisattva"], *bodhi* refers to the sphere of the mind, reality, the limit of the real. Because he exerts himself and strives to achieve that, he is a hero contemplating enlightenment [*bodhisattva*]. Because he has left the two obstructions aι a great distance, he is a Superior. Regarding "Avalokita," because he looks on all sentient beings with compassion in the manner of non-observation (*anupalambha*) from among the three types of compassion, he is one looking down [*avalokita*]. Because he has found the ability himself to dispel the sufferings of sentient beings, he is the capable one [Īśvara]. . .

> Wisdom [in "perfection of wisdom"] is of three types: there is the sword of wisdom that cuts the nets of the five aggregates, there is the thunderbolt of wisdom that smashes the aggregates of suffering, and there is the lamp of wisdom that dispels the darkness of ignorance. In brief, the non-conceptual wisdom that realizes the emptiness of all phenomena in all ways is called "wisdom." Because that wisdom takes one beyond, it is called "perfection" [literally, "gone beyond" (*pāramitā*)]. There are three types of perfection: mundane perfection, supramundane perfection, and supramundane ultimate perfection. The mundane perfection is the state of having abandoned the suffering of the three paths [of śrāvaka, pratyekabuddha, and Bodhisattva]. The supramundane perfection is the state of having abandoned the cycle of birth and death and attained the nirvāṇa that is one-sidedly peaceful. Regarding the supramundane ultimate perfection, because the three realms are like a dream, there is no wish even for nirvāṇa. Because sentient beings are like illusions, there is no hope even for the fruition of Buddhahood. Because all phenomena are naturally beyond sorrow, the unlocated nirvāṇa is attained. This is the ultimate perfection.
>
> To [answer the question of] what the perfection of wisdom is, it says, "practice of the profound." The profound is non-production and non-cessation. "Practice" refers to the meaning. Non-production and non-cessation is called the perfection of wisdom.
>
> "Viewing"[59] is to observe the meaning of non-production and non-cessation. Not only is the meaning of non-production and non-cessation observed, but the five aggregates, such as form, are also seen to be empty.
>
> Emptiness is of two types: the emptiness of unconditioned space and the emptiness that is the lack of subject and object, which is understood individually by a Superior's wisdom of the ultimate. He was viewing the emptiness that is lack of subject and object in the aggregates. There are three kinds of views: the views of common beings and heretics, the views of śrāvakas and pratyekabuddhas, and the views of Bodhisattvas and Tathāgatas. Common beings and heretics view the five aggregates as a living being, a self, and a person. Śrāvakas and pratyekabuddhas view the five aggregates as origins and sufferings [among the four truths]. Bodhisattvas and Tathāgatas view the five aggregates and see that they are empty of inherent existence.[60]

Praśāstrasena provides several important comments here that both illuminate the meaning of key terms and aid in identifying his doctrinal affiliations. He says that Avalokiteśvara looks on all sentient beings with compassion in the manner of non-observation (*anupalambha*) from among the three types of compassion. The three types of compassion are delineated by Candrakīrti in the first chapter of his *Madhyamakāvatārabhāṣya.* The first is the compassion observing sentient beings "who are powerless like a bucket travelling in a well" (*Madhyamakāvatāra*, I.3), bound by the rope of contaminated actions and afflictions, wandering in the great well of saṃsāra from the Peak of Cyclic Existence (*bhavāgra*) to the Most Tortuous Hell (*avīci*), moving naturally downward, moving upward only with great exertion. The second compassion is called compassion observing phenomena in which the Bodhisattva observes sentient beings subject to impermanence and momentary disintegration, and feels compassion for them. Compassion of the unobservable is the compassion for sentient beings that observes them to be qualified by emptiness; they are unobservable as truly existent. All three of these compassions are conjoined with the wish to attain perfectly the state of a Buddha, the friend of all transmigrators.[61] According to Praśāstrasena, Avalokiteśvara observes sentient beings with this third type of compassion.

Praśāstrasena also provides a threefold division of perfections of wisdom. The first is liberation from suffering and rebirth via the path of the śrāvaka, pratyekabuddha, or Bodhisattva. The second, which he calls a supramundane perfection, has a very different meaning from the perfection that Candrakīrti describes with the term. For Praśāstrasena, it is the perfection sought by the Hīnayāna. It is liberation from rebirth and the attainment of the nirvāṇa, which he disparagingly refers to as "one-sidedly peaceful." The best of all perfections is what he calls the ultimate supramundane perfection, which is the unlocated nirvāṇa of a Buddha, according to the Mahāyāna. Here, with the understanding of the emptiness of all phenomena of saṃsāra and nirvāṇa, there is attachment to neither, for both are like illusions. Understanding that all persons are also empty of inherent existence, the Buddha has no hope of achieving Buddhahood for the sake of sentient beings who are intrinsically real. Rather, abiding in neither the saṃsāra of befuddled sentient beings nor the one-sidedly peaceful nirvāṇa of the Hīnayāna, the Buddha abides in the unlocated nirvāṇa, fully active in the world for the welfare of others while in full cognition of reality, aware each instant that all phenomena are naturally empty, or as he says, naturally passed beyond sorrow.

In his description of emptiness, Praśāstrasena implies affinities with the Yogācāra school, which held that there is no external world, and hence emptiness is the lack of any ontological difference between subject and object. He says that emptiness is the lack of the five aggregates' being either subject or object. He thus implicitly denies the assertion of the other Buddhist schools that the form aggregate is an object and the consciousness aggregate is a subject.

Chapter 4

The Question and the Answer

Then, by the power of the Buddha, the venerable Śāriputra said this to the Bodhisattva, the Mahāsattva, the Superior Avalokiteśvara: "How should a son of good lineage train who wishes to practice the profound perfection of wisdom?"

The Bodhisattva, the Mahāsattva, the Superior Avalokiteśvara said this to the venerable Śāriputra: "Śāriputra, a son of good lineage or a daughter of good lineage who wishes to practice the profound perfection of wisdom should view [things] in this way: They should correctly view those five aggregates also as empty of inherent existence.

The actual sūtra, the marvelous doctrine, begins with the question of Śāriputra. Avalokiteśvara's answer comprises the body of the sūtra and that answer has a brief and extended version. The brief answer is given first.

Up until this point in the sūtra, Śākyamuni has been referred to with the term *bhagavan*. Here he is called "the Buddha." The verbal root *budh* from which Buddha is derived means both awaken and open, as does the bud of a flower. Candrakīrti says in his *Triśaraṇasaptati:*

> He is liberated from the paths of the three times.
> He has opened his awareness to objects of knowledge.
> He has destroyed the sleep of ignorance.
> Therefore, a Buddha is expansive, like a lotus.
>
> One who has cut through the sleep of ignorance
> And has seen the emergent perfect wisdom
> Is a Buddha,
> Like a person who has awakened from sleep.[1]

The Tibetan translation encompasses both senses of the root *budh*, rendering *buddha* as *sangs rgyas*, "awakened or purified-spread"; he has awakened from slumber of ignorance with his perfect knowledge and has purified his mind of the two obstructions and he has spread his awareness to all objects of knowledge.

Among the many ways of classifying the word of the Buddha, there is the threefold classification according to the primary cause of the statement. The first of these is words from the Buddha's mouth, that is, words spoken directly by the Buddha. The second is words that are spoken as a result of permission given by the Buddha. The words "Thus did I hear at one time," and the identification of the place and audience of a given sūtra would be included in this category. The third category is words that are the result of the Buddha's blessing. These blessings sometimes empower a Bodhisattva or śrāvaka to teach the doctrine or may cause the words of the doctrine to issue magically from musical sounds, from the sky, or from a pleasant breeze. Such blessings may be conveyed physically, as when the Buddha places his hands on the head of the prospective speaker; the blessings may be conveyed verbally; or they may be conveyed mentally, as when the Buddha enters a state of deep contemplation. This occurs in the *Heart Sūtra*.[2] When the sūtra says, "Then, by the power of the Buddha," it implies that both Śāriputra's question and Avalokiteśvara's answer occur as a result of the Buddha's empowerment.

Śāriputra and Maudgalyāyana are the best-known disciples of the Buddha, and are often portrayed flanking the Buddha in painting and statuary. Maudgalyāyana was the most adept of the disciples in magical power (*ṛddhi*); Śāriputra was unexcelled in wisdom, the master of the Abhidharma. His conversion is recounted in the *Vinaya*, the *Mahāvastu*, and the *Mahāprajñāpāramitāśāstra*.[3] He was the son of Tiṣya and the beautiful Śārī and thus is known sometimes as Upatiṣya but more often as Śāriputra, the son of Śārī, the most intelligent woman of Magadha. That Śāriputra inherited his mother's intellectual acumen is evident from the story of his conversion to the doctrine of the Buddha. Encountering the monk Aśvajit, one of the Buddha's five original disciples, Śāriputra was impressed by his composed countenance and asked him whether he was a master or a disciple. Upon learning that he was a disciple, he asked Aśvajit what his master's teaching was. Aśvajit demurred, saying that he was of little learning and could provide only a simple summary. Aśvajit then delivered one of the most famous lines in Buddhist philosophy, "The Tathāgata has proclaimed the causes of those phenomena that arise from causes and he also has proclaimed their cessation. So has spoken the great renunciate." (*ye dharmā hetuprabhāvā hetun teṣāṃ tathāgato āha teṣāṃ ca yo nirodho evaṃvādī mahāśramaṇaḥ*). (This statement in Sanskrit later became used as a formula of blessing and in fact appears as such at the end of Śrīmahājana's *Heart Sūtra* commentary.[4]) Upon merely hearing these words, Śāriputra became a streamwinner (*srotāpanna*), gave up false views, doubt, and perplexity and asked, "Where is the master staying?"

Hence, his appearance in the Mahāyāna sūtras carries with it an intentional irony. He is a common interlocutor of the Buddha in the sūtras, asking the Buddha to expound the sublime Mahāyāna doctrine. Sometimes he is portrayed as a dignified arhat. Elsewhere, as in the *Vimalakīrtinirdeśa*, he is portrayed as the fool. In either case, the point made by the author of the sūtra is not difficult to grasp: the wisest of the Buddha's Hīnayāna disciples must have the sublime teachings of the Mahāyāna explained to him, sometimes repeatedly. Therefore, the Mahāyāna is more profound than anything contained in the Hīnayāna canon; the Hīnayāna arhat has more to learn. Śāriputra is the master of the Abhidharma, which Vasubandhu defines as stainless wisdom.[5] It would seem, then, that Śāriputra has wisdom but lacks the perfection of wisdom. That he will eventually win the perfection of wisdom and the full path is intimated in the third chapter of the *Lotus Sūtra*, where the Buddha prophesies that in the future Śāriputra will become the Buddha Padmaprabha.

Śāriputra is called *āyuṣmant*, roughly rendered here as "venerable." The term literally means "endowed with life," and was a common form of polite address among Buddhist monks. "Venerable" is a somewhat misleading translation because the term was used by elder monks to address their juniors. This causes bsTan-dar-lha-ram-pa to observe that such an understanding of the term is not suitable in this context because it would imply that Śāriputra was junior in training to the compiler of the sūtra, presumably Ānanda. Therefore, he etymologizes the term in accordance with its literal meaning of "endowed with life," saying that it means that Śāriputra was endowed with a life in which the afflictions had been abandoned and which is free from birth and death.[6]

Without being empowered by the Buddha, Śāriputra would not ordinarily have been able to fully comprehend the unfathomable activities of sentient beings; he asks his question upon being blessed to understand the minds of others. It is only appropriate, however, that he ask the question, not that he provide the answer. Because he is a śrāvaka, and hence of lesser awareness, the world does not believe that Śāriputra is liberated into the understanding of the profound. Hence, the Buddha empowered him only to ask the seminal question. Knowing that Avalokiteśvara is endowed with great intelligence and great compassion, the world believes that he is capable of teaching the perfection of wisdom, the mother of the Conquerors, in accordance with the capacities of those of lesser wisdom, such as Śāriputra. Therefore, it is Avalokiteśvara to whom the question is directed.[7]

Śāriputra asks how a son of good lineage should practice the perfection of wisdom. The blessing of the Buddha causes him to recall sentient beings of the three realms and fills him with boundless courage, inspiring him to ask Avalokiteśvara his question for the sake of those having some interest in the profound thought of the Buddhas of the three times.[8] The good lineage is not that of a biological family, but of the family of the Tathāgatas; a son or daughter of good lineage is a Bodhisattva, a child of the Conqueror (*jinaputra*) born from the Mahāyāna scriptures.[9] Vajrapāṇi comments that although Avalokiteśvara speaks in his answer of male and female, the nature of the mind is the same, the difference is merely apparent, as in a dream.[10] Children of good lineage are those who have the Mahāyāna lineage. In this lineage, there are those who are not interested in the profound meaning and who are frightened by it. There are also those who have interest in and seek the perfection of wisdom, who simply by hearing the profound doctrine experience happiness and joy.[11] Śrīmahājana comments that a son or daughter of good lineage is a Bodhisattva on the first of the five Mahāyāna paths, the path of accumulation (*saṃbhāra-mārga*).[12] The Mahāyāna lineage to which the son and daughter belong has great power, protecting them from suffering through their progressive cultivation of such practices as the mindful establishments (*smṛtyupa-sthāna*) and providing them refuge through their allegiance to the Mahāyāna, the cause of abandoning suffering. The lineage also endows them with the aspiration for nirvāṇa because they create the aspiration to achieve the enlightenment that has the nature of wisdom and compassion, with compassion being their practice of merit (the first five perfections of giving, ethics, patience, effort, and concentration) and wisdom being their cultivation of the wisdoms that arise from hearing, thinking, and meditation.[13]

The term "practice" (*caryā*) encompasses many activities. Śrīmahājana cites Maitreya's *Madhyāntavibhāga* (V. 9), where ten ways to practice the dharma are enumerated: writing, making offerings, giving gifts, listening, reading, studying, explaining, reciting, contemplating, and meditating.[14] He notes that in the context of the sūtra, "practice" refers to the accumulation of the collections of merit and wisdom.[15]

In glossing the term "perfection of wisdom" in this context, Praśāstrasena provides yet another division of wisdom, this time into the wisdom knowing the conventional and the wisdom knowing the ultimate. The wisdom of the conventional is the understanding that all pnenomena are like illusions, mirages, and dreams. The wisdom of the ultimate is the wisdom that all phenomena are inexpressible and inconceivable, like the surface of space. It is the wisdom of the ultimate that is the perfection of wisdom.[16] To ask how to practice the perfection of wisdom is to inquire how one should enter into the perfection of wisdom through hearing, contemplation, meditation.[17]

Avalokiteśvara answers that a son or daughter of good lineage who wishes to practice the profound perfection of wisdom should view the five aggregates to be empty of inherent existence. In explaining the key phrase "emptiness of inherent existence," Praśāstrasena says:

> There are five types of emptiness: the emptiness of what did not exist before, the emptiness of what does not exist upon being destroyed, the emptiness of the utterly non-existent, the emptiness of one not existing in the other, and the emptiness of entityness.[18] Regarding that, the lack of yogurt in milk is the emptiness of what did not exist before, the lack of milk in yogurt is the emptiness of what does not exist upon being destroyed, the lack of horns on a rabbit's head is the emptiness of the utterly non-existent, the emptiness of an ox in a horse is the emptiness of one not existing in the other, and the non-inherent existence of all phenomena is the emptiness of entityness. Since among the five types of emptiness, the five aggregates are empty in the sense of being without entityness, they should be analyzed as empty.[19]

Thus, according to Praśāstrasena, this emptiness of entityness is what Avalokiteśvara means when he says that the five aggregates are empty of inherent existence (*svabhāvaśūnya*). Praśāstrasena does not provide an example of this fifth and most difficult kind of emptiness. bsTan-dar-lha-ram-ba does, saying that the emptiness of entityness is like the non-existence of a human in a cairn that is mistaken from a distance to be a human.[20]

The five kinds of emptiness presented by Praśāstrasena do not appear to be mutually exclusive. It is clear from the examples of milk and yogurt that the first two, the emptiness of what did not exist before and the emptiness of what does not exist upon being destroyed, are simply cases of the absence of manifest effect at the time of the cause and the absence of the manifest cause at the time of the effect. Hence, the first two kinds of emptiness deal with the relationship between cause and effect. The next, the emptiness of the utterly non-existent is illustrated by the absence of horns on a rabbit's head. The horns of a rabbit is one of the most famous examples in Buddhist philosophy of something that does not exist, along with the diadem of a frog, a cloak of tortoise hairs, the son of a barren woman, and a flower in the sky. The example is one of an existent attribute that never occurs as the quality of a given object. It is called the utterly non-existent perhaps because the particular conjunction of the object and the attribute never occurs, nor would it ever be considered that it could occur. bsTan-dar-lha ram-pa provides a different example of the emptiness of the utterly non-existent, the absence of a pot in a place where there is no bulbous container for water.[21] This is an example not of object and attribute but of definiendum and definition; where there is no water, there is no H_2O. Although he uses a different example, the emptiness of the utterly non-existent is also a case of the absence of an object that would never be mistakenly considered present. The emptiness of one not existing in the other is illustrated by the absence of a horse in an ox. This is a case of two existent and different objects that are mutually exclusive; an ox cannot be a horse, nor a horse an ox. The first four kinds of emptiness are the emptiness or absence of something that exists but is absent at a particular time or in a particular place. The emptiness of entityness is different; it is the emptiness of something that does not exist at all, in that an ultimately existent entity has not, does not, and will not exist anywhere or at any time. The fifth kind of emptiness also differs from the other four in that it possesses a deceptive quality; it appears to be present but is not. Milk does not appear to be present in yogurt or yogurt in milk, a rabbit does not appear to have horns, and a horse is rarely mistaken for an ox. The emptiness of entityness is illustrated by bsTan-dar-lha-ram-pa with the example of a cairn and a human being.[22] Both exist and are mutually exclusive, but unlike the horse and the ox, a cairn when viewed from a distance can easily be mistaken for a human, whereas upon closer inspection, there is nothing whatsoever that is human about a pile of stones. A human is utterly absent there. A rope mistaken for a snake would seem to be another example of the emptiness of entityness.

In his commentary to Āryadeva's *Catuḥśataka* (*Four Hundred*), Candrakīrti says that inherent existence means not relying on another.[23] That is, persons and phenomena are ignorantly conceived to exist in and of themselves, to exist autonomously, to exist objectively, to exist in their own right, to exist by way of their own character, without depending on causes and conditions, without depending on their parts, without depending on designation by terms and thoughts. Persons and phenomena are ignorantly conceived to be endowed with some inherent existence, some entityness, some substance, some thingness, some intrinsic nature, some own-being discoverable under analysis. To be empty of inherent existence is to utterly lack such hypostatized qualities, superimposed onto persons and phenomena by ignorance. Hence, although Praśāstrasena says that it is the fifth kind of emptiness, the emptiness of entityness that is the referent of Avalokiteśvara's statement, there are also affinities between the emptiness of the utterly non-existent and the emptiness of inherent existence. Inherent existence is an attribute that never qualifies persons or phenomena. In this sense, it is like the horns of a rabbit.

If things do not exist in that way, how do they exist? They are merely imputed by thought. The *Upālipariprcchā Sūtra* says:

> These alluring blossoming flowers of many colors
> And these delightful palaces of gleeming gold have no maker here.
> They are posited by the power of thought;
> The world is imputed by the power of thought.[24]

And Nāgārjuna, the greatest philosopher of the Perfection of Wisdom, said in his *Yuktiṣaṣṭikā* (37):

> The Buddhas have said
> That the world is conditioned by ignorance.
> Therefore, how is it infeasible
> That this world is a conception?[25]

In making a similar point, Candrakīrti invokes the example of the rope-snake. He says in his commentary to Āryadeva's *Catuḥśataka:*

> It is certain that those things whose very existence is only due to thought and which do not exist without thought are not established by way of their own entity, like a snake that is imagined in a rope.[26]

A coiled rope in a dark corner may appear to be a snake, and based on that misperception, a person may become frightened and agitated and pursue a variety of strategies to either evict or destroy the snake. Despite what a person may believe, at that very moment there is nothing whatsoever about the rope that is a snake; the snake is merely imagined. With proper illumination of the corner, it is easy to discern that there is no snake. In the same way, inherent existence or self is falsely imputed to the five aggregates, for example, and based on that misperception a variety of activities is engaged in, motivated by desire and hatred, to nurture and protect that non-existent self. There is no "I" that is not merely imputed to the aggregates by thought.[27]

Thus, all phenomena are empty of inherent existence and exist only due to thought. This is the meaning of the perfection of wisdom. What is the relationship, however, between this emptiness of inherent existence and the persons and phenomena that are merely imputed by the power of thought? That question points to the heart of Avalokiteśvara's answer.

Chapter 5

Form is Emptiness; Emptiness is Form

Form is emptiness; emptiness is form. Emptiness is not other than form; form is not other than emptiness. In the same way, feeling, discrimination, compositional factors, and consciousnesses are empty. Śāriputra, in that way all phenomena are empty, without characteristic, unproduced, unceased, stainless, not stainless, undiminished, unfilled.

This statement is the heart of the *Heart Sūtra*, the most famous and the most problematic section of the text. Traditional Tibetan commentators divide it into two sections. "Form is emptiness; emptiness is form. Emptiness is not other than form; form is not other than emptiness," is known as the fourfold profundity. The remainder of the statement, delineating eight characteristics of phenomena (including "without characteristic"), is known as the eightfold profundity.

The Fourfold Profundity

Form is the first of the five aggregates, the most basic of the many Buddhist dissections of the psychophysical continuum called the person. According to the Abhidharma systems, form encompasses visible form, including all color and shape, as well as sound, odor, taste, and tangible objects. The category of form also includes the five sense powers (*indriya*), the subtle matter that provides the physical capacity for sight, hearing, smell, taste, and touch. According to Praśāstrasena, form is mentioned first because it is the most easily recognizable of the five aggregates and because, as the only physical aggregate, it provides the material support for the other four.[1] Form is like a vessel; the other four aggregates are like the water contained in that vessel. When the vessel is destroyed, the water is easily dispersed. In the same way, when it is understood that form is empty, it is easy to understand that the other four aggregates are also empty.

Like all phenomena, form is empty of inherent existence. This emptiness is not a quality that form gains in the course of its existence, but is rather present from the moment of its creation; that which appears as form is devoid of any intrinsic entity or nature of form. Thus, form is empty. The sūtra says, however, that form is emptiness. There is a critical difference between form being empty and form being emptiness; this is explored below. Emptiness, which according to the Perfection of Wisdom sūtras is the final nature of reality, does not exist apart from the phenomena that it qualifies and is not to be sought as something separate. Furthermore, although emptiness is the mode of being of form, emptiness does not negate the conventional appearance of form. Thus, emptiness is form. Emptiness is, in this sense, dependent upon the form that it qualifies.

Having considered the meaning of the passage in this general way, it is useful to consider the explanations provided by the Indian commentators in order to gain some sense of the wealth of meaning with which this statement was invested in Pāla India.

The most straightforward commentary is provided by Jñānamitra. He writes:

> "Form" is a word that conventionally designates the form that is seen and conceived by those with mistaken minds who have not understood the nature of emptiness. Regarding "emptiness", because emptiness is the nature of form, [form] is without characteristic and unobservable in the past and is without characteristic and unobservable in the present and the future. Therefore, since it does not abide anywhere or in anything, [the sūtra] says "emptiness". "Emptiness is form" conventionally designates with words that even emptiness [has] an unobservable nature [like] form. Because it does not abide apart from that [form], emptiness is form. Regarding "Emptiness is not other than form, form is not other than emptiness," that very thing which is form is the inexpressible emptiness; [when] form is abandoned, emptiness is not to be found. Therefore, it is said that emptiness is not other than form. That very thing which is the inexpressible emptiness does not exist and is not found apart from that which is conventionally designated with the word "form." Therefore, it is said that form is not other than emptiness.[2]

Pointing out that all these words are merely conventional designations, Jñānamitra adopts an ultimate perspective to describe the final nature of form. It is without any inherently existent characteristics and thus is not observable as inherently existent. It is empty of such qualities. Thus, Jñānamitra seems actually to say that form is empty rather than that form is emptiness. This becomes clear from his gloss of "Emptiness is form," where he temporarily avoids a radical identification of the two, preferring to interpret the line to say that emptiness does not abide separate from form; where there is form, there is emptiness. However, in reading "Emptiness is not other than form, form is not other than emptiness", he identifies the two, saying that form itself is the inexpressible emptiness. But emptiness is not identical with form; again, it simply does not exist separate from it. Jñānamitra seems to say, then, that form is emptiness in that it shares the quality of ultimate unfindability that is emptiness. Emptiness, however, is form not because it shares the qualities of form, such as color, shape, mass, and dimension, but because it, in a sense, is coextensive with form and is not to be discovered apart from it.

Śrīmahājana says:

> "Form is emptiness; emptiness is form" is the brief teaching. "Emptiness is not other than form; form is not other than emptiness" is the extensive explanation. Regarding that, some assert that emptiness is the destruction of form. The answer to that is that form is emptiness.[3] It is said that emptiness is not other than form because dependent natures (*paratantrasvabhāva*), which are wrongly imagined [to be independent], are empty of the nature of duality that is imputed [by ignorance]. The nature of form is the emptiness of duality in the manner of an affirming negative (*paryudāsapratiṣedha*). Some say that form and so forth turn into the nature of the dharmadhātu, like an illusion. In response to that it is said that only emptiness is form. "Form is not other than emptiness" [means] that dependent forms are only emptiness, that is, they have the nature of the dharmadhātu. . . . [4]

Śrīmahājana begins by making the point that emptiness is not the destruction of form, a point that he will return to. Form exists, but form is emptiness. Emptiness is not the elimination of form but rather the lack of a falsely imagined intrinsic nature in form.

He describes the meaning of "Emptiness is not other than form" in terms of the Yogācāra doctrine of the three natures (*trisvabhāva*). Imaginary natures (*parikalpitasvabhāva*) are of two types, the real and the unreal. The real include permanent phenomena, such as space. The more important category, unreal imaginaries, comprise the non-existent, such as a self of persons and external objects—objects external to the consciousness perceiving them. Dependent natures (*paratantra-svabhāva*) include all impermanent phenomena, those things that are dependent on causes and conditions. The most important of these causes in the Yogācāra school are the seeds (*bīja*) that fructify to simultaneously create consciousnesses and their objects. The third of the three natures is the consummate (*parinișpanna*), the ultimate truth of the Yogācāra school. This is the emptiness of a difference of entity of subject and object, the negation of the existence of external objects. All phenomena are qualified by this emptiness.[5] Thus, Śrīmahājana says that all dependent natures are empty of the duality of subject and object; that is, the final nature of all existence is the consummate nature, which is the emptiness of duality. This, he says, is the meaning of "Emptiness is not other than form."

This nature of form is an affirming negative (*paryudāsapratiședha*). Two types of negation are set forth in the canons of Buddhist logic, the affirming negative and the non-affirming negative (*prasajya-pratiședha*).[6] A negative is a phenomenon that is understood upon the explicit elimination of something else. An affirming negative is one which implies the existence of some other phenomenon in the place of that which is eliminated. A famous example of an affirming negative is that expressed by the statement, "The fat Devadatta does not eat during the day," implying, of course, that his fasting ceases at sunset. A non-affirming negative eliminates without implying the existence of anything in the place of that which was eliminated. An example is the selflessness of persons (*pudgalanairātmya*). Śrīmahājana seems to be saying here that the emptiness of duality of subject and object is an affirming negative, negating the existence of form as an object external to consciousness but implying the existence of form as of the nature of emptiness in its place; this is the meaning of "Form is emptiness." He sees form being negated on the one hand and affirmed on the other, arguing against those who would say that the conventional existence of form is somehow lost in emptiness, dissolving into the dharmadhātu. The statement, "emptiness is form," upholds the conventional nature of form. Śrīmahājana continues:

> It might be said that if blue and so forth had a nature of not losing their entity and not being encompassed in the dharmadhātu, then blue and so forth and that [dharmadhātu] would be in direct and mutual contradiction, like the mottle of a butterfly. In that case, even the dharmadhātu would be damaged by the contradiction of singularity and plurality and would thereby become deceptive (*saṃvṛti*). Blue and so forth, however, do not attain this status. Thus, it is said that form is not other than emptiness. "Other" means that blue and so forth would be endowed with a mode of existence whose entity was not encompassed by the luminous and clear nature of the mind. . . .[7]

Form is emptiness in the sense that the lack of duality of subject and object is the final nature of form, and emptiness is form in the sense that the appearance of form is not negated by emptiness, that form is not lost in emptiness. Śrīmahājana considers the relationship of form and emptiness further, raising the question of whether form and emptiness would be in contradiction if form (in his example, blue) maintained some distinct character without being superceded by the dharmadhātu. Would not blue be one thing and reality another, like the different colors on the wings of a butterfly? Each phenomenon would have its own entity and reality would consequently be multiple. Śrīmahājana concludes that this is not the case because the sūtra says that form is not other than emptiness. Form can be discrete without being endowed with an entity contradictory to emptiness. From a Yogācāra perspective, for form to be other than emptiness, it would have to be of an entity other than that of consciousness, whose nature is one of clear light. Because form is of the nature of consciousness, it is endowed with that quality and is thus not ultimately other than emptiness. He continues:

> Therefore, this directly indicates the character of emptiness of being free from superimposition (*āropa*) and derogation (*apavāda*). The superimposition of existence onto form and the superimposition that emptiness has the nature of negating that [form], which is a misconception of objects, are eliminated by "Form is emptiness . . . Emptiness is not other than form." The derogation of the existence of the ultimate [occurs] by asserting that the dharmadhātu, like form, is a conventionality. Derogation through asserting non-existence, that is, that because its entity is not a conventional entity, the final nature does not exist, entails the superimposition of conceiving form to be endowed with a mode of being [leading to the position] that it is correct [to hold] that the dharmadhātu is not the nature of form. This is dispelled by "Only emptiness is form and form is not other than emptiness."[8]

Emptiness is free from the extreme of superimposition of false qualities onto it and the extreme of the derogation of it as being nothingness. The statements, "Form is emptiness. Emptiness is not other than form," eliminate the superimposition of some independent existence onto form. Those statements also dispel the misconception that emptiness is the utter negation of objects of consciousness. "Emptiness is form. Form is not other than emptiness." dispel the derogation of the ultimate that occurs when it is held that emptiness, the dharmadhātu, is a mere conventionality or when it is held that reality does not exist at all. Both of these denigrations of reality entail a consequent hypostatization of form as having its own mode of being apart from emptiness.

Praśāstrasena provides a more detailed commentary on the lines:

> In the statement, "Form is emptiness," "form" refers to earth, water, fire, and wind. "Emptiness" is the ultimate, the dharmadhātu. Due to the character of emptiness, those forms are emptiness. The character of emptiness is non-dual in the sense of being beyond enumeration and enumerator and is the state of having abandoned I and mine. It is free from object and subject. Therefore, it is the character of the non-dual reality. Phenomena are not the composite of many types of emptiness. Therefore, even the four—earth, water, fire, and wind—are without characteristic, without entity, without self, without [the Sāṃkhya] principal (*pradhāna*).
>
> It is not the case that things become emptiness when they are smashed to pieces; they are naturally empty. Therefore, "Form is emptiness." That very thing which is the natural emptiness of form is the ultimate emptiness itself; the ultimate emptiness does not exist apart from the natural emptiness of form. Therefore, "emptiness is form." That is, the words say that the ultimate emptiness is itself form's nature of emptiness.
>
> What is the evidence that the emptiness of form is the ultimate emptiness? The *Akṣayamatinirdeśa Sūtra* says:
>
>> Bodhisattvas, the dharmadhātu [which is the object] of the wisdom that enters the dharmadhātu is the elements—earth, water, fire, and wind. The dharmadhātu, however, is not the character of hardness, moisture, heat, and motility. The dharmadhātu and all phenomena are similar. Why? Because they are similar in emptiness.
>
> Thus, it should be known that the emptiness of form is the ultimate emptiness. [This is] the twofold emptiness of form.[9]

Praśāstrasena's reading of "Form is emptiness; emptiness is form," considers not so much the relationship of the conventional and the ultimate as it does the relationship between the final nature of form and the final nature of reality. Form is emptiness because emptiness is its final nature. Although there are a variety of forms, they are all qualified by the same emptiness. And that emptiness, which he calls "the natural emptiness of form" is identical with the emptiness that is the final nature of reality, the dharmadhātu, the "ultimate emptiness." That ultimate emptiness is not to be found apart from the emptiness of form; indeed, they are identical. Therefore, "emptiness is form," which to Praśāstrasena seems to mean "[the ultimate] emptiness is [the emptiness of] form."

Having discussed the identity of the natural emptiness of form and the ultimate emptiness, Praśāstrasena goes on to discuss a threefold division of form and its relation to emptiness.

> The three aspects of form are imaginary form (*parikalpitam rūpam*), designated form (*vikalpitam rūpam*), and the form of reality (*dharmatā rūpam*). The imputation of the characteristic of hardness to earth, etc. by childish common beings is imaginary form. The form that is the object engaged by a correct consciousness is designated form. The characteristic of reality free from imaginary form and designated form is the form of reality. Since the form of reality lacks imaginary form and designated form, it is said that form is empty. To those who wonder whether the reality of form—emptiness—is something that exists apart from imaginary form and designated form, it is said that emptiness is form, meaning that the form of reality—emptiness—has the same character as imaginary form and designated form.[10]

The *locus classicus* for the three types of form enumerated here is the "Questions of Maitreya" chapter of the *Pañcaviṃśatisāhasrikā-prajñāpāramitāsūtra.*[11] The sūtra says, "Maitreya, view imaginary form (*parikalpitam rūpam*) as without substantial existence (*adravyam*). View designated form (*vikalpitam rūpam*) as substantially existent because thought substantially exists, not because it arises independently. View the form of reality (*dharmatā rūpam*) as neither without substantial existence or substantially existent; [view it as] distinguished by [being] the ultimate."[12] The sūtra later provides a fuller description of each of the three. Regarding imaginary form, it says:

> Maitreya, this complete imagination of an entityness of form through [the use of the] name, discrimination, designation, or convention "form" for this or that conditioned thing, from "This is an imaginary form" to "This is an imaginary Buddha" [is imaginary form].[13]

Imaginary form is, then, the inherently existent form mistakenly conceived by ignorance and imputed onto phenomena throught the use of names, designations, and so forth. It does not exist. Regarding designated form, the sūtra says:

> Conditioned things are expressed through designations that abide in a reality that is merely designated. Designated form is that which is [expressed by] the name, discrimination, designation, or convention, from "this is form," "this is feeling," this is discrimination," "this is compositional factors," "this is consciousness," to "these are the qualities of the Buddha."[14]

That the very use of terminology and designation is not being prohibited is evident here, where designated forms are identified as all conventional phenomena. Unlike imaginary forms, designated forms exist, but only through the power of designation by terms and thoughts. They are conventional truths, existent and valid, but empty. Their emptiness is the form of reality. The sūtra says:

> [The reality of form] is the permanent and eternal sole entitynessless, the selflessness of phenomena, the thusness, and the limit of reality, [that is, the emptiness] of imaginary form in designated form, from "this is the reality of form" to "this is the reality of the qualities of the Buddha."[15]

The form of reality is emptiness, designated form's lack of the falsely imagined inherent existence of imaginary form. Thus, Praśāstrasena says that common worldly beings ignorantly impute some intrinsic quality of hardness to the earth element, some intrinsic wetness to the water element, and so forth. This non-existent nature is the thoroughly imagined form. Designated form is the conventionally existent form observed by correct consciousnesses, and the form of reality is emptiness, free from both of the other kinds of form. In this context, "form is emptiness" can be taken to mean that the form of reality, which is emptiness, is empty of thoroughly imagined form and designated form. "Emptiness is form" means that the form of reality has the same final nature as the other kinds of form; they are all empty.

Thus far, then, Praśāstrasena has adopted a rather conservative stance in interpreting the lines of the *Heart Sūtra*, saying little more than that form is empty of inherent existence and emptiness, whether it is called the ultimate or the form of reality, has the same character as the emptiness of more ordinary forms. He continues:

> That very thing which is form is emptiness. Emptiness is also form. Regarding the statement that emptiness does not exist apart from form, the emptiness that is the characteristic of form and the ultimate emptiness are not different but one. Therefore, it says that emptiness does not exist apart from form. Why are they not different? Because there is no difference in the character of emptiness, which is the nature of having abandoned augmentation, diminishment, separation, and the two extremes. Saying that that which is form is emptiness is a way of saying that that which is the characteristic of form is also the characteristic of emptiness. Saying that that which is emptiness is form is a way of saying that that which is the characteristic of emptiness is also the characteristic of form.

Therefore, this is taught: Sentient beings, debased and childish, cycle in the five evil paths in the beginningless cycle of birth and death. Through acquaintance with the five aggregates and familiarity with the eighteen elements, they become attached and attracted to them and conceive of them to be real and solid. If [they think] that, because the Tathāgata teaches [that forms are] naturally empty, the characteristic of form is destroyed in emptiness, they believe that the antidote, emptiness, exists apart. [Consequently] they are attached to the nirvāṇa of a śrāvaka, who is biased toward peace. Thus, "that which is form is emptiness" is set forth as an antidote that prevents falling into the extreme of saṃsāra through being attached to form. "That which is emptiness is form" is set forth as an antidote to falling into the extreme of nirvāṇa for śrāvakas who enter into the selflessness of persons and create signs of emptiness, [thinking] that form is destroyed in emptiness.

Form and emptiness are to be abandoned because they do not exist. Regarding that, when emptiness is taught in order that [sentient beings] abandon the conception that form has signs [of inherent existence], they come to think that emptiness has signs. Signs are the observation of signs [of inherent existence] with regard to anything. Therefore, because it obstructs the realization of reality, the conception that emptiness is real is a sign. Hence, both form and emptiness are to be abandoned. For example, a person with poor vision was travelling. Along the right side of the path were thorns and ditches. Along the left side of the path were ravines and precipices. If a person with faultless vision had said, "There are thorns and ditches [on the right]," the person would have fallen into the ravines and off the precipices. If he had said, "There are ravines and precipices [on the left]," the person would have fallen into thorns and ditches. However, [a person with faultless vision] indicated that the middle path was pleasant and without the slightest obstacle. [The person with poor vision] arrived at his home. In accordance with that example, the person with poor vision is [both] the common being (*pṛthagjana*) impeded by the afflictive obstructions (*kleśāvaraṇa*) and the śrāvaka obstructed by the obstructions to omniscience (*jñeyāvaraṇa*). The thorns and ditches are attachment to the signs of persons, forms, and so forth, that is, falling to the extreme of saṃsāra. The ravines and precipices are attachment to the nirvāṇa of the śrāvakas, that is, falling to the extreme of emptiness. The person with vision is the Tathāgata. Because he sees with the clear eyes of wisdom that form is naturally empty, he does not abandon saṃsāra, because it is like an illusion. Because [he sees that] the three realms are like a dream, he does not even seek the qualities of nirvāṇa. Because he enters the middle path with signlessness (*animitta*), wishlessness (*apraṇihita*), and emptiness (*śūnyatā*), he arrives at the abode of the nonabiding nirvāṇa (*apratiṣṭhitanirvāṇa*).

> Therefore, since he taught that apprehending signs is a precipice and a fault, signs are not to be held regarding existence or non-existence.[16]

Here Praśāstrasena explores the soteriological purport of "Form is emptiness; emptiness is form." To discourage sentient beings from becoming attached to form and consequently indulging in activities that will cause them to continue wandering in the realms of gods, humans, animals, hungry ghosts, and hell-beings, the Buddha taught that form is emptiness. Even this statement, however, can be taken to an extreme, as evidenced by the Hīnayāna śrāvakas, who believe that emptiness destroys form and who become attached to emptiness, endowing it with signs of inherent existence. The belief that emptiness is ultimately real is as detrimental as the belief that form is ultimately real because, whereas the latter leads to the extreme of saṃsāra, the former leads to the extreme of nirvāṇa, the static, solitary peace of the Hīnayāna; there are dangers on both sides of the road home. Hence, to counter the misconception that emptiness is something autonomous and other, the Buddha teaches, "Emptiness is form." The Buddha neither abandons saṃsāra nor covets nirvāṇa, knowing both to be like a dream, equally empty. He abides in neither the cycle of rebirth or the nirvāṇa of the Hīnayāna, but in the unlocated (literally "non-abiding") nirvāṇa that is the *summum bonum* of the Mahāyāna.

Praśāstrasena concludes with a brief discussion of the emptiness of the other four aggregates. He begins by noting that form is the only aggregate that is physical. The physical provides a basis for the mental, such that if the basis is destroyed, that which it supports is also dissipated. Therefore, the sūtra focuses first on form, the support, before turning to the remaining four aggregates, the supported. The second of the five aggregates, feeling (*vedanā*) is defined by Asaṅga as, "that which has the character of experience, that is, the entity of experience that experiences individually the fruitions that are the effects of virtuous and non-virtuous actions."[17] Feelings are of three types: pleasurable, painful, and neutral, and may occur either with one of the five sense consciousnesses or with the mental consciousness. The third aggregate, discrimination (*saṃjñā*), is the mental factor that apprehends the uncommon signs of an object, allowing consciousness to distinguish one object from another. Discrimination accompanies both the sense consciousnesses and the mental consciousness. Feeling and discrimination are mental factors but are separated from the other mental factors, which are grouped under compositional factors, because they are roots of disputation in that discrimination causes attachment to opinions and feeling causes attachment to pleasure, and because they are causes of rebirth.[18] It is said that mental factors (*caitta*) are treated in three of the five aggregates because it is the unanalyzed mass of mental factors, many of which would be considered emotions, that appear to be the self. In order to break down this conception, special attention is devoted to the analysis of mental factors.[19] The fourth category, compositional factors (*saṃskāra*), comprises those factors associated with the person that do not fall into any of the other four headings. These include forty-eight mental factors as well as factors that are neither form nor consciousness, numbered as either fifteen or twenty-four. This latter group of non-associated factors (*viprayuktasaṃskāra*) includes such things as time, area, the life faculty, and the person. The final aggregate, that of consciousness (*vijñāna*), is composed of the six main consciousnesses: the eye consciousness, ear consciousness, nose consciousness, tongue consciousness, body consciousness, and mental consciousness. The five sense consciousnesses are necessarily non-conceptual (*nirvikālpaka*) whereas the mental consciousness may be either non-conceptual, as in the case of yogic direct perception (*yogī-pratyakṣa*), or conceptual, as in the case of thought (*kalpanā*). These are the four aggregates, all of which are non-physical, that the sūtra deals with, having proclaimed that "Form is emptiness; emptiness is form. Emptiness is not other than form; form is not other than emptiness."

> [The sūtra] says, "In the same way, feeling, discrimination, compositional factors, and consciousness are empty." Earlier, it said that [Avalokiteśvara] saw that the five aggregates are empty. The emptiness of form was stated, it was taught that form is emptiness, and it was taught that emptiness and form are not different. . . .
>
> Those phenomena [the remaining four aggregates] are the continuum of the mind. The mind has the character of the emptiness of the formless; it is based on the form aggregate upon the maturation of predispositions (*vāsanā*). For example, it is similar to an empty vessel; the vessel is a support. If the vessel is destroyed, there is no place for the supported; it is not different from the great voidness [of space]. Like that, by analyzing the form aggregate and [finding it to be] empty, there is no place for the mental aggregates; they are not different from the ultimate, the sphere of reality.
>
> What is the evidence that the five aggregates are empty of inherent existence? The *Akṣayamatinirdeśa Sūtra* says:
>
> > The form aggregate is like a ball of foam; it cannot withstand being held and separated. The feeling aggregate is like a water bubble; because it is momentary, it is impermanent. The aggregate

> of discrimination is like an mirage because it is mistakenly apprehended by the thirst of attachment. The aggregate of compositional factors is like the stalk of a lotus; when it is destroyed it has no core. The aggregate of consciousness is like a dream; it is mistakenly conceived. Therefore, the five aggregates are not a self, not a person, not a sentient being, not a life, not a nourished being, not a creature. The five aggregates are naturally empty of I and mine, unproduced, unarisen, non-existent, the sphere of space, unconditioned, and naturally passed beyond sorrow.[20]

Unlike the other commentators, Vajrapāṇi does not provide a philosophical exegesis of the line, but rather discusses it in terms of the practice of meditation. He says:

> In order to become accustomed to viewing persons and phenomena as selfless, one becomes accustomed to not finding the self by investigating and examining the minute particles of all internal and external phenomena. As a result, when [the mind] is placed in meditative equipoise (*samāhita*), it does not observe anything or conceive of anything. When one has the goal of placing the mind there for a prolonged period, one is in a state of meditative equipoise observing the clear and joyous mind. At the time of subsequent attainment, all phenomena are observed to be like illusions, like dreams, like mirages, like echoes, like a moon in water, like rainbows, like a city of the *gandharvas*, like the wheel of a firebrand, like matted hair, like Indra's net, and the aspect of an emanation. For the sake of persons who, having done that, have interest in the arising of the mind [that realizes] the union of the varieties [of phenomena] and emptiness, it is said, "Form is emptiness, emptiness is form. Emptiness is not other than form, form is not other than emptiness."[21]

Vajrapāṇi begins by emphasizing the central place of analysis in meditation on emptiness. To realize the selflessness of persons and other phenomena, it is necessary to examine their parts in search of a self. Having investigated and found no self, a mere vacuity of self appears to the mind, and the mind is placed in equipoise (*samāhita*) on that vacuity. Nothing appears to that mind except emptiness. Thus, "Form is emptiness." In the subsequent state (*pṛṣṭhalabdha*), one rises from meditative equipoise on emptiness and the varieties of phenomena again appear. Due to the impact of the prior realization of emptiness, however, these forms do not appear to be real. Rather, they appear as illusions, dream objects, mirages, and so forth. They seem to appear out of emptiness. Thus, "emptiness is form."

Vimalamitra chooses not to deal directly with the relationship of form and emptiness in his commentary, preferring instead to iterate the traditional Mādhyamika critique of causation that occurs most prominently in the first chapter of Nāgārjuna's *Mūlamadhyamakakārikā*. If causation inherently exists, then a cause must exist either at the same time as its effect or at some other time. Simultaneity of cause and effect is untenable because cause and effect would be indistinguishable and there could be no progression over time. If cause and effect were temporally distinct, they would remain discrete with no relation between them, leaving three possibilities, all of which are unacceptable: things would arise causelessly, things would remain static and unchanging, or things would not exist at all. Vimalamitra cites sūtras to present the correct position: that cause and effect do not exist by way of their own entity but arise in dependence upon one another. To be produced by causes and conditions is to be unproduced by an entity that is either inherently the same or different from the product. Production, which only exists conventionally, can only take place in dependence upon causes and conditions. Vimalamitra says:

> Here it is said that because the aggregates, constituents (*dhātu*), and sources (*āyatana*) are dependently arisen, the position that they are causeless or impermanent is dispelled. There are two analyses of the position that they arise from causes: that when things are produced they are produced simultaneous with their cause or at a different time. According to the first position, cause and effect and all conjunctions of the prior and the subsequent would be observed at one time in which case cause and effect would be indivisible and an aeon would be just one year. According to the second position, since cause and effect would not come together at the same time, there would be no potency. Therefore, there would be the consequence [that things would arise] causelessly. If there is no cause, there are the consequences that [things would] be permanent or would be non-existent because there would be nothing other on which to depend [for production]. If they were dependent, things would be occasional. There is no third possibility because [occurring] at the same time and at different times are mutually exclusive. Therefore, those which appear as forms and so forth are empty of their own entity, like the water of a mirage. Those things that are thought to arise in dependence on this and that are deceptive. Therefore, the Transcendent Victor said in the *Lalitavistara:*
>
> Śākyaputra, upon seeing that dependently arisen phenomena
> Are without their own entities
> One is endowed with the space-like mind and
> Is not moved by seeing the demons and their hosts.

The *Ratnolkā* says:

> Those which are produced from conditions are not [produced]
> by way of their own entities.
> The body of phenomena is the body of the Conquerors.
> Reality abides forever, like space.
> When this is taught, one attains the purity of phenomena.

The *Sarvabuddhaviṣayāvatārajñānālokālaṃkāra* says:

> One does not stir from the nature of phenomena. One who does not stir from the nature of phenomena, attains the nature of phenomena. One who attains the nature of phenomena is not involved with the slightest [conceptual] elaboration. Why? Because [phenomena] are produced from causes and conditions. That which is produced from causes and conditions is utterly unproduced. That which is utterly unproduced is definitely attained. That which is definitely attained does not abide together with taking any phenomena to mind.

There are such statements. Therefore, the Superior Nāgārjuna says:

> That which is dependently arisen
> Is not inherently produced.
> How can you say that that which is not inherently produced
> Is "produced"?
>
> The utterly unwise
> Who impute production
> Even to very subtle things
> Have not seen the meaning of conditional arising.[22]

Vimalamitra next considers the status of the wisdom that understands emptiness. Does not it, at least, ultimately exist? The wisdom itself, like all other phenomena, is dependently arisen. It has also passed beyond the extremes of inherent existence and utter non-existence. He identifies the nihilistic tendencies of the latter position and quotes Nāgārjuna to demonstrate that the understanding that phenomena do not exist in a certain manner does not entail that they do not exist at all; because there is no water in a mirage does not mean that water does not exist. Buddhahood and omniscience are possible without their being ultimately existent, for to see things as they truly are means not seeing them as they are perceived by ignorance; as the *Samādhirāja* says: "To not see anything is to see all phenomena."[23]

But if it is not asserted that the wisdom of the non-duality of object and subject ultimately exists, why is it not non-existent? It is not; it is asserted to be dependently arisen conventionally and it has passed beyond being ultimately existent or non-existent. Existence is overcome. The conception of non-existence, the view that nothing exists in that way is the extreme of annihilation; father does not exist, mother does not exist, this world does not exist, the next world does not exist, the fructifying of auspicious and faulty actions does not exist. If such derogatory characterizations of the [four] truths and the [three] jewels and so forth are sinful, what is the appropriate view in the system of the exceedingly pure Mādhyamikas? The *Ratnāvalī* [I.55, 60] says in response:

> Having thought a mirage to be
> Water and then having gone there,
> It would be simply foolish to hold that [in general]
> "Water does not exist."
>
> Those who rely on enlightenment
> Have no nihilistic thought,
> Assertion, or behavior.
> How can they be considered nihilists?[24]

Objection: Because existence is refuted, is non-existence not entailed? Because non-existence is refuted, why is existence not entailed? If those who assert that the knowledge of non-duality ultimately exists apprehend their consciousnesses of those things which involve different causes, how is it non-dual? Then, if it is not held to be ultimately existent, how can it be omniscience? You have a similar fault.

Answer: It is not the case. To not see ultimate existence is to see reality; not seeing water in a mirage is not a case of being endowed with ignorance. As it is said, "To not see form is to see form," and the *Samādhirāja* says, "To not see anything is to see all phenomena." In the same way, it is taught that the aggregates, from feeling to consciousness, like form, are, in brief, empty of their own entity. Thus, it is to be understood in this way: feeling is emptiness, emptiness is feeling. Emptiness is not other than feeling, feeling is not other than emptiness. This is to be applied in the same way to discrimination. Having taught that the aggregates are empty of their own entity, it is taught also concerning the sources and constituents.[25]

The Relationship of Form and Emptiness

The general position expressed by the Indian commentators in explaining the fourfold profundity is that form is emptiness in the sense that emptiness is the final nature of form and that emptiness is form in that emptiness is not to be discovered apart from form. They do not take up, however, the problems that occur when the statement, "Form is emptiness; emptiness is form," is read literally. The commentators would not want to say that form, the object of the eye consciousness, is the ultimate truth, emptiness. Nor would they want to say that emptiness, the permanent and unchanging nature of reality, is identical with the impermanent phenomenon and conventional truth, which is form. Form is a positive phenomenon and impermanent; emptiness is a negation and permanent in the sense that it is not in constant flux. Although this problem is not addressed by the *Heart Sūtra* commentators, it is considered explicitly by other Indian Buddhist thinkers. The classic formulation of the problem is found in the *Saṃdhinirmocana Sūtra*, where it is demonstrated that form, or conditioned things, and emptiness, or the ultimate, cannot be different and cannot be the same:

> Suviśuddhamati, if the nature of conditioned things and the nature of the ultimate were different, then even those who see the truth would not be free from the signs of conditioned things. Due to not being free from the signs of conditioned things, seeing the truth would not release them from the bonds of signs. If they were not released from the bonds of signs, they would not be released from the bonds of assuming unfortunate states. If they were not released from those two bonds, those who see the truth also would not achieve the nirvāṇa that is unsurpassed bliss. They would also not become completely purified in the unsurpassed perfect and complete enlightenment. . . . Suviśuddhamati, if the natures of conditioned things and nature of the ultimate were different, then the nature of the ultimate would not be the general nature of all conditioned things. . . . Suviśuddhamati, if the natures of conditioned things and the nature of the ultimate were different, then the mere selflessness and entitynessless of conditioned things would not be the ultimate nature. Also, afflicted natures (*saṃkliṣṭa*) and pure natures (*vyavadāna*) would be established as different natures simultaneously [in the continuum of a Buddha].[26]

A number of important points are made here. The first is that if form and emptiness were different, discrete entities, then enlightenment could not occur because it would be impossible to destroy the conception that form exists in and of itself. Form would be one thing and emptiness would be another, such that understanding emptiness would have no adverse effect on ignorant conceptions about form. Hence, "seeing the truth would not release them from the bonds of signs," ignorance would continue and would not be destroyed and replaced by wisdom, and liberation would be impossible. Furthermore, it is suggested that if the form and emptiness were different, then emptiness could not be the final mode of being of form; emptiness would be one thing, the final nature of form, another. A further problem is that if form and emptiness were different in entity, then the elimination of the self or intrinsic nature falsely attributed to form would not be the final nature of form; the selflessness of form would be one thing and its ultimate nature would be something else. Finally, the sūtra argues that if form and emptiness were different entities, then it would be possible that both the misconception that form exists by way of its own entity and the wisdom realizing the emptiness of inherent existence could exist simultaneously in the mind of the Buddha because the realization of emptiness would not adversely affect the conception that form is real. Hence, a Buddha would have both wisdom and ignorance.

Later Tibetan doxographers find in the previous quotation four absurd consequences that would be entailed if the two truths were two different entities:

> it would absurdly follow that by understanding the mode of being of form, the misconception that form inherently exists would not be eliminated;
>
> it would absurdly follow that the emptiness of a form would not be the form's final mode of being;
>
> it would absurdly follow that the mere elimination of inherent existence with respect to form would not be the reality of form;
>
> it would absurdly follow that ignorance, the conception of inherent existence, and wisdom, the realization of the lack of inherent existence, would exist simultaneously, even in the mind of a Buddha.[27]

All this would suggest that form and emptiness are not different entities, that indeed they are the same, as the *Heart Sūtra* seems to suggest. The *Saṃdhinirmocana*, however, argues just as forcefully that undesired consequences would be entailed if form and emptiness were identical.

> Suviśuddhamati, if the nature of conditioned things and the nature of the ultimate were not different, then all childish common beings would see the truth. While only common beings, they would attain the nirvāṇa that is unsurpassed enlightenment and bliss. They would become completely purified in the unsurpassed, complete, perfect enlightenment. . . . Suviśuddhamati, if the natures of conditioned things and the nature of the ultimate were not different, then just as the natures of conditioned things are included in the category of the afflicted, the nature of the ultimate would also be included in the category of the afflicted. . . . Suviśuddhamati, if the natures of conditioned things and the nature of the ultimate were not different, then just as the nature of the ultimate in all conditioned things is without particularities, so all natures of conditioned things would be without particularities. Yogis would not seek an ultimate that surpasses how conditioned things are seen, how they are heard, how they are differentiated, and how they are known.[28]

Again, several problems are identified. First, if form and emptiness were not somehow different, then anyone who saw a form would, perforce, see emptiness. A farmer who looked at his cow or a dog who regarded a tree would directly perceive emptiness and thereby achieve enlightenment. As attractive as this might sound to those inclined toward Zen, there is something distinctly inappropriate, even unseemly, about such a proposition to the Indian Buddhist scholastic's sensibility. A related problem is that if form and emptiness were not different, then emptiness would become the object of afflicted states of mind, such as desire, hatred, pride, greed, and jealousy. Since certain forms, such as gold, for example, are often the objects of such negative emotions, emptiness, being identical with form, would also be their object. Consequently, the observation of emptiness, rather than serving as an antidote to the afflictions and the sufferings they produce, could serve as an object of those afflictions, thus increasing suffering. Furthermore, if the form and emptiness were not different, the varieties of form would be effaced. That is, because emptiness is invariable and undifferentiated in the myriad phenomena that it qualifies, were form and emptiness identical, form would also share in that. The other alternative, not suggested by the sūtra but equally troublesome, would be that emptiness would be as variegated as form. Finally, related to the first point that common beings would see emptiness in their ordinary and unmotivated experience is the problem that yogis would have no reason to pursue the path to enlightenment. There would be little reason to pursue the truth because there would be no truth beyond sense experience.

Tibetan doxographers also discern four consequences here:

it would absurdly follow that even common beings would directly realize emptiness, the ultimate truth;

it would absurdly follow that emptiness could be observed by consciousnesses contaminated by the afflictions (*kleśa*);

it would absurdly follow that there would be no need to seek the path to enlightenment;

it would absurdly follow that the varieties of form would not exist.[29]

These statements from the *Saṃdhinirmocana* would lead to the conclusion that it is the position of the sūtra that form and emptiness are not different and are not not different; and, indeed, that is exactly what the sūtra says in a concluding stanza:

The conditioned constituents and the ultimate characteristic
Have a nature lacking sameness and difference.
Those who imagine them to be either the same or different
Do not abide in that which is correct.[30]

Thus, it would seem to be incorrect that form is emptiness and emptiness is form; that emptiness is not other than form and form is not other than emptiness.[31] In dGe-lugs-pa expositions of the problem of the relationship of the two truths, the conventional (*saṃvṛti*) and the ultimate (*paramārtha*), a statement from the *Bodhicittavivaraṇa*, a work traditionally attributed to Nāgārjuna, is often cited:

Suchness is not observed to be
Different from the conventional.

The conventional is explained to be emptiness,
Emptiness is only the conventional,
Because it is certain that without [one the other] does not occur,
Like product and impermanent thing.[32]

The stanza adds little to what the *Heart Sūtra* itself says, with the exception of the last line, which suggests that the relationship between the conventional and the ultimate is like that which pertains between product (*kṛta*) and impermanent thing (*anitya*). These two terms are synonyms, such that everything that is a product is an impermanent thing and vice versa. It is not this relationship of product and impermanent thing that Nāgārjuna is indicating, because it is not the case, at least according to the *Saṃdhinirmocana*, that whatever is a form is emptiness and whatever is emptiness is form. Rather, in the context of the stanza, Nāgārjuna seems to illustrate that the conventional does not exist without the ultimate, just as wherever there is a product there is also invariably an impermanent thing.

The Yogācāra master Dignāga makes further progress on the problem. In his *Prajñāpāramitāpiṇḍārtha* (40-41), he explicitly rejects what is said in the *Heart Sūtra:*

> Because they are mutually exclusive,
> It is not feasible that form is emptiness.
> Emptiness lacks inherent existence [whereas]
> Form is endowed with aspects [such as color and shape].
>
> Therefore, the idea that they are the same is damaged.
> Because there is no way in which
> Form could be other than emptiness,
> The idea of difference is refuted.[33]

His commentator, Triratnadāsa, expands:

> "Form is emptiness" is the conviction that [they are] exactly the same. To the idea of sameness is applied this statement of the mother, the Perfection of Wisdom, "That which is the emptiness of form is not form." Therefore, the expression that sets forth the statement refuting the idea of sameness is, "because they are mutually exclusive," and so forth. It is not correct that form is emptiness. Why? Because they are mutually exclusive in that emptiness and form are mutually damaging. Why are they contradictory? Because emptiness is just without inherent existence, it is without entity, like a lotus in the sky. The "ness" of entityness denotes emphasis; it means that it is only without entity. "Form is endowed with aspects" means that form has aspects such as white and blue. Lacking entityness and having entityness are contradictory, "therefore the idea that they are the same" [is damaged]. "Therefore" is a term meaning a reason. Thus, the idea that they are the same is damaged; the text clearly states that the emptiness of form is not form. Therefore, this puts an end to the disturbing idea that they are the same.
>
> To refute the idea of difference, that "form is other than emptiness," this statement is made in the mother, the Perfection of Wisdom itself, "Emptiness is not other than form." What is this statement? It is a

> refutation and an elimination. What is it eliminating? The idea of difference. Why? Because there is no way in which form could be other than emptiness, that form having the character of the aggregates could be other in terms of emptiness. However, form is only emptiness; it does not differ from emptiness in the slightest, nor could it. This clearly indicates the disturbing quality of difference.[34]

Dignāga reiterates that form could not be other than emptiness and he says that form and emptiness also are not the same because form has its own entity while emptiness does not. Here, entityness does not seem to mean anything more than physical attributes. Triratnadāsa quotes the *Aṣṭasāhasrikāprajñāpāramitā* ostensibly to contradict the *Heart Sūtra* with the statement, "That which is emptiness is not form." Form and emptiness are, he says, in fact, mutually exclusive such that there can be nothing that is both form and emptiness. Hence, the two are not identical, nor are they synonyms, like product and impermanent thing. Triratnadāsa, however, also supports the position that form and emptiness are not different, going so far as to say that form does not differ from emptiness in the slightest.

One solution, at least doctrinally speaking, of this consequential conundrum is offered by the Tibetan scholar Tsong-kha-pa and his followers.[35] Before turning to their delineation, however, it is useful to attempt to delimit the meaning of the terms "same" and "different" that figure so prominently in the discussion.

There developed in Tibet a genre of monastic literature called "collected topics" (*bsdus grwa*) in which were gathered together technical vocabulary, primarily from the works of Dignāga and Dharmakīrti but also from the Abhidharma, and in which it was attempted to provide systematic and consistent definitions and illustrations of key terms. The most famous of these works is the fifteenth century *Rwa stod bstus grwa* (*Collected Topics of Rwa-stod*) by 'Jam-dbyangs-phyogs-lha-'od-zer. In the second section of the work, the "intermediate path of reasoning" (*rigs lam 'bring*), there is a chapter dealing with contradiction and relationship (*'gal be dang 'brel ba*), where a number of important terms germane to a discussion of the relationship between form and emptiness are defined.

In this chapter, contradiction is defined as "abiding in mutual discord,"[36] which can be understood to mean that if two things are contradictory they must be different and it must be observed that there occurs no common locus of the two things.[37] Contradictions are of two types: contradiction in the sense of mutual abandonment (Sanskrit: *anyonyaparihāravirodha*; Tibetan: *phan tshun spang 'gal*) and contradiction in the sense of not abiding together (Sanskrit: *sahānavasthā-virodha*; Tibetan: *lhan cig mi gnas 'gal*). The first, contradiction in the sense of not abiding together, is defined as "abiding discordantly in the sense of exclusion and inclusion".[38] It is this type of contradiction that seems to denote what is meant by mutual exclusivity, where the inclusion of one excludes the other, there being nothing that is both. The second type of contradiction, that of not abiding together, is defined as "not abiding together in the sense of continually [acting as] eliminator and eliminated".[39] From the examples of hot and cold, the mistaken belief in self and the wisdom realizing selflessness, and the perennial feathered foes, the owl and the crow[40], this type of contradiction involves actual displacement of one thing by the other; the two cannot inhabit the same place, be it a consciousness or the limb of a tree.

From these definitions and illustrations, it can be surmised that in these terms, form and emptiness are contradictory in the sense that they are terminologically different and there is no common locus of the two; there is nothing that is both form and emptiness. They are also contradictory in the sense of mutual abandonment, where the fact that something is form eliminates the possibility that it is emptiness. They are not contradictory in the sense of not abiding together because the *Heart Sūtra* commentators repeatedly make the point that emptiness is not to be found apart from form; form and emptiness abide together.

Two types of relationship (Sanskrit: *saṃbandha*; Tibetan: *'brel ba*) are discussed in the works on the "Collected Topics." The relationship of identity (Sanskrit: *tādātmyasaṃbandha*; Tibetan: *bdag gcig 'brel*) entails two things being terminologically different but being related in such a way that if one is absent the other must also be absent. The other type is relationship in the sense of arising (Sanskrit: *tādutpattisaṃbandha*, Tibetan: *de byung 'brel*), which pertains between an effect and its substantial cause (*upādāna*).[41] Form and emptiness are related in the sense of being the same entity, because the commentators make it clear that emptiness could not exist without form.

Thus, form and emptiness are mutually exclusive and contradictory in the sense that nothing can be both form and emptiness but are the same entity in the sense that one cannot exist without the other. Form serves as the basis of emptiness; without form there could be no emptiness. Emptiness is the final nature of form; if emptiness did not exist, there would be no single reality in all phenomena. In an earlier period of Tibetan thought, it was said that the two truths had a difference that negated identity (*gcig bkag ba'i tha dad*); that is, that ultimate truths and conventional truths were different only in the sense that they were not identical. From the time of Tsong-kha-pa (1357-1419), however, the standard description of the relationship between the two truths, between form and emptiness, was that they were *ngo bo gcig ldog pa tha dad*, literally "the same entity and different opposites of the negative," more broadly translated as "ontically the same and conceptually different."[42]

The Tibetan term *ldog pa* (Sanskrit: *vyatireka*) means "change," "return," "reverse." It is a technical term in Tibetan Buddhist philosophy meaning the opposite of the negative.[43] The opposite of the negative of table is non-non-table, that is, table, the table-in-itself. An instance of table, an oak table, for example, is not the table-in-itself, a synonym of table is not the table-in-itself, and the definition of table is not the table-in-itself. The only thing that is the opposite of the negative of table, the table-in-itself is table. Anything that appears to thought as different in any way from table is not the opposite of the negative of table. Thus, two things may be the same entity but they cannot be the same opposite of the negative. Two things that are synonymous are the same entity; a universal and its instances are the same entity. The only thing, however, that is the opposite of the negative of form is form; the only thing that is the opposite of the negative of emptiness is emptiness. If two things have different names, they are different opposites of the negative in that they are not expressed by the same term and are not objects of the same thought consciousness; the name of one cannot evoke understanding of the other. The notion of opposite of the negative has to do with how things appear to thought (*kalpanā*); if two things appear separately to thought, they are different opposites of the negative. The notion of entity has to do with how they appear to direct perception (*pratyakṣa*); if two things do not appear separately to direct perception, they are said to be the same entity. Therefore, form and emptiness are mutually exclusive and different opposites of the negative but the same entity, intimately related and occupying the same place.

The length of this exegesis of the relationship of form and emptiness seems, in the end, to suggest the startling and radical profundity of the essential statement of the *Heart Sūtra*, "Form is emptiness; emptiness is form. Emptiness is not other than form; form is not other than emptiness."[44]

The Eightfold Profundity

Śāriputra, in that way all phenomena are empty, without characteristic,[45] *unproduced, unceased, stainless, not stainless, undiminished, unfilled.*

Here the implications of the aggregates being empty are drawn out. All phenomena in the universe are empty. They are without characteristic in the sense that they lack the characteristic of having their own entity or being established by such an entity. Production is the arising of that which did not exist before and cessation is the present non-existence of something that existed at a prior moment. Both production and cessation exist conventionally but neither is analytically findable. Hence, phenomena are not ultimately produced or ceased. Because all phenomena are empty, they are not intrinsically stained by saṃsāra. But because nirvāṇa is also empty of inherent existence, phenomena are also not intrinsically stainless. Because ultimately neither saṃsāra nor nirvāṇa exist, phenomena are not diminished by faults or filled with good qualities.[46]

Three of the *Heart Sūtra* commentators provide glosses of the eightfold profundity that warrant consideration. Jñānamitra says:

> "Śāriputra" is a term of address [meaning], "Listen undistractedly and well." "In that way, all phenomena are empty," [means] that just as it was explained with regard to the five aggregates, he should also know that all [mundane and] supramundane phenomena, from the six sources to the knowledge of all aspects (*sarvākārajñāna*), are empty. "Without characteristic" means that just as space is without characteristic, [phenomena] are without the characteristic of affliction, as well as without the characteristic of purity. "Unproduced, unceased" means that such production is the coming into existence subsequently of what did not exist before. Cessation is the becoming non-existent of what existed before. Because emptiness is unobservable, it is not produced before. Since it is not produced, it does not cease later. Regarding "stainless, not stainless," "stain" is the activity of consciousness that apprehends objects. Since the activity itself transcends consciousness, it is stainless. Regarding "not stainless," because stains do not exist, [stainlessness] is also lacking. With respect to "undiminished, unfilled," the diminished is sentient beings. The "filled" is the Buddha. "Not" means that since sentient beings and Buddhas are not found when sought, the diminished and the filled do not exist.[47]

Jñānamitra says that all phenomena, from the six sources to the knower of all aspects, are empty. He refers to 108 phenomena that the Perfection of Wisdom sūtras enumerate as being empty. These phenomena are divided into two broad classes, the afflicted (*saṃkliṣṭa*), of which there are fifty-three phenomena, and the pure (*vaiyavadānika*), of which there are fifty-five phenomena. "All phenomena, from form to the knower of all aspects," is the phrase that commonly appears, with form being the first of the fifty-three phenomena of the afflicted class and the knower of all aspects, the Buddha's omniscient mind, being the last of the fifty-five phenomena of the pure class. The phenomena of the afflicted class are the five aggregates, the six sense powers (*indriya*), which Jñānamitra calls the six sources (*āyatana*), the six consciousnesses (*vijñāna*), the six objects of consciousness, the six contacts (*sparśa*), the six feelings (*vedanā*), the six elements (*bhūta*), and the twelve branches of dependent arising (*pratītyasamutpāda*). The fifty-five phenomena of the pure class are the six perfections (*pāramitā*), the eighteen emptinesses, the thirty-seven harmonies of enlightenment (*bodhipakṣa*), the four truths, the four concentrations (*dhyāna*), the four immeasurables (*apramāṇa*), the four formless absorptions (*ārūpya-samāpatti*), the eight liberations (*vimokṣa*), the nine serial absorptions (*samāpatti*), the paths of insight, the five superknowledges (*abhijñā*), the four meditative stabilizations (*samādhi*), the four doors of retention (*dhāraṇī*), the ten powers (*bala*), the four fearlessnesses (*vaiśāradya*), the four sciences (*vidyā*), great love (*mahāmaitrī*), great compassion (*mahākaruṇā*), the eighteen unique qualities of a Buddha (*āveṇika*), Stream Enterers (*srotāpanna*), Once Returners (*sakṛdāgāmin*), Never Returners (*anāgāmin*), arhats, pratyekabuddhas, the knower of bases (*āśrayajñāna*), the knower of paths (*mārgajñāna*), and the knower of all aspects (*sarvākārajñāna*).[48] When the sūtra says that all phenomena are empty, these are the phenomena it implies.

Having referred to the phenomena of the afflicted class and the pure class, Jñānamitra says in the next line that "without characteristic" means that phenomena cannot be so classified as intrinsically afflicted or pure. For the remaining six profundities, Jñānamitra shifts his attention away from phenomena in general, to apply the profundities to specific phenomena. Thus, it is emptiness that is unproduced and unceased. The diminished are sentient beings, the filled are Buddhas. Because both are analytically unfindable, they are undiminished and unfilled. For Jñānamitra, "stain" refers to the activity of consciousness that perceives objects. Because that activity itself is not observable as something real, the sūtra says "stainless."

Praśāstrasena provides a different reading of the eight. He writes:

> Regarding "All phenomena are empty," "all phenomena" refers to that which is based on the aggregates, that is, the sense powers, their objects, the constituents (*dhātu*), the sources (*āyatana*), dependent arising (*pratītyasamutpāda*), and so forth. By understanding that the

> aggregates are empty, their branches are also known to be of the character of emptiness. For example, if one understands that the primary part of the body is empty, it will implicitly be known that the feet and arms [are empty]. Regarding "without characteristic," because all phenomena are beyond signs, they are without characteristic. Regarding "unproduced and unceased," the subsequent existence of what did not exist before is production. The subsequent non-existence of what existed before is cessation. The Buddha nature, the dharmadhātu, is the ultimate emptiness. Because this is beginningless, its end is not to be found. Therefore, it is said to be unproduced and unceased. Even when sentient beings cycle on the five paths [of rebirth], the Buddha nature does not become stained. Therefore, it is said to be pure. Even the Buddhahood which is unsurpassed, perfect, complete enlightenment is without a purity that surpasses the Buddha nature. Therefore, it is without purity. Because the Buddha nature exists even in the bodies of ants and beetles without becoming smaller, it is undiminished. Because it exists even in the Truth Body without increasing, it is unfilled. Why? Because it is beyond thought and expression; it is not encompassed by measures.
>
> Because the dharmadhātu is not produced in the two ways, by actions or afflictions, it is unproduced. If it is not produced, it is not destroyed. Therefore, it does not cease. Because the dharmadhātu is naturally pure, it is without purity. Therefore, it is not pure. Although it is naturally pure, the adventitious afflictions do not make it impure. Therefore, it is pure. Because it is the state of having abandoned the completely afflicted class, the dharmadhātu is undiminished. Hence, it is undiminished. Because the dharmadhātu does not increase when purity increases, it is not filled.[49]

After explaining what is entailed by the term "all phenomena" and how all phenomena are without characteristic because no phenomenon is marked with signs of inherent existence, Praśāstrasena chooses to explain the remaining six profundities not in terms of all phenomena, but in terms of the Buddha nature and dharmadhātu. He thus evinces the cataphatic approach to emptiness that is characteristic of the later Mahāyāna, when the most important of the works on tathāgatagarbha, the *Ratnagotravibhāga*, was incorporated into Mādhyamika thought.[50] He suggests that the Buddha nature, the dharmadhātu, and the ultimate emptiness are identical. This Buddha nature, this emptiness, is beginningless and endless. It remains unstained as it abides in the minds of sentient beings who wander through the five realms of gods, humans, animals, hungry ghosts, and hell beings. Because it is naturally and forever pure, it is not purified in the process of enlightenment. Being inconceivable and inexpressible and beyond all attempts to delimit its extent or fathom its depth, it does not decrease in size in order to abide in even the tiniest of sentient beings nor does it grow to encompass the limitless Truth Body (*dharmakāya*) of the Buddha. The dharmadhātu is described in similar terms, being unproduced and unceased because it is not created by actions and afflictions, as are the phenomena of saṃsāra. Because it is naturally pure and thus cannot be purified or tainted by anything, it cannot be said to be either pure or impure. It is neither decreased by the afflictions nor increased by their purification. Praśāstrasena's gloss of "undiminished, unfilled" is very much reminiscent of the famous statement in the *Ratnagotravibhāga* (I.154-55):

> There is nothing to be removed from it;
> There is nothing whatsoever to be added.
> Reality should be viewed correctly.
> When reality is seen, one is liberated.
>
> The element [of the Tathāgatha] lacks the adventitious,
> Which are by nature divisible,
> But it does not lack the unsurpassed qualities,
> Which have a nature of indivisibility.[51]

It is exactly such paeans to emptiness as the Buddha nature and the dharmadhātu that caused the Hīnayāna schools to accuse the Mahāyāna of rejecting the doctrines of impermanence and selflessness and replacing them with a thinly veiled eternalism. Among the Hīnayāna charges listed by Bhāvaviveka in their argument that the Mahāyāna is not the word of the Buddha is that the Mahāyāna does not abandon the conception of self because it teaches that the tathāgatagarbha is all-pervasive.[52] The apparent substantialism embodied in the notion of the tathāgathagarbha was a problem to which the authors of the Mahāyāna sūtras and śāstras were not insensitive; it is taken up in such sūtras as the *Śrīmālādevīsiṃhanāda*, the Mahāyāna *Mahāparinirvāṇa* and the *Laṅkāvatāra* and in such śāstras as the *Ratnagotravibhāga* and the *Madhyamakāvatāra.*

The fullest sūtra exposition of the tathāgatagarbha occurs in the *Śrīmālādevīsiṃhanāda*, where the four inverted views of permanence (*nitya*), pleasure (*sukha*), self (*ātman*), and purity (*śubha*) about conditioned phenomena, which are, in fact, impermanent, miserable, selfless, and impure, become, through double negation, the four perfect qualities (*guṇapāramitā*) of the tathāgatagarbha. The sūtra, however, explicitly states that the tathāgatagarbha is not the *ātman* of the non-Buddhists.[53] The *Mahāparinirvāṇasūtra* also describes the tathāgatagarbha as endowed with the four perfect qualities and goes on to designate it with the term *ātman*.[54] But the sūtra also says:

> O child of good lineage, the Buddha nature is not in reality self; it is for the sake of sentient beings that it is spoken of as self. Child of good lineage, due to the existence of causes and conditions, the Tathāgata has spoken of the selfless as self, but in reality there is no self. Though he has spoken in this way, it was not false. Child of good lineage, it is because of causes and conditions that the self is said to be selfless. Even though self exists in reality, it is for the sake of the world that it has been said that there is no self. But that was not false.[55]

The apparent paradox of this statement is remedied later when the Buddha explains that both the views of self and selflessness are untenable as dogma.

> Child of good lineage, because you are endowed with wisdom most profound, I will teach you well how to enter the tathāgatagarbha. If what is called "self" were an eternally permanent phenomenon, there would be no freedom from suffering. If what is called "self" did not exist, the practice of purity (*brahmacarya*) would have no beneficial purpose. If it is said that all phenomena are selfless, it is a nihilistic view. If it is said that they are eternally permanent, it is a view of permanence. . . . Non-duality is reality: self and selflessness are naturally without duality.[56]

The most extensive śāstric delineation of the theory of the tathāgatagarbha occurs in the *Ratnagotravibhāga*. The subtitle of the text is the *Uttaratantra*, the "subsequent or superior continuation" of the teaching of the *Prajñāpāramitā*, which because of its apophatic language, is in a danger of being misconstrued (I.160-161):

> Furthermore, this superior continuation,
> In order to abandon the five defects,
> Teaches that the [Buddha] element exists.
>
> Due to not hearing that [teaching] in this way,
> Those who are not timid
> Will not create the aspiration to enlightenment
> Because they will wrongly despise themselves.[57]

In the commentary to the *Ratnagotravibhāga* traditionally ascribed to Asaṅga, the *Mahāyānottaratantraśāstravyākhyā*, is found perhaps the clearest explanation of how the four perfect qualities differ from the four inverted views and of how the tathāgatagarbha differs from the self that the non-Buddhists hold to exist:

> The fourfold perfect qualities of the dharmakāya of the Tathāgata are seen as antidotes, the opposite of the fourfold inversion, respectively. Regarding that, there is the discernment that impermanent things, such as form, are permanent and the notions that the miserable is pleasureable; the selfless, self; and the impure, pure. This is called the fourfold inversion. The opposite of this is known as the fourfold non-inversion. What are these four? They are the discernment that those very things, such as form, are impermanent, the discernment that they are miserable, the discernment that they are selfless, the discernment that they are impure. This is the opposite of the fourfold inversion. Moreover, here, in terms of the dharmakāya of the Tathāgatha who has the character of permanence and so forth, [these] are held to be inverted. As an antidote to that, the four perfect qualities of the dharmakāya of the Tathāgata are set forth: the perfection of permanence, the perfection of bliss, the perfection of self, and the perfection of purity.[58]

The author goes on to explain the causes of the four perfected qualities of the Tathāgata. The perfection of purity is the result of the Bodhisattva's cultivation of belief in the Mahāyāna, having turned away from, and thus being opposed to the great delight taken by those of great desire (*icchāntika*) in the impurities of saṃsāra. The Bodhisattva attains the perfection of mundane and supramundane bliss by cultivating various samādhis, such as the "sky treasury" (*gaganagañja*), having turned away from, and thus being opposed, to the desire of śrāvakas, who fear the sufferings of saṃsāra and seek a mere pacification of suffering. The perfection of permanence, whereby the Tathāgata works for the benefit of sentient beings as long as the world exists, is the result of the Bodhisattva's practice of great compassion, having turned away from, and thus being opposed to, the delight taken by pratyekabuddhas in remaining aloof, without considering the welfare of sentient beings. On the perfection of self, the commentary says:

> It is to be seen that the attainment of the perfection of the supreme self is the effect of cultivating the perfection of wisdom, turning away from, [and thus being opposed to], the delight taken in a non-existent self by the others, the non-Buddhists, who see self in the five appropriated aggregates. For all the others, the non-Buddhists, assert that things which do not have that nature, such as form, to be self. Those things as they conceive them are always selfless because they are deceived by the nature of self. The Tathāgata has found perfection of the supreme selflessness of all phenomena with the wisdom that correctly [sees pheno-

> mena] just as they are. The selflessness which he sees is always held to be self because he is not deceived by the nature of what does not actually exist. The selflessness is itself taken as self; as it is said, "He abides in a manner of not abiding."[59]

In the *Laṅkāvatara*, Mahāmati asks the Buddha how the tathāgatagarbha, which is described as naturally radiant and primordially pure, differs from the self propounded by the *tīrthikas*, which they describe as permanent, pervasive, and immortal. It should be noted that Mahāmati also describes a tathāgatagarbha possessing the thirty-two marks of a Buddha as present in the bodies of all sentient beings. This latter qualification is idiosyncratic; the other major texts do not appear to conceive of the Buddha nature as a fully developed Buddha lying hidden in the bodies of all sentient beings, "like a precious gem wrapped in a dirty cloth," but rather as a seed or potentiality for the eventual attainment of Buddhahood. Nonetheless, the Buddha's answer to Mahāmati is instructive. He says:

> Mahāmati, the tathāgatagarbha that I teach is not similar to the self propounded by the *tīrthikas*. Mahāmati, the completely perfect Buddhas, the arhat Tathāgatas, teach that emptiness, the limit of reality, nirvāṇa, the unproduced, signlessness, wishlessness, and so forth are the tathāgatagarbha. The entry into the tathāgatagarbha is taught so that the childish will abandon the state of being frightened by selflessness, thereby indicating [to them] the non-conceptual state, the sphere of non-appearance. Mahāmati, Bodhisattvas, Mahāsattvas of the future and the present should not conceive of it as self.[60]

Here the Buddha identifies the tathāgatagarbha with emptiness, as Praśāstrasena does earlier. The sūtra, however, takes the further step of identifying the teaching of the tathāgatagarbha as provisional (*neyārtha*), a cataphatic gloss of emptiness for those who are frightened by the apparent nihilism of the doctrine of selflessness. This appears also to be the view of later scholastics such as Candrakīrti.

Finally, Vimalamitra's interpretation of the eightfold profundity should be considered.

> Having taught that [all phenomena] are to be seen to be empty of their own entity, [the sūtra] teaches that they are to be seen to be empty of characteristic. Therefore, it says, "without characteristic." A characteristic is that which defines or that which is defined. Thus, the general characteristic of the form aggregate is that which is suitable as form. Therefore, it is form. The general characteristic of the feeling aggregate

is experience. Therefore, it is feeling.

Question: What are the particularities of this [general characteristic] apart from [the object's] own entity?

Answer: Particularities are constituted by specific and general characteristics. The specific characteristic is [the object's] own entity; that which is the unique entity of such things as blue. All phenomena of the aggregates, the sources, and the constituents lack those general characteristics. Therefore, they are without characteristic. The very fact that they are without characteristic also refutes that they [have] their own entity. Therefore, it is not necessary to force the issue.

Question: If all phenomena are empty and without characteristic, how are they produced in accordance with their own conditions and how do they cease through the cessation of their own conditions?

Answer: They are composed by the conditions of ignorance (*avidyā*) in that way. The branches of mundane existence, such as "consciousness," are created by the conditions of composition (*saṃskāra*), and composition is ended by putting an end to ignorance. By ending composition, the branches of mundane existence end, "consciousness ends," etc. [The sūtra] is teaching that those [cessations] do not exist in this perfection of wisdom. Therefore, it is said "unproduced, unceased."

Question: If that is the case, how are the thoroughly afflicted as well as the completely pure four truths of Superiors, [both of which] involve cause and effect, possible?

Answer: [The sūtra] says "stainless and not stainless."[61] Because they lack an entity that is stained by the affliction, all phenomena are stainless. Since they are without purity from the standpoint of the elimination of stains, they are said to be "not stainless" because all phenomena are naturally clear light.

Question: If that is the case, how do faults diminish through abiding spontaneously and signlessly in order to abandon the fault of signs on the immovable stage [the eighth Bodhisattva stage]?[62] How is it feasible that earlier [on the path] the afflictions of the bad realms, such as total obscuration, were abandoned?

Answer: [The sūtra] says "undiminished"; here it is seen [to mean] that faults [are not] ultimately diminished. Similarly, on the three [pure stages], such as the ninth stage, one attains respectively the individual correct knowledge, the great superknowledge (*abhijñā*), as well as the wisdom of non-obstruction. Therefore, [the sūtra] says "unfilled" in order to teach that there is no filling with good qualities. Here, one should affix "with good qualities" [to unfilled] because this is what is said in the *Ratnakaraṇḍaka Sūtra*.

Question: Why are there only eight aspects and why are they set forth in that order?

Answer: What is explained here is the heart of the perfection of wisdom; the heart is the supreme and the primary among the other parts. The primary meaning of the perfection of wisdom is the three doors of liberation, such as emptiness. These eight aspects are included in those [three]. Those aspects are ordered here in this way: emptiness and without characteristic are [included] in the samādhi on emptiness; the ones in the middle, the refutations of production, cessation, affliction, and purity, are the samādhi of signlessness; and the last two are the samādhi of wishlessness, called wishless here because it puts an end to wishing for the abandonment of faults or the attainment of good qualities.[63]

Vimalamitra explains the eightfold profundity by providing four questions from a hypothetical questioner, one question dealing with "without characteristic" and three dealing with the remaining three pairs.

He discusses "characteristic" (*lakṣaṇa*) in terms of the general characteristics (*sāmānyalakṣaṇa*) of phenomena rather than explicitly dealing with the notion of specific characteristic (*svalakṣaṇa*), a rather common object of Mādhyamika refutation. He describes the general characteristic as that which defines or identifies an object. Thus, the general characteristic of form is its definition, "that which is suitable as form," and that which defines feeling is its definition, "experience." Vimalamitra argues that all phenomena are devoid of such general characteristics, and being empty of general characteristics they are perforce empty of specific characteristics.

Such a radical denial of any character of the varieties of phenomena evokes the question as to how, then, things are produced by causes and conditions and how things cease to exist. That is, without general and specific characteristics, what is the mechanism of production and cessation? Vimalamitra answers that production and cessation take place via the operation of ignorance, which conditions all phenomena. In the twelvefold sequence of dependent arising (*pratītyasamutpāda*), it is ignorance that causes conditioned action (*saṃskārakarma*), which in turn causes consciousness (*vijñāna*), the third of the twelve links in the chain of mundane existence, which are consequently produced in sequence. Hence, it is ignorance and the action that it motivates that create the world. By putting an end to ignorance, conditioned action ceases, and then consciousness, and then all of the constituents of mundane existence. But in the perfection of wisdom, ignorance is absent so that no such production or cessation takes place. Thus, all phenomena are "unproduced, unceased."

Adhering to the notion of cause and effect as real, the hypothetical questioner turns his attention away from the general production and cessation of phenomena to the process of how the mind becomes defiled by the afflictions and how it becomes purified by understanding the four truths. How do defilement and purification take place if there is no cause and effect? Vimalamitra answers that all phenomena are naturally pure and thus cannot be tainted in any real way by the adventitious afflictions. In the same way, because all phenomena are naturally and beginninglessly of the nature of clear light, it is impossible that they somehow acquire purity. Hence, all phenomena are "stainless, not stainless."

The questioner persists, asking whether it is not the case that as a Bodhisattva progresses through the ten stages (*bhūmi*) that certain faults, such as seeds for rebirth in the realms of animals, hungry ghosts, and hell beings, are abandoned and certain knowledges and wisdoms are attained. Vimalamitra concedes that this indeed takes place, but will not admit that this occurs as the result of any inherent diminishment of faults or acquisition of good qualities. Thus, all phenomena are "undiminished and unfilled."

Finally, the questioner asks about the order of the eightfold profundity. Vimalamitra answers that they are listed in that sequence because they are to be summarized under the three headings of emptiness (*śūnyatā*), signlessness (*animitta*), and wishlessness (*apraṇihita*), the renowned three doors of liberation (*vimokṣamukham*).

The Doors of Liberation

The samādhis on the three doors of liberation are described in a number of ways in Buddhist Sanskrit literature. In the *Abhidharmakośa* (VIII.24-27), Vasubandhu explains the three samādhis in terms of the sixteen aspects of the four truths. The four aspects of the first truth, the truth of suffering (*duḥkhasatya*) are impermanence, misery, emptiness, and selflessness. The four aspects of the truth of origin (*samudayasatya*) are cause, origin, strong production, and condition. The aspects of the third, the truth of cessation (*nirodhasatya*) are cessation, pacification, auspicious exaltedness, and definite emergence. The four aspects of the truth of the path (*mārgasatya*) are path, suitability, achievement, and deliverance.[64] According to Vasubandhu, the samādhi of signlessness is similar to the four aspects of the truth of cessation, such as peace. It is called signless because the cessation which is nirvāṇa is free of ten signs: form, sound, odor, taste, tangibility, male, female, production, abiding, and cessation. The samādhi of emptiness observes selflessness and emptiness, two of the four aspects of the truth of suffering. The samādhi of wishlessness observes the remaining ten aspects, those of origin and path and the remaining two of the truth of suffering. Thus Vasubandhu says at VIII.24:

> The signless is the aspect of peace.
> Emptiness engages in selflessness and emptiness.
> The wishless [has similarity] with the aspects
> Of the truths other than those.[65]

The terms emptiness, signlessness, and wishlessness appear together in a number of Mahāyāna sūtras. For example, the *Kāśyapaparivarta* says:

> Phenomena are not made empty by emptiness; phenomena themselves are empty. Phenomena are not made signless by signlessness; phenomena themselves are signless. Phenomena are not made wishless by wishlessness; phenomena themselves are wishless. The individual knowledge of those, Kāśyapa, is the middle path, the correct individual knowledge of phenomena.[68]

The *Āryarāṣṭrapālaparipṛcchā* says:

> Transmigrators wander because they do not understand
> Emptiness, peace, and non-production.
> The Compassionate One guides them with method
> And with hundreds of reasonings.[67]

A Tibetan commentator explains that emptiness in the stanza refers to the lack of a truly existent entity of all phenomena. Peace is signlessness, which is the emptiness of a truly existent cause. Wishlessness means that effects lack truly existent production. Because they do not understand the three doors of liberation, sentient beings, under the influence of the conception of I and mine, engage in a variety of actions. As a result, they cycle in the ocean of suffering of saṃsāra. The Buddha, whose nature is compassion, considers these beings mercifully and teaches them with a variety of methods and reasonings, causing them to enter the three doors of liberation.[68]

Two more interpretations occur in the eighteenth chapter of Maitreya's *Mahāyānasūtrālaṃkāra.* The first identifies the objects of the three samādhis, the second their causes. Regarding the objects of the three, the text says:

> The objects of the three samādhis
> Are the two selflessnesses,
> The basis which is viewed as a self,
> And the eternal pacification of that.[69]

Here, it is said that the samādhi on emptiness realizes the selflessness of persons and phenomena, the samādhi on wishlessness views the five aggregates, which serve as the basis for the conception of self, as faulty, and the samādhi on signlessness views nirvāṇa, which is the complete pacification forever of the aggregates.[70]

The second aligns the samādhis on the doors of liberation with the four seals that certify a doctrine as Buddhist, identifying the latter as causes of the former:

> It is explained to Bodhisattvas
> That the fourfold summary of the doctrine
> Is a cause of the three samādhis.[71]

According to Vasubandhu's commentary, "All conditioned things are impermanent" and "All contaminated things are miserable" are the cause of the samādhi on the door of liberation of wishlessness. "All phenomena are selfless" is the cause of the samādhi on the door of liberation emptiness. The fourth seal, that "Nirvāṇa is virtuous and peaceful", is cause of the samādhi on the door of liberation wishlessness.[72]

Haribhadra's presentation in the *Sphuṭārtha* is similar to that of Vasubandhu in the *Abhidharmakośa.* The samādhi of emptiness is the wisdom that directly realizes emptiness and selflessness. Because this is the actual antidote to the view of self, it is the first door of liberation. The samādhi of signlessness takes as its object the entities of the eight aspects of the truths of cessation and path. It serves as the antidote to the misconception of signs that causes the view of self. This is the second door of liberation. The samādhi of wishlessness is the wisdom that directly realizes impermanence and suffering (the two remaining aspects of the truth of suffering) and the four aspects of true origins.

This serves as an antidote to the wish for a final object of attainment in the three realms of saṃsāra. It is the third door of liberation.[73]

Asaṅga provides at least two descriptions of the three doors of liberation, both of which differ from that of his sibling, Vasubandhu. In the *Mahāyānasaṃgraha*, he says that the doors of liberation of emptiness, wishlessness, and signlessness are posited in dependence on the imaginary, dependent, and thoroughly established natures, respectively.[74] In the *Bodhisattvabhūmi*, he says that the samādhi of emptiness is the Bodhisattva's state of mind that sees that everything has a nature of inexpressibility (*nirabhilapyasvabhāva*). The samādhi of wishlessness is the wishless state of mind, which sees that many sins are created by the afflictions that result from mistakenly conceiving the inexpressible nature. The samādhi of signlessness is the state of mind that removes all the signs of conceptual elaboration of the inexpressible nature.[75]

It is clear, then, that although the terms emptiness, wishlessness, and signlessness often appear together in Sanskrit literature, there is little consensus concerning their order, much less their meaning. It is unclear from a survey of these various definitions exactly what Vimalamitra means by the three doors of liberation and why he grouped the eight profundities under the three doors in the way that he did. Fortunately, an explanation of Vimalamitra's intention is provided in the *Heart Sūtra* commentary of Atīśa. He says:

> The emptiness of entityness of phenomena is the door of liberation emptiness. "Emptiness" and "without characteristic" explain [that phenomena] lack a specific entity and a general entity [respectively]. Because all meanings of emptiness are included in those two perspectives, [the inclusion of "emptiness" and "without characteristic" under the door emptiness] is explained. Signlessness is the lack of causes and causes are posited in terms of effects. "Unproduced, unceased, stainless, not stainless" [are included under the door of liberation signlessness] because they include the cause and effect of the thoroughly afflicted and the cause and effect of the completely pure. Regarding wishlessness, there are two effects that are objects of wishes: the wish to be separated from faults and the wish to be endowed with good qualities. Separation from these two [wishes] is wishlessness.[76]

Thus, "emptiness" and "without characteristic" demonstrate that phenomena lack both a specific or general nature of inherent existence. They are included under the heading of the door of liberation emptiness, which negates the existence of an inherently existent nature of phenomena. "Unproduced," "unceased," "stainless," and "not stainless" are encompassed by the door of liberation signlessness, which negates the inherent existence of causes. Causes are posited in terms of effects, so it is permissible that the negation of any inherent existence in the process of cause and effect that occurs in both the afflicted class and the pure class be included under signlessness. The door of liberation wishlessness demonstrates that effects do not inherently exist. In the case of the path to liberation, the desired effects are the abandonment of faults and the acquisition of good qualities. The emptiness of these is implied by "undiminished" and "unfilled."

Atīśa concludes by saying that the Sugata teaches emptiness, wishlessness, and signlessness in all sūtras as an antidote to attachment to the view, behavior, and fruit of Buddhahood.

Chapter 6

The Negations and Enlightenment

Therefore, Śāriputra, in emptiness there is no form, no feeling, no discrimination, no compositional factors, no consciousness, no eye, no ear, no nose, no tongue, no body, no mind, no form, no sound, no odor, no taste, no object of touch, no phenomenon. There is no eye constituent, no mental constituent, up to and including no mental consciousness constituent. There is no ignorance, no extinction of ignorance, up to and including no aging and death and no extinction of aging and death. Similarly, there are no sufferings, no origins, no cessations, no paths, no wisdom, no attainment, and also no non-attainment.

Therefore, Śāriputra, because Bodhisattvas have no attainment they depend on and abide in the perfection of wisdom and their minds are without obstruction and without fear. Having completely passed beyond all error they go to the completion of nirvāṇa. All the Buddhas who abide in the three times have been fully awakened into unsurpassed, perfect, complete enlightenment through relying on the perfection of wisdom.

Here Avalokiteśvara proclaims the negation of all phenomena in the face of emptiness. He does not, however, simply say that in emptiness there are no phenomena. Rather, he systematically negates the categories of phenomena formulated by the Hīnayāna Abhidharma masters, of whom Śāriputra is supreme. Before considering the meaning of Avalokiteśvara's negation, it is useful to identify those categories.

The first of the classifications of phenomena is the five aggregates. The Bodhisattva then says, "no eye, no ear, no tongue, no body, no mind, no form, no sound, no odor, no taste, no object of touch, no phenomenon." This is the negation of the twelve sources (*āyatana*) of consciousness, comprising the six senses (*indriya*) and their six objects. The five senses (eye, ear, nose, tongue, body) are forms of subtle matter, included in the form aggregate, that provide the physical bases for the generation of the sense consciousnesses. In order for consciousness to occur, there must be three conditions: the dominant condition (*adhipatipratyaya*), which is the sense; the object of observation condition (*ālambanapratyaya*), the object that the consciousness will apprehend; and the immediately preceding condition (*samanantarapratyaya*), any former moment of consciousness, insuring the existence of the unbroken continuum of consciousness. The mental consciousness has no physical sense as its dominant condition. Its dominant condition is the mental sense (*mana indriya*), which can be the prior moment of any of the six consciousnesses. Hence, the dominant condition and the immediately preceding condition of a mental consciousness are the same.

The six objects of the six consciousnesses are the objects of the five sense consciousnesses and the object of the mental consciousness. The objects of the sense consciousness are forms (here referring to color and shape perceived by the eye consciousness, rather than the larger category of the form aggregate), sounds, odors, tastes, and objects of touch. The object of the mental consciousness can be any object of knowledge, permanent or impermanent, physical or mental. Hence its object is "phenomena." Technically speaking, this final category includes all objects of knowledge not comprised by the other eleven categories, namely, feeling, discrimination, compositional factors, non-revelatory forms, and all permanent phenomena. The six sense powers and the six objects are aligned as follows:

Senses	*Objects*
eye	forms
ear	sounds
nose	odors
tongue	tastes
body	tangible objects
mental sense	phenomena

Because the object of the mental consciousness can be any object of knowledge, the classification of the twelve sources includes all phenomena in the universe. To delineate clearly, however, the three-fold division into senses, objects, and the consciousnesses they generate, the eighteen constituents (*dhātu*) are set forth. This classification simply adds the six consciousnesses to the twelve sources. This is what the sūtra refers to when it says, "no eye constituent, no mental constituent, up to and including no mental consciousness constituent." The eighteen constituents may be arranged as follows, with the names of the constituents specifically mentioned in the sūtra capitalized:

Senses	*Objects*	*Consciousnesses*
EYE CONSTITUENT	form constituent	eye consciousness constituent
ear constituent	sound constituent	ear consciousness constituent
nose constituent	odor constituent	nose consciousness constituent
tongue constituent	taste constituent	tongue consciousness constituent
body constituent	tangible object constituent	body consciousness constituent
MENTAL CONSTITUENT	phenomena constituent	MENTAL CONSCIOUSNESS CONSTITUENT

A detailed presentation of the five aggregates, twelve sources, and sixteen constituents occurs in the first chapter of Vasubandhu's *Abhidharmakośa.*

Avalokiteśvara then says, "There is no ignorance, no extinction of ignorance, up to and including no aging and death and no extinction of aging and death." He refers to the twelvefold dependent arising (*pratītyasamutpāda*) of saṃsāra and its twelvefold extinction. The chain of dependent arising is an ancient doctrine of Buddhism; in some accounts its realization constitutes the Buddha's enlightenment at Bodhgāyā. It describes the manner in which ignorance gives rise eventually to birth and death. The original significance of the specific chain of cause and effect remains somewhat uncertain. Later scholastics, however, provided a variety of explanations whereby the sequence of the twelve links occurs over the course of two or three lifetimes.[1] The twelvefold order is as follows:

ignorance (*avidyā*)
action (*saṃskārakarma*)
consciousness (*vijñāna*)
name and form (*nāmarūpa*)
sources (*āyatana*)
contact (*sparśa*)
feeling (*vedanā*)
attachment (*tṛṣṇā*)
grasping (*upādāna*)
existence (*bhava*)
birth (*jāti*)
aging and death (*jarāmaraṇa*)

The sūtra mentions the first and last, indicating the process by which the cycle of rebirth functions, and mentions the extinction of the first and last, indicating the process by which the cycle of rebirth is destroyed. By putting an end to ignorance, action ceases. When action ceases, consciousness ends, and so on. The twelve links of the chain of dependent arising are often depicted as a circle, the beginning of which, ignorance, can only be discerned by a Buddha.[2]

The sūtra next lists the four truths: "Similarly, there are no sufferings, no origins, no cessations, no paths." The Buddha is said to have taught the four truths in his first sermon at Sarnath. The varieties of experience that are qualified by suffering are to be identified; the origins of those sufferings, such as desire, hatred, and ignorance, are to be abandoned; the cessation of suffering, nirvāṇa, is to be actualized; and the paths to nirvāṇa are to be cultivated.[3] According to Vasubandhu, the order of the four truths follows the medical model of disease, diagnosis, prognosis, and cure.[4]

Finally, Avalokiteśvara turns to the consciousness that understands these categories and the results of that understanding, saying, "no wisdom, no attainment, and no non-attainment."

Responding to the apparent contradiction of the sūtra saying that emptiness is form and then saying that in emptiness there is no form, a Tibetan commentator takes this section of the sūtra to refer to meditation on emptiness on the fourth of the five Mahāyāna paths, the path of meditation (*bhāvanāmārga*). Here, the Bodhisattva enters repeatedly into equipoise on emptiness in which the only thing that appears is emptiness, the utter vacuity of inherent existence. No conventional phenomena appear at that time, such that there is "no form, no feeling, no discrimination."[5] This interpretation is implicitly supported by Vimalamitra, who says, "Seeing emptiness thoroughly is to be understood as thoroughly not seeing form; not to see any phenomenon is to see emptiness.[6] With such an interpretation, it is not necessary to say that the statement, "in emptiness, there is no form" means, "in emptiness there is no *inherently existent* form" because in meditative equipoise on the mode of being of form, form would have to appear if it inherently existed in that its inherent existence would be the final mode of being of form. To say that "in emptiness there is no form" implies that form does not inherently exist without suggesting that form is non-existent.[7] Other interpretations, however, are possible. Consider those of Jñānamitra and Praśāstrasena.

Jñānamitra appears to read the statement *śūnyatāyāṃ na rūpaṃ*, "in emptiness there is no form" or "when there is emptiness, there is no form" as "emptiness is not form". He says:

Regarding "emptiness is not form", form has the characteristic of disintegration whereas emptiness is without characteristic. Therefore, emptiness is not form. It is not feeling in the same way [because] feeling has the characteristic of experience. It is not discrimination [because] discrimination has the characteristic of apprehension. It is not compositional factors [because] compositional factors have the characteristic of composition. It is not consciousness [because] consciousness has the characteristic of apprehending individual particularities whereas emptiness is unobservable. Therefore, it is not consciousness. It is not those [aggregates] because the five aggregates have the characteristic of contamination (*sāsrava*); emptiness is not the aggregates.

It is not the eye [because] the eye has the characteristic of sight, but because emptiness is without characteristic, it is not the eye. It is not the ear similarly [because] the ear has the characteristic of hearing. It is not the nose [because] the nose has the characteristic of smelling. It is not the tongue [because] the tongue has the character of experiencing tastes. It is not the body [because] the body has the character of touching. It is not the mind because the mind has the nature of distinguishing particularities, and because emptiness is without characteristic, it is not the mind. Thus, the six senses have the characteristic of apprehending, but because emptiness is without characteristic, it is not the six senses.

It is not form. Form has the characteristic of color and shape, but because emptiness is without characteristic, it is not form. It is not sound similarly [because] sound has the characteristic of the pleasant or unpleasant. It is not odor because odor has the characteristic of scent. It is not taste because taste has the characteristic of flavor. It is not tangible objects because tangible objects have the characteristic of being rough or smooth to the touch. It is not phenomena because phenomena have the characteristic of particular aspects, but emptiness is without characteristic; therefore, it is not phenomena. Thus, objects have the characteristic of conditions that cause observation, but emptiness is without characteristic. Therefore, it is not the objects.

It is not the eye constituent, the mental constituent, up to and including the mental consciousness constituent. The eighteen constituents have the characteristic of viciousness, but emptiness is without characteristic. Therefore, it is not the eighteen constituents.

It is not ignorance, it is not aging and death, it is not the extinction of ignorance, up to and including, it is not the extinction of aging and death. The twelvefold dependent arising from ignorance to aging and death has the characteristic of upholding saṃsāra, but because emptiness

> is without characteristic, it is not ignorance up to and including aging and death. The extinction of ignorance up to and including the extinction of aging and death have the characteristic of purification, but because emptiness is without characteristic, it is not the extinction of ignorance up to and including the extinction of aging and death.
>
> It is not suffering, origin, cessation, or path. Suffering has the characteristic of affliction. Origin has the characteristic of appropriation (*upādāna*), cessation has the characteristic of peace, and path has the characteristic of knowledge, but emptiness is without characteristic. Therefore, emptiness is not the four truths.
>
> It is not wisdom. Wisdom has the characteristic of directly perceiving all phenomena, but because emptiness is without characteristic, it is not wisdom. It is not attainment, it is not non-attainment. Attainment is the unsurpassed, perfect, complete enlightenment. Non-attainment is the non-attainment of the unsurpassed by sentient beings. "Is not" [means] that the characteristic of emptiness is without unsurpassed enlightenment as well as [without] sentient beings. Therefore, it is not attainment and it is not non-attainment. These enumerations teach the emptiness of inherent existence with regard to all phenomena, saying that "emptiness is like that." This [section sets forth] the characteristic of emptiness.[8]

Jñānamitra sees this section as delineating the distinctiveness of emptiness: how it is not any of the various categories of conventional phenomena because it lacks their defining characteristics. Emptiness is thus seen as beyond definition and expression. He does not relate his interpretation here that emptiness is without characteristic to the statement early in the sūtra that all phenomena are without characteristic because they are empty.

Praśāstrasena provides a somewhat more interesting reading of the section. He writes:

> It was taught above that the individual divisions of the five aggregates are empty. Consequently, if the five aggregates, which are [mistakenly] thought to have signs, are empty, it is unsuitable to designate them with names such as "form," because they are indivisible from emptiness. Thus, in order to dispel signs which are [mis]conceptions about the names, it says "when [there is] emptiness, form is not, feeling is not", etc. The five aggregates are empty of entityness, that is, they have the characteristic of indivisibility [from emptiness] beyond names and designations. Therefore, because the signs imputed to form and so forth do not exist, there are the words, "form is not, feeling is not"; that is, "no form, no feeling." Furthermore, in emptiness, "form" is not

expressed as a name and "feeling" is not expressed.[9]

Here, Praśāstrasena considers some of the implications of the aggregates being empty of inherent existence. If form, as well as the other four aggregates, are emptiness, it is inappropriate to designate them with names that imply the existence of signs that distinguish them in some ultimate manner. Emptiness is indivisible and beyond expression and so must be the aggregates. The signs by which the aggregates are differentiated do not inherently exist. Therefore, the sūtra says, "In emptiness, there is no form, no feeling," and so forth. Also, although form is emptiness, form is not a name for emptiness. Hence, "when emptiness, no form," can be taken to mean that the name "form" cannot be used to express emptiness. Emptiness is beyond names and designations and because form is emptiness, it is equally inexpressible. Praśāstrasena continues:

> "Not eye, not ear, not nose, not tongue, not body, not mind." This is the six senses. The six senses depend on the five aggregates. Therefore, if the five aggregates do not exist so do not the six senses because they are not other than the five aggregates. "Not form, not sound, not odor, not taste, not touch, not phenomena." This is the six objects. They are the fructifications of predispositions (*vāsanā*) due to the power of ignorance. A polluted mind holds that that which is established as [these] conditioned effects exists. Because ultimately they are empty of entityness, [they] "do not exist." "Not the eye constituent to not the mental constituent." This is the eighteen constituents. If the six internal senses do not exist, the bases of the six consciousnesses do not exist. Therefore, because six external objects do not exist, the abodes of the six consciousnesses do not exist. Because nothing arises, the six consciousnesses also do not exist. Therefore, the eighteen constituents do not exist.[10]

Here, Praśāstrasena emphasizes the interdependence of the six senses, the six objects, and the six constituents. The five physical senses are included in the form aggregate and the mental sense is included in the consciousness aggregate. Hence, the demonstration of the emptiness of the five aggregates entails the emptiness of the six senses. He adopts something of a Yogācāra perspective toward the six objects, calling them the fructification of predispositions, implying that the six objects do not exist as external objects but are merely appearances that are falsely perceived as real due to the power of ignorance; the six objects do not inherently exist. If the senses, which serve as the physical bases—the dominant conditions—of the six consciousnesses, do not exist and the six objects that serve as the objects—the observed object conditions—of the six consciousnesses do not exist, then consciousness also does not exist; its causes are lacking. Because all phenomena are dependent in this or some other manner, nothing exists objectively, autonomously, inherently. As Nāgārjuna says in his *Mūlamadhyamakakārikā* (XXIV.19):

> Because there are no phenomena
> That are not dependent arisings,
> There are no phenomena
> That are not empty.[11]

It is significant that Praśāstrasena says that the six objects "ultimately are empty of entityness." This indicates that he recognizes that the negations of this section, "form does not exist," and so forth, are not negations of the existence of the five aggregates, the twelve sources, and the eighteen constituents, but rather are negations of their existing by way of their own entity ultimately. It has already been pointed out by Jñānamitra that utter non-existence is an extreme to be avoided. According to dGe-lugs-pa presentations of Mādhyamika theories of scriptural interpretation, the statement in the *Heart Sūtra*, "no form" requires interpretation (*neyārtha*) according to the Svātantrikas because the qualification "ultimately existent" (that is, "no ultimately existent form") is not explicit. According to the Prāsangikas, however, the statement is definitive (*nītārtha*) because the qualification "inherently existent" occurs earlier in the sūtra (when Avalokiteśvara sees that the five aggregates are empty of inherent existence) and thus is implied in this context. Furthermore, in the *Śatasāhasrikāprajñāpāramitā*, the Buddha says that when he says that things do not exist, "this is for the conventions of the world, not ultimately."[12]

Praśāstrasena goes on to consider the twelvefold dependent arising:

> "Ignorance is not, the extinction of ignorance is not, aging and death are not, the extinction of aging and death are not." This is the sphere of those who have entered the vehicle of pratyekabuddhas. Saying "ignorance" is the brief statement of the teaching [of the other eleven branches] up to and including aging and death; from action conditioned by ignorance are seen consciousness, name and form, the six sources, contact, feeling, attachment, grasping, existence, birth, and aging and death. Ignorance arises from the view of self. The conception of self arises from that which does not exist. Therefore, ignorance also does not exist. For example, by lighting a lamp in a house that has long been dark, [the darkness] becomes non-existent in an instant and its non-

> existence does not appear as something real. In that way, investigation with the lamp of wisdom makes non-existent in an instant the thick darkness of ignorance [that has obscured] sentient beings beginninglessly. Its non-existence does not appear as something real. What is called "knowledge" is just the designation for the opposite of ignorance; because ignorance does not exist, not even the name of knowledge is established. Therefore, "ignorance is not and the extinction of ignorance is not." Because the entity of ignorance does not exist, ignorance does not exist. Because its non-existence does not appear as something real, its extinction does not exist.[13]

In this section, Praśāstrasena emphasizes the invalidity of saṃsāra, the house of cards that rests on the foundation of ignorance. Ignorance is the conception of self. Because the object of ignorance does not exist, it can be said that ignorance also does not exist in the sense that it is utterly unfounded. All the other eleven branches of the chain of dependent arising are derived ultimately from ignorance. Thus, if the non-existence of ignorance can be established, the chain is broken. Ignorance is dispelled by the light of wisdom, and having been dispelled is not to be found anywhere; it does not appear. Knowledge is simply the extinction of ignorance, but if ignorance never existed, there is no extinction of it. Thus, the sūtra says that there is no ignorance and no extinction of ignorance.

He turns next to the four truths:

> "Suffering, origin, cessation, and path are not." This is the four truths, the sphere of those who have entered the vehicle of śrāvakas. The truths are of three types: the mundane, the supramundane, and the ultimate supramundane truths. Regarding that, the mundane truths are understanding that the five aggregates are origins and that aging and death are suffering. The supramundane truths are understanding suffering, origin, cessation, and path. Regarding the [ultimate] supramundane truths of Superiors, the understanding that the aggregates are not produced is the understanding of the truth of suffering. The understanding of the truth of origin is that by which mundane existence is destroyed. The understanding that ignorance and the insidiosities (*anuśaya*) are without entityness is the understanding of the truth of cessation. Not making superimpositions about anything due to the equality of phenomena is the understanding of truth of the path. Thus, because the truths also are ultimately without entityness, [the sūtra says they] do not exist. What is the evidence that the truths lack entityness? The *Akṣayamatinirdeśa Sūtra* says:
>
> > How does a Bodhisattva become skilled in the truths? The aggregates

> are suffering. The understanding of how [the aggregates] are empty of the signs of suffering is called the Superiors' truth of suffering. The aggregates arise from the cause of attachment and the cause of [wrong] view. That which does not grasp and does not superimpose the cause of attachment and the cause of [wrong] view is called the Superiors' truth of origin. The understanding that the aggregates do not arise earlier and do not depart later and do not abide in the present is called the Superiors' truth of cessation. That which is placed in equipoise on the non-dual wisdom and understands that the four truths are emptiness is the Superiors' truth of path.[14]

It is not surprising at this juncture to learn that the four truths are also empty. Praśāstrasena concludes with a discussion of the emptiness of Bodhisattva's wisdom.

> "Wisdom is not, attainment is not, non-attainment is not." This is the sphere of one who has entered the great vehicle of the Bodhisattva. "Wisdom" is the non-dual wisdom which is the state of having abandoned the afflictive obstructions and the obstructions to omniscience. Because it is not wisdom ultimately, it says, "no wisdom." Attainment is the attainment of what did not exist before. If attainment exists, it also is empty; if there is fruition, it will disintegrate. Therefore, the Buddha nature abides equally in all sentient beings and is not absent in the beginning or attained in the end. Even the levels of the ten stages that are mentioned are just the gradual purification of the predispositions of ignorance on the ālayavijñāna; upon purifying the predispositions of ignorance, the dharmadhātu that is the mirror-like wisdom of a Buddha [is attained]. Regarding [the dharmadhātu], there is nothing to be called attainment or non-attainment. Therefore, [the sūtra] says, "no attainment, no non-attainment." The *Saptaśatikā-prajñāpāramitā* (*Perfection of Wisdom in Seven Hundred Stanzas*) says, "Not practicing any signs is the practice of the perfection of wisdom. Not attaining anything is the attainment of unsurpassed enlightenment."[15]

Praśāstrasena's discussion here centers on the impossibility of attaining or not attaining that which has never been lost, the dharmadhātu, the Buddha nature, that abides naturally in all sentient beings. Although it is said that predispositions are gradually eradicated from the mind and purity gradually achieved, there is no attainment of anything that is not empty. How these negations relate to enlightenment is taken up in the next section of the sūtra.

Therefore, Śāriputra, because Bodhisattvas have no attainment they

> *depend on and abide in the perfection of wisdom and their minds are without obstruction and without fear. Having completely passed beyond all error they go to the completion of nirvāṇa. All the Buddhas who abide in the three times have been fully enlightened into unsurpassed, perfect, complete enlightenment through relying on the perfection of wisdom.*

This section sets forth the good qualities (*guṇa*) of the perfection of wisdom. Praśāstrasena concedes that, "although the unsurpassed enlightenment of yogis has a nature of emptiness, it is not the case that there is no effect of the perfection of wisdom; there is. In order to create joy, [its] good qualities are explained." Yet he reminds us that to abide in and rely on the perfection of wisdom means not to abide in any signs.[16] Praśāstrasena again adopts a Yogācāra perspective in describing the obstructions of which the Bodhisattva's mind is free; they are internal predispositions and all signs of external objects. When he glosses the error that Bodhisattvas have passed beyond, he says, "Viewing non-existent external objects in a variety of ways due to predispositions of ignorance on the ālayavijñāna is error."[17]

Vimalamitra identifies the obstructions as the twenty-two obscurations (*sammoha*) and the eleven assumptions of bad states (*dauṣṭhulya*), which are abandoned over the eleven stages—the ten Bodhisattva stages and the stage of Buddhahood. On each stage, two obscurations and one assumption of bad states is overcome.[18]

Vajrapāṇi provides a more extensive discussion of the nature of error which Bodhisattvas pass beyond.

> Error is not having interest in reality and seeing phenomena as real, thinking that sentient beings of the three realms exist ultimately. The sentient beings of the three realms are mistaken; the happiness and suffering of the sentient beings of the three realms are like seeing a magician's illusion in a dream or seeing a rope as a snake in a dream or a virgin seeing the birth and death of her son in a dream. Error is mistakenly seeing the unmistaken ultimate truth. For example, some people on ships see mountains and cliffs move and tremble. In the same way, people without a spiritual friend (*kalyāṇamitra*) mistakenly see the profound and unmistaken reality. For example, young lions drink lion's milk that if drunk by others will crack the body and poison them. Similarly, the profound meaning of the perfection of wisdom is to be taught to those of the Mahāyāna lineage with very pure minds. If it is taught to those of the Hīnayāna lineage, they will be frightened with terror and fear. For example, if a person with a phlegm [disorder] is given milk to drink, it will not dispel the malady and will poison him.

In the same way, the profound reality is not to be taught to those who are not vessels. Furthermore, if, however, that [milk] is made into yogurt and whey and given to the person with a phlegm [disorder], it will be beneficial. In the same way, when the profound reality which is the perfection of wisdom is mixed with the [other] five perfections, such as giving, and is taught to Hīnayānists, it will be beneficial. For example, suppose that many blind people are separated from their hometowns and from their mothers and wander in cities and towns. Upon returning, although they encounter their hometowns and their mothers, they do not recognize them. Similarly, Hīnayānists become separated from the city of omniscience and the mother, the perfection of wisdom, and wander through the cities of saṃsāra. Upon returning, although they encounter the city of omniscience and the mother, the meaning which is the heart of the perfection of wisdom, they do not recognize it. They will [only] understand the heart through the examples and meanings taught by a spiritual friend endowed with method and wisdom. For example, some people who wished to take jewels from a jewel mine were told by a mistaken person that the footprint of an ox was a source of jewels. If they believed what they heard, they would be impeded. In the same way, those of the Mahāyāna lineage who cast aside the meaning of the heart of the perfection of wisdom are impeded if they look at and believe other sūtras.

Therefore, excellent persons who rely completely and in all ways on the instructions on the meaning of the heart of the perfection of wisdom bring together the meanings of the four: action, view, meditation, and fruition. Repeatedly viewing the meaning of the unmistaken heart of the Buddha's word and being mindful by mixing the mind with that [heart of his word], without being separated from emptiness, is the meaning of the action. The actual teaching of abiding in emptiness, supreme and inconceivable, is the meaning of the meditation. Non-production and non-cessation, upon freeing oneself by not seeing thoroughly afflicted phenomena and completely pure phenomena as real is the meaning of the view. Because Buddhas have no object of meditation and sentient beings have no object of awareness, the stains of objects of knowledge do not exist and the non-conceptual wisdom does not exist. Therefore, there is nothing to attain and nothing to be lost. This is the meaning of the fruition.[19]

This section of the sūtra defines the existence of all phenomena in terms of their non-existence in the face of emptiness. Śāriputra is then instructed that Bodhisattvas abide in and rely on this perfection of wisdom, the lack of inherent existence of all phenomena from form to Buddhahood. The benefit of such reliance is that by understanding the meaning of emptiness one's mind is freed from all obstruction and all reasons for fear. Having passed beyond the mistaken conception of self, the Bodhisattva also passes beyond the nirvāṇa sought by śrāvakas and pratyekabuddhas and arrives at the end, Buddhahood. This perfection of wisdom is the sole path travelled by all the Buddhas of the past, present, and future.

Chapter 7
The Mantra

Therefore, the mantra of perfection of wisdom is the mantra of great knowledge, the unsurpassed mantra, the mantra equal to the unequalled, the mantra that thoroughly pacifies all suffering. Because it is not false it should be known to be true. The mantra of the perfection of wisdom is stated:

tadyathā oṃ gate gate pāragate pārasaṃgate bodhi svāhā

The next line of the sūtra is, "Śāriputra, Bodhisattva Mahāsattvas should train in the perfection of wisdom in that way." This line would follow quite naturally after the previous section of the sūtra; the section on the mantra seems stylistically out of place, breaking the flow of Avalokiteśvara's discourse. The "therefore" that begins the section does not provide a logical connection to what precedes it. Although mantras and dhāraṇīs are often appended to some Mahāyāna sūtras, such as the *Laṅkāvatāra* and occur in texts such as the *Ratnaketudhāraṇī* (which was translated into Chinese in the fifth century), they are for the most part absent from the earlier, longer Perfection of Wisdom sūtras. Mantras are common, however, in the shorter, tantric Perfection of Wisdom texts of a much later period (c. 600-1200). The mantra in the *Heart Sūtra*, which appears in both versions of the text, may be an interpolation or may indicate a transition from the longer Perfection of Wisdom sūtras to the shorter tantric Perfection of Wisdom sūtras.[1]

The Indian commentators on the *Heart Sūtra*, all writing at a time when tantric Buddhism was in full flower, find varying degrees of significance in the mantra.

For Praśāstrasena, the mantra is stated to prevent downfall.

> Because it completely clears away all the predispositions of internal consciousness, it is the mantra of the perfection of wisdom. Because it naturally understands and clears away all of the signs of external objects[2], it is the mantra of great knowledge. Because it clears away all the signs of both the internal and the external, it is the unsurpassed mantra. Because it brings about the fruition of Buddhahood, it is the

> mantra equal to the unequalled. Because it causes the abandonment of the bad realms and fulfills the welfare of sentient beings, it is the mantra that pacifies all suffering.
>
> "It is true, not false." Because it is not spoken with words, it is wishless. Therefore, it is verbally true. Because it is not practiced with the body, it is signless; it is physically true. Because it is inconceivable by the mind, it is emptiness; it is mentally true. Thus, it does not contradict the three doors of liberation of Superiors. The perfection of wisdom accords with the conceptual door that clears away all mental signs and causes simultaneous entry into the ultimate. Therefore, it is true, not false.
>
> "It is to be known" means that the perfection of wisdom is to be known as the cause of going to Buddhahood. The mantra of the perfection of wisdom is stated thus, "Tadyathā gate gate pāragate pārasaṃgate bodhi svāhā." This mantra of the perfection of wisdom serves as the cause of mundane and supramundane merit. Mundane merit is effectively able to prevent harm and protect one from afflictions, demons, and obstacles. Regarding supramundane merit, relying on this dhāraṇī serves as a cause of wisdom and knowledge.[3]

Praśāstrasena, thus, does not consider the meaning of the mantra, concentrating his attention instead on the meaning of its epithets. Jñānamitra adopts a similar approach. His glosses of the epithets differ from those of Praśāstrasena. For example, he takes the phrase "equal to the unequalled" to mean that the perfection of wisdom is not equal to the deeds of worldly beings, śrāvakas, and pratyekabuddhas, but is equal to the wisdom of all the Buddhas. It is the mantra that completely pacifies all sufferings because reciting the perfection of wisdom, bearing it in mind properly, and explaining it to others destroys all diseases and brings one under the protection of Buddhas, deities, and nāgas, and practicing the perfection of wisdom overturns the bad realms and the entire ocean of saṃsāra.[4]

Śrīmahājana, whose commentary on the *Heart Sūtra* is in large part an attempt to correlate the words of the sūtra to late Indian Mahāyāna delineations of the path, finds such a correlation in the words of the mantra. He says:

> *Gate gate pāragate* means the path of seeing, with the nature of having abandoned the six places of rebirth. Therefore, one goes beyond by going from the path of great desire to the path of accumulation. One goes beyond by going from the path of accumulation to the path of preparation. Going even beyond those is *gate gate pāragate*. *Pārasaṃ*

> means abiding in the path of meditation. *Gate* is different and means abiding in the path of no more learning. *Bodhi* is the fruition. *Oṃ* and *svāhā* are words of blessing for achieving the effect of repetition.[5]

The mantra can be translated as "Gone, gone, gone beyond, gone completely beyond, enlightenment." Śrīmahājana says that the first "gone" refers to proceeding from the state of a worldly being, involved in great desire, to the path of accumulation, the first of the Bodhisattva paths. The second "gone" refers to moving from the first path to the second, the path of accumulation. "Gone beyond" indicates moving from the path of preparation to the path of seeing. It is with the attainment of the path of seeing that emptiness is seen directly for the first time, making the Bodhisattva a Superior (*ārya*) and destroying the seeds for future rebirth as an animal, hungry ghost, or hell being. Because of the special qualities of this path, it merits "gone beyond" rather than a simple "gone." *Pārasaṃgate* means "gone completely beyond." Śrīmahājana chooses to divide the word in two with *pārasaṃ* (completely beyond) referring to the fourth path and *gate* referring to the final path, the path of no more learning, which is Buddhahood. Thus, he says, the final *gate* does not mean "gone", apparently because there is no place further to go, but rather means "abide." *Bodhi* means enlightenment. Later Tibetan commentators arrived at a somewhat more straightforward correspondence, following Śrīmahājana's explanation through the path of seeing, but then explaining that "go completely beyond" refers to the path of meditation and "enlightenment" (*bodhi*) to Buddhahood, the path of no more learning.[6]

Vimalamitra and Vajrapāṇi evince a greater interest in the tantric implications of the mantra, with Vimalamitra quoting the *Vairocanābhisambodhitantra* at length and paraphrasing the etymology of *mantra* found in the *Guhyasamājatantra* (XVIII.69b-70a):

> Minds arising dependent on a sense and an object
> Are said to be *man*. *Tra* means protection.[7]

Vimalamitra goes on to consider the ways in which the perfection of wisdom itself may be considered a secret mantra. It is secret in the sense that even if it is taught to those of dull faculties, they are not able to see it; it remains hidden from them. Furthermore, to say that the perfection of wisdom is to be taught secretly suggests its great profundity. Finally, looking at the term *mantra* as meaning protector of the mind, Vimalamitra states that the perfection of wisdom protects those whose minds abide in it; those who are capable of doing so should think about the perfection of wisdom constantly.[8]

Atīśa distinguishes the audience of the sūtra into those of dull faculties and those of sharp faculties. The former require the full teaching of all of the characteristics of the five paths, whereas the latter understand merely through a statement of the major headings. This abbreviated teaching for those of sharp faculties becomes a secret mantra for those of dull faculties because they cannot understand it. "Being secret or not being secret exists in the mind; in actuality there is no difference in what is taught. The Teacher does not have a closed fist."[9]

The most substantial consideration of the nature of the *Heart Sūtra* mantra is made by Vajrapāṇi. He writes:

> Many sets of tantras are taught[10] for the sake of those of sharp faculties who have interest in the secret Mahāyāna. The outer secret mantra teaches such things as pacification and increase, and the inner secret mantra teaches the bliss of body and mind in dependence on the channels, winds, and so forth. Having been taught through secret mantra to abide for a long time in samādhi, there is Buddhahood in one instant or in one lifetime or in the intermediate state or after seven lifetimes.
>
> Someone may have doubts concerning whether this instruction on the meaning of the heart of the perfection of wisdom is of the Definition Vehicle or the Mantra Vehicle. Although it appears to be different to the perception of sentient beings, there is no difference in the profound reality. Therefore, this mantra of the perfection of wisdom is the heart of the meaning of all secret mantras.[11]
>
> The mantra of the perfection of wisdom is not a mantra for pacification, increase, power, or wrath. What is it? By merely understanding the meaning of this mantra, the mind is freed. The first four syllables of this mantra [*tadyathā oṃ*] are the arising of action, the meaning of the middle four syllables [*gate gate*] is to teach clearly, and the end summarizes the meaning of the mantra in four aspects. What are the four meanings? The illusion-like, emptiness, signlessness, and wishlessness. *Tadyathā* means "like this." *Gate, gate,* "gone, gone" [means] all mindfulness has gone [to be] like illusions. *Pāragate*, "gone beyond," [means] that beyond mindfulness, one goes beyond to emptiness. *Pārasaṃgate*, "gone completely beyond," [means] that beyond the illusion-like and emptiness, one goes beyond to signlessness. *Bodhi svāhā*, "become enlightened," [means] that having purified the afflictions and all objects of knowledge, one transcends awareness.[12]

Vajrapāṇi begins by repeating the common claim that through the practice of Highest Yoga Tantra (*anuttarayogatantra*), the path to Buddhahood can be traversed and completed in as little as one instant or as much as seven lifetimes, a period much shorter than the three periods of countless aeons required by the path of the Perfection Vehicle (*pāramitāyāna*), also referred to by tantrists as the Definition Vehicle (*lakṣaṇayāna*). He then raises the question of whether the *Heart Sūtra* itself, because it contains a mantra, is to be considered a sūtra or a tantra. He answers that emptiness is undifferentiated, suggesting perhaps that such questions are inappropriate, but adds that the mantra of the *Heart Sūtra* is the heart or essence of all mantras. Earlier in his commentary, he said that the *Heart Sūtra* is the heart or essence of all sūtras.

As appealing as this statement may be, it does not directly address the question of how to deal with the presence of a mantra in a sūtra, because the practice of the Vajrayāna has traditionally been considered superior to and distinct from the sūtra practices of the Perfection Vehicle (*pāramitāyāna*). Does the presence of a mantra make the *Heart Sūtra* a tantra? If not, is the mantra an authentic mantra of the Vajrayāna? In arranging the texts that constitute the Tibetan canon, the encyclopedic scholar Bu-ston included the *Heart Sūtra* in both the Perfection of Wisdom section and in the tantra section.

There is a wide range of opinion in Indian Mahāyāna and Tibetan thought as to what distinguishes the Secret Mantra Vehicle from the Perfection Vehicle. In an oft-quoted statement from his *Nayatraya-pradīpa*, Tripiṭakamāla says:

> Though the aim is the same, the Mantra Vehicle
> Is superior due to [being for] those who are not obscured,
> Having many skillful methods, not being difficult,
> And being designed for those of sharp faculties.[13]

According to Tsong-kha-pa, the goal of the vehicles is the same in that they both are directed toward the same Buddhahood. The wisdom is the same because both set forth emptiness as the final mode of being of phenomena. The motivation for practice in both vehicles is the aspiration to enlightenment out of compassion for all sentient beings. What distinguishes the Secret Mantra Vehicle from the Perfection Vehicle is the practice of deity yoga (*devatāyoga*), in which the mind understanding emptiness appears as the form body (*rūpakāya*) of a Buddha.[14] The *Heart Sūtra* clearly does not delineate such practices.

To complicate the matter further is the existence of two tantric *sādhanas* on the *Heart Sūtra*, one ascribed to Nāgārjuna and the other to Dārikapa, one of the eighty-four siddhas.[15] The greater part of the sādhana ascribed to Nāgārjuna is devoted to the performance of obeisance, offering, confession, and so forth before it describes a *maṇḍala* in which Śākyamuni Buddha appears in the center. In the east is the goddess Prajñāpāramitā, described as "the mother," in a two-armed form. She is golden in color, adorned as a *sambhogakāya*, her right hand in the *mudrā* of teaching the doctrine, her left hand holding a text. In the south is Vajrapāṇi, in the west is Śāriputra, and in the north Avalokiteśvara. Apart from these references to three of the principals of the sūtra (Śākyamuni, Śāriputra, and Avalokiteśvara), the only connection to the sūtra is the statement, "If you are tired, recite the mantra of truth, saying *gate gate pāragate pārasaṃgate bodhi svāhā*, adding *tadyathā* and *oṃ*."[16]

The sādhana attributed to Dārikapa is more directly related to the sūtra. It is translated here in its entirety.

> Having paid homage to the mother of the Conquerors,
> Who, through acting in the past,
> [Achieved] peace and omniscience,
> One should take to mind the rite of the sādhana.
>
> In a place isolated and pleasant
> Sitting on a comfortable cushion,
> [Imagine that] on a sun in the center of a lotus at the heart
> There is a *maṃ* from which light radiates
>
> Inviting the conquerors with their children from the ten directions.
> Imagine that they abide in the direction of the space [in front].
> Make offerings and confess faults,
> Admire [virtues] and entreat [them to remain and teach].
>
> Go for refuge and create the aspiration [to Buddhahood]
> And dedicate [all this] to the great enlightenment.
> Cultivate the abodes of purity: love, compassion,
> Joy, and equanimity.
>
> Recite fully this secret mantra:
> *oṃ svabhāva śuddha sarva dharma svabhāva śuddho 'haṃ.*
> Be mindful that everything, the moving and the unmoving,
> Is naturally empty from the beginning.

After paying homage to the goddess Prajñāpāramitā, the mother of the Buddhas, the meditator imagines a lotus at his or her heart upon which is a horizontal sun disc. Standing upright on the sun disc is the letter *maṃ* from which light radiates, inviting Buddhas and Bodhisattvas from throughout the universe, imagining that they stand arrayed in the space in front of him. The meditator then performs a series of preliminary practices derived from the opening stanzas of the *Bhadracarī* (*Deeds of Samantabhadra*) prayer of the *Avataṃsaka Sūtra* by presenting marvelous imagined offerings to the assembled Buddhas and Bodhisattvas, revealing his faults to them, admiring his own and others' virtues, and entreating them to teach the doctrine and not pass into nirvāṇa. The meditator then goes for refuge to the Three Jewels, creates the aspiration to achieve Buddhahood for the welfare of all sentient beings, and dedicates the merit accumulated from the foregoing and subsequent practices toward that end. The meditator next cultivates the four pure abodes (*brahmavihāra*) of love, compassion, joy, and equanimity. His mind imbued with love and compassion and aspiring toward Buddhahood, he then meditates on emptiness, reciting the famous mantra, *oṃ svabhāva śuddha sarva dharma svabhāva śuddho 'haṃ*, "Oṃ, naturally pure are all phenomena, naturally pure am I," understanding that emptiness is the primordial nature of everything, the unmoving world and the sentient beings who move upon it. Out of this emptiness, the meditator next creates the maṇḍala.

After that, from the nature of emptiness
Imagine the four elements as *yaṃ raṃ baṃ laṃ*.
From *suṃ* arises Mount Meru.
On it, from *bhruṃ* a beautiful palace
Expansive and ornamented.

In the center of it is a lion throne
Where, seated on lotus and sun,
Is the orange mother of the Conquerors; her body golden.
Full-bodied, with one face and four arms.

Imagine that her two right hands hold a vajra and bestow protection,
Her two left hands hold a text and teach the doctrine.
She is endowed with the ornaments of a *saṃbhogakāya*.

In the east, on a moon on a lion [throne]
Is a *sa*, from which the Conqueror Śākyamuni is created.
He is a *nirmāṇakāya*, the color of refined gold,
And has a crown protrusion.

Imagine that in the west, on a lotus and moon
Is a *hrīḥ*, from which Lokeśvara [arises],
Very white and beautifully adorned;
He sits in the cross-legged posture of a [Bodhi]sattva.

Imagine that in the south, from a *maṃ*, is Śāriputra.
He is dressed as an ascetic, his body is light red.
He is kneeling and the palms of his hands are joined.
His body is very beautiful.

In the north, create Ānanda, born from *da*.
He is red, [seated] on a lotus,
In the mode of respecting the Conqueror.

Having thus completed the creation,
Light radiates from the *maṃ* at one's own heart,
Drawing forth the wisdom beings.
Make offerings. Through *ja hūṃ baṃ hoḥ* they enter
[the residents of the maṇḍala].

The Conquerors confer initiation on them
With the names Vairocana, Akṣobhya,
Ratnasambhava, Ananta, and Jinatva
And bless them with the three syllables.

The meditator next creates an imaginary universe out of emptiness. First a grey *yaṃ* appears, from which a wind maṇḍala in the shape of a bow appears. On top of this is a red *raṃ* from which a red fire maṇḍala appears. Atop the maṇḍala stands a white *baṃ*, from which a circular water maṇḍala appears. Above the water maṇḍala, a yellow *laṃ* arises, from which a square earth maṇḍala appears. The maṇḍalas of the four elements having been created, a *suṃ* appears from which Mount Meru arises and atop the mountain, a palace appears from the syllable *bhruṃ*. In the center of the palace is a throne supported on the backs of lions where, on cushions of lotus and sun disc, sits the goddess Prajñāpāramitā, the embodiment of the knowledge of emptiness. She has four arms; one holds a *vajra*, another holds a text, another is in the gesture of bestowing protection, while the fourth is in the mudrā of teaching the doctrine. She is surrounded on thrones in the four cardinal directions by the *dramatis personae* of the *Heart Sūtra*, each of whom arises from a seed syllable: Śākyamuni Buddha, Avalokiteśvara, Śāriputra, and Ānanda, the unidentified *rapporteur* of the sūtra. It is rare for Śākyamuni to appear in a maṇḍala in his historical nirmāṇakāya form rather than in his tantric form as Vajradhara. It is highly unusual for Hīnayāna śrāvakas such as Śāriputra and Ānanda to be seen frequenting such an esoteric domain.

Having created this scene, the meditator now animates the residents of the maṇḍala by causing the Buddhas and Bodhisattvas assembled in space, referred to as "wisdom beings" (*jñānasattva*), to merge with Prajñāpāramitā, Śākyamuni, Avalokiteśvara, Śāriputra, and Ānanda. Light radiates from the *maṃ* at the meditator's heart, drawing the wisdom beings to the maṇḍala where, through offerings and the recitation of the mantra *ja hūṃ baṃ hoḥ*,[17] they are caused to enter the residents of the maṇḍala. Other Buddhas then confer initiation on the five residents of the maṇḍala with the names of the Buddhas of the five families: Vairocana, Akṣobhya, Ratnasambhava, Ananta [Amitābha], and Jinatva [Amoghasiddhi].[18] The residents are then blessed or "transformed into magnificence" with the three syllables; a white *oṃ* at the crown of the head, a red *ā* at the throat, and a blue *hūṃ* at the heart.

> Imagine that the Conqueror [Śākyamuni] is drawn to
> the heart of the Mother
> And enters into samādhi.
> [Avalokiteśvara] gives answers to [Śāriputra's]
> question about the meaning of emptiness
> For all those surrounding.

With the preliminary visualization now complete, the stage is set for the central meditation of the *sādhana*. It begins with the sūtra being inserted into the tantric rite as Śākyamuni enters into samādhi. Unlike the sūtra, however, he here is drawn to the heart of goddess Prajñāpāramitā at the center of the maṇḍala. It is this that seems to then empower Avalokiteśvara "to give answers to [Śāriputra's] question about the meaning of emptiness"; that is, to set forth the *Heart Sūtra*. Presumably the meditator would also listen, contemplating the meaning of emptiness.

> In this way, all of the retinue who are elaborated
> Out of the pacification of all phenomena are drawn into the Mother.
> Observe the letter [*maṃ*] in the samādhi with signs
> Clearly and without conception.
>
> All phenomena, originally peaceful,
> Appear mistakenly through the power of conditions.
> When reality [is realized], they are pacified,
> When they are pacified, they appear like illusions.
>
> Do not be devoid of not conceiving of the four extremes.
> The basic mind, without abiding in laxity or excitement

> Is clear light, not meditating on anything.
> This is the perfection of the signless yoga.
>
> Because the Conqueror said that [all phenomena] are peaceful
> And because of the lack of being one or many, etc.
> Elaborations cease and the non-conceptual is known.
> Think completely and realize reality.

Through Avalokiteśvara's teaching of emptiness, all the residents of the maṇḍala and the surrounding Buddhas and Bodhisattvas are drawn into the heart of the central figure, Prajñāpāramitā. The meditator then turns to the practice of the signed and signless samādhis, also referred to in the *kriyā, caryā,* and *yoga* tantras as the yoga with signs and the yoga without signs. According to Tsong-kha-pa, a yoga with signs refers to visualization of a deity and mantra repetition that does not explicitly involve meditation on emptiness.[19] Here, in the samādhi with signs, the meditator concentrates on the letter *maṃ* at his heart in order to induce mental stability. Next the meditator understands that all phenomena are originally peaceful, only appearing to be real through the influence of adventitious conditions, such as ignorance. When the emptiness of phenomena is understood, they become peaceful, appearing like illusions. With this understanding, he passes on to a yoga without signs, a visualization that directly involves meditation on emptiness. By not conceiving of the four extremes (*catuṣkoṭi*, that things exist, do not exist, both exist and do not exist, neither exist nor not exist), the basic mind, the nature of clear light, is free from laxity (*laya*) and excitement (*auddhatya*), the chief impediments to mental clarity and quiescence, and the mind does not meditate on anything, abiding in emptiness. "This is the perfection of the signless yoga." The nature of emptiness is established by scripture (*āgama*), as when the Buddha proclaimed that all phenomena are peaceful, and by reasoning (*yukti*), such as the argument that phenomena do not inherently exist beause of not being truly one or many. The elaborations of inherent existence spawned by ignorance cease and the state beyond conception is attained.

> When you are tired, repeat, *tadyathā oṃ gate gate pāragate pārasaṃgate bodhi svāhā.*

The final reference to the *Heart Sūtra* occurs here, although the mantra holds a somewhat less exalted place here than it does in the sūtra. No comments are made concerning the meaning or significance of the mantra. Rather, it is to be recited near the end of the session, when the main visualization and contemplation have been completed. The recitation of mantra as a means of resting at the end of a session is a common feature of tantric sādhanas.[20]

> Light rays of [the letters] of the mantra surrounding [*maṃ*]
> Around the center [of the lotus at one's heart]
> Are emitted and withdrawn, performing the [two] purposes.
> Make offerings to the wisdom beings and [invite them to] leave.
>
> Speak the eighteen kinds of emptiness;
> All the pledge beings and palace become unobservable.

The meditator visualizes the letters of the *Heart Sūtra* mantra standing upright in a circle around the *maṃ* in the center of the lotus at his heart. Rays of light shine forth from the letters performing the two purposes of making offerings to the Buddhas and Bodhisattvas and alleviating the suffering of all beings. The light then returns to the letters and the meditator makes mental offerings to the assembly before inviting them to leave. The meditator then recites the eighteen emptinesses,[21] at which point the entire visualization, the palace, and its residents, called pledge beings (*samayasattva*), dissolve into emptiness.

> [I] have written this excellent rite, a supreme
> technique, based on the words of the Conqueror and
> the statements of Nāgārjuna,
> For the sake of those with interest and to discipline myself.
> May scholars be tolerant of the stains of my mind.
> By the roots of virtue of my work here
> May transmigrators understand the meaning of the
> completely pure essence
> And thoroughly attain the state of a Conqueror;
> May transmigrators be set on the path of peace.

The sādhana ends with a traditional statement of the sources for the work, an apology for any mistakes, and a dedication of the merit accrued through composing the work to the welfare of all beings.

This is, then, a tantric sādhana, very typical of its genre in content and style, distinguished by its allusions to the *Heart Sūtra*. These are three: first, Śākyamuni, Avalokiteśvara, and Śāriputra reside in the maṇḍala; second, the plot of the sūtra is reflected in the two stanzas in which Śākyamuni enters into samādhi and Avalokiteśvara answers Śāriputra's question about emptiness; and finally, the repetition of the mantra is prescribed in the final stages of the rite.

The question still remains of the exact function of the mantra within the sūtra, because the sūtra provides no such explanation and the sādhanas make only perfunctory references to the mantra. When the commentators speak of the mantra, they could just as easily be speaking of the perfection of wisdom itself: for Praśāstrasena the mantra clears away obstacles and causes wisdom; Vajrapāṇi says that by understanding the mantra the mind is freed; Vimalamitra explains how the perfection of wisdom itself is secret because of its profundity and a mantra because of its capacity to protect the mind.

The fullest discussion of the status of the mantra occurs in the Tibetan commentary of Gung-thang, who sees the mantra as authentically tantric for a number of reasons. First, following Vimalamitra, he calls the mantra secret in the sense that its meaning is cryptic, remaining hidden, and thus secret from all but Bodhisattvas of the sharpest faculties. The sūtra explicitly teaches emptiness, but does not clearly indicate how to practice emptiness over the course of the path. Gung-thang creatively reads the mantra as an exhortation by Avalokiteśvara: "Proceed, proceed, proceed beyond, proceed completely beyond, be founded in enlightenment." The mantra is thus the hidden teaching of the stages of the path for the most brilliant Bodhisattvas, who are capable of understanding the entire path merely through this veiled reference to the five paths. His argument, then, is that because the Mantrayāna is something that is taught in a secret or hidden manner and because the stages of the path are said to be the hidden meaning of the Perfection of Wisdom sūtras, then the *Heart Sūtra* mantra, which he sees as secretly teaching the stages of the path, merits inclusion in the Mantrayāna.

Gung-thang also sees the mantra as authentically tantric because there are tantric sādhanas that employ it. Thus, the mantra is a secret mantra of the Vajrayāna for those who are capable of making use of it as such through the practice of sādhanas such as that of Dārikapa. Gung-thang would not identify the *Heart Sūtra* itself as a tantra simply because it contains a mantra; a tantra must set forth methods for achieving Buddhahood that do not occur in sūtras. Nonetheless, Gung-thang sees the inclusion of an authentic mantra in the famous sūtra as another example of the Buddha's skillful methods (*upāya*), subtly mixing the taste of tantra into the sūtra for those who currently are incapable of practicing the tantric path and who would be intimidated by a more direct exposition of the Vajrayāna, the vehicle that all will eventually enter in order to become enlightened.[22]

Chapter 8
The Epilogue

Śāriputra, Bodhisattva Mahāsattvas should train in the profound perfection of wisdom in that way.
Then the Transcendent Victor rose from that samādhi and said to the Bodhisattva, the Mahāsattva, the Superior Avalokiteśvara, "Well done." "Well done, well done. Child of good lineage, it is just so. Child of good lineage, it is like that; the profound perfection of wisdom should be practiced just as you have taught it. Even the Tathāgatas admire this." The Transcendent Victor having so spoken, the venerable Śāriputra, the Bodhisattva, the Mahāsattva, the Superior Avalokiteśvara, and all those surrounding and those of the world, the gods, humans, demigods, and gandharvas, were filled with admiration and praised the words of the Transcendent Victor.

Avalokiteśvara completes his answer to Śāriputra's question with an exhortation to Bodhisattvas to practice the perfection of wisdom, at which point the Buddha rises from his meditative absorption. It was by the power of his entering into samādhi on the profound that Śāriputra was able to ask his question and that Avalokiteśvara was able to provide his answer. With that now completed, the Buddha rises.[1] The Buddha alone can explain the meaning of the perfection of wisdom; others cannot. Avalokiteśvara explained and Śāriputra listened through the blessing of the Buddha's samādhi.[2] The Buddha praises what Avalokiteśvara has said, saying "Well done" twice to express his pleasure, thus dispelling the doubts of any who might question the validity of what has been taught. "Child of good lineage, it is like that," he says, indicating that if the profound reality is understood, the mind is freed.[3] Even the Tathāgatas, the Buddhas who have thus come and thus gone, who have understood reality and taught it accordingly, are delighted by what Avalokiteśvara has taught.

Everyone, Avalokiteśvara, Śāriputra, and the entire audience was filled with admiration. Some say that even the Buddha shared in this admiration because he saw his disciples had grasped the main meaning of the perfection of wisdom.[4] Of the audience, Vimalamitra says:

Because all the Bodhisattvas, monks, laymen, and laywomen were sitting there, it says, "all those surrounding." The gods are the four royal lineages, and so forth. Humans are well-known. Demigods (*asura*) are so-called because they gave up the beer (*sura*) that arose when the ocean of milk was churned. They are also [called] *daityas* and *dānavas*. The gandharvas are the divine musicians and the protectors of the country. The world is the gods, humans, demigods, and gandharvas who are seated with the gods. Because they [the gods] are primary, they are named first. Because it disintegrates, it is the world [literally, "disintegrating base"]; its nature is the five aggregates. "The words of the Buddha" is the entity of the explanation itself. "Praised" means that they had clear joy and were grasped with joy.[5]

Chapter 9

The Structure of the Sūtra and the Structure of the Path

A number of the commentators provide outlines of the sūtra. Jñānamitra and Praśāstrasena divide the sūtra according to subject matter, providing sevenfold and tenfold divisions, respectively. Kamalaśīla, Atīśa, and Śrīmahājana undertake the more difficult task of aligning the structure of the sūtra with the structure of the five paths.

Jñānamitra's Structure

The Introduction

This did I hear at one time. The Transcendent Victor was sitting on Vulture Mountain in Rājagṛha together with a great assembly of monks and a great assembly of Bodhisattvas.

The Entry into Wisdom

At that time the Transcendent Victor was absorbed in a samādhi on the enumerations of phenomena called "perception of the profound." Also at that time, the Bodhisattva, the Mahāsattva, the Superior Avalokiteśvara was contemplating the meaning of the profound perfection of wisdom and he saw that those five aggregates also are empty of inherent existence. Then, by the power of the Buddha, the venerable Śāriputra said this to the Bodhisattva, the Mahāsattva, the Superior Avalokiteśvara, "How should a son of good lineage train who wishes to practice the profound perfection of wisdom?"

The Bodhisattva, the Mahāsattva, the Superior Avalokiteśvara said this to the venerable Śāriputra: "Śāriputra, a son of good lineage or a daughter of good lineage who wishes to practice the profound perfection of wisdom should view [things] in this way: They should correctly view those five aggregates also as empty of inherent existence.

The Definition of Emptiness

Form is emptiness; emptiness is form. Emptiness is not other than form; form is not other than emptiness. In the same way, feeling, discrimination, compositional factors, and consciousnesses are empty. Śāriputra, in that way, all phenomena are empty, that is, without characteristic, unproduced, unceased, stainless, not stainless, undiminished, unfilled. Therefore, Śāriputra, in emptiness, there is no form, no feeling, no discrimination, no compositional factors, no consciousness, no eye, no ear, no nose, no tongue, no body, no mind, no form, no sound, no odor, no taste, no object of touch, no phenomenon. There is no eye constituent, no mental constituent, up to and including no mental consciousness constituent. There is no ignorance, no extinction of ignorance, up to and including no aging and death and no extinction of aging and death. Similarly, there are no sufferings, no origins, no cessations, no paths, no exalted wisdom, no attainment, and also no non-attainment.

The Sphere of Wisdom

Therefore, Śāriputra, because Bodhisattvas have no attainment, they depend on and abide in the perfection of wisdom and their minds are without obstructions and without fear.

The Qualities of Wisdom

Having completely passed beyond all error they go to the completion of nirvāṇa.

The Fruition of Wisdom

All the Buddhas who abide in the three times have been fully awakened into unsurpassed, perfect, complete enlightenment through relying on the perfection of wisdom.

The Dhāriṇī of Wisdom

Therefore, the mantra of the perfection of wisdom is the mantra of great knowledge, the unsurpassed mantra, the mantra equal to the unequalled, the mantra that thoroughly pacifies all suffering. Because it is not false, it should be known to be true. The mantra of the perfection of wisdom is stated:

> tadyathā oṃ gate gate pāragate pārasaṃgate bodhi svāhā

Śāriputra, Bodhisattva Mahāsattvas should train in the profound perfection of wisdom in that way.

Praśāstrasena's Structure

The Name of Wisdom

The Heart of the Transcendent and Victorious Perfection of Wisdom Sūtra

The Prologue

This did I hear at one time. The Transcendent Victor was sitting on Vulture Mountain in Rājagṛha together with a great assembly of monks and a great assembly of Bodhisattvas.

The Absorption

At that time the Transcendent Victor was absorbed in a samādhi on the enumerations of phenomena called "perception of the profound."

The Transition[1]

Also at that time, the Bodhisattva, the Mahāsattva, the Superior Avalokiteśvara was contemplating the meaning of the profound perfection of wisdom and he saw that those five aggregates also are empty of inherent existence.

The Entry into Wisdom

Then by the power of the Buddha, the venerable Śāriputra said this to the Bodhisattva, the Mahāsattva, the Superior Avalokiteśvara, "How should a son of good lineage train who wishes to practice the profound perfection of wisdom?"

The Definition of Wisdom

The Bodhisattva, the Mahāsattva, the Superior Avalokiteśvara said this to the venerable Śāriputra: "Śāriputra, a son of good lineage or a daughter of good lineage who wishes to practice the profound perfection of wisdom should view [things] in this way: They should correctly view those five aggregates also as empty of inherent existence. Form is emptiness; emptiness is form. Emptiness is not other than form; form is not other than emptiness. In the same way, feeling, discrimination, compositional factors, and consciousnesses are empty.

The Sphere of Wisdom

Śāriputra, in that way, all phenomena are empty, that is, without characteristic, unproduced, unceased, stainless, not stainless, undiminished, unfilled. Therefore, Śāriputra, in emptiness, there is no form, no feeling, no discrimination, no compositional factors, no consciousness, no eye, no ear, no nose, no tongue, no body, no mind, no form, no sound, no odor, no taste, no object of touch, no phenomenon. There is no eye constituent, no mental constituent, up to and including no mental consciousness constituent. There is no ignorance, no extinction of ignorance, up to and including no aging and death and no extinction of aging and death. Similarly, there are no sufferings, no origins, no cessations, no paths, no exalted wisdom, no attainment, and also no non-attainment.

The Qualities of Wisdom

Therefore, Śāriputra, because Bodhisattvas have no attainment, they depend on and abide in the perfection of wisdom and their minds are without obstructions and without fear. Having completely passed beyond all error they go to the completion of nirvāṇa.

The Fruition of Wisdom

All the Buddhas who abide in the three times have been fully awakened into unsurpassed, perfect, complete enlightenment through relying on the perfection of wisdom.

The Dhāraṇī of Wisdom

Therefore, the mantra of the perfection of wisdom is the mantra of great knowledge, the unsurpassed mantra, the mantra equal to the unequalled, the mantra that thoroughly pacifies all suffering. Because it is not false, it should be known to be true. The mantra of the perfection of wisdom is stated:

tadyathā oṃ gate gate pāragate pārasaṃgate bodhi svāhā

Śāriputra, Bodhisattva Mahāsattvas should train in the profound perfection of wisdom in that way.

Beginning in the Gupta period, the Perfection of Wisdom sūtras were mined for a delineation of the Bodhisattva path as well as for their proclamation of the doctrine of emptiness. The structure of the path, which was said to be the implicit or hidden teaching of the Perfection of Wisdom sūtras was made explicit in Maitreya's *Abhisamayālaṃkāra*, which schematized the path to Buddhahood in terms of eight categories and seventy topics. Attempts to expand upon Maitreya's often cryptic work and to identify its topics with actual statements in the longer Perfection of Wisdom sūtras resulted in scores of commentaries to the *Abhisamayālaṃkāra*, twenty-one of which remain extant.[2]

Atīśa notes in his commentary to the *Heart Sūtra* that all the topics of the Perfection of Wisdom sūtras can be condensed into two: topics of realization (*abhisamaya*) and topics of the essence, by which he presumably means emptiness. The realizations that occur on the path are set forth primarily in the Perfection of Wisdom sūtras in 100,000,

25,000, and 8000 stanzas, which teach the topic of the essence only implicitly. The shorter Perfection of Wisdom sūtras, such as that in 700 stanzas, primarily teach the essence, although implying the realizations that occur on the path.[3]

Kamalaśīla, Atīśa, and Śrīmahājana attempt to delineate the structure of the path that is implicit in the *Heart Sūtra*, with Kamalaśīla providing the briefest exposition and Śrīmahājana the most extensive. They all describe the process of enlightenment in terms of the five paths: those of accumulation, preparation, seeing, meditation, and no more learning. The path of accumulation begins with the creation of the aspiration to become enlightened (*bodhicittotpāda*) for the sake of all sentient beings. A person becomes a Bodhisattva with the commencement of the path of accumulation. Over the course of this path, the Bodhisattva gains a conceptual understanding of emptiness and cultivates a level of concentration called calm abiding (*śamatha*), whereby the mind can be placed one-pointedly on its object effortlessly for long periods of time. The Bodhisattva also accumulates merit over this period through the practice of the perfections.

The path of preparation commences with the acquisition of special insight (*vipaśyanā*), a conceptual understanding of emptiness with the strength of calm abiding. The path of preparation is divided into four parts: heat, peak, forbearance, and supreme mundane quality. The path of preparation is the time of refining the understanding of emptiness until it finally becomes non-conceptual. The initial direct, non-conceptual vision of emptiness, marks the beginning of the path of seeing. This state of equipoise (*samāhita*) has two parts: an uninterrupted path, the period when afflictions are actually abandoned, and a path of release, the subsequent state of having abandoned the afflictions on that particular level of the path. From this point on the path, all subsequent progress will occur in states of meditative equipoise, each of which will have an uninterrupted path and a path of release. The attainment of the path of seeing marks achievement of the first of the ten Bodhisattva stages (*bhūmi*).

The path of meditation comprises the second through tenth Bodhisattva stages and marks a long period of repeated entry into direct realization of emptiness alternating with the practice of the perfections in states subsequent to meditative equipoise (*pṛṣṭalabdha*). The final uninterrupted path of the path of meditation, called the diamond-like samādhi (*vajropamasamādhi*), destroys the last of the obstructions to the achievement of Buddhahood, and with the attainment of the path of release in the next moment, the Bodhisattva is a Buddha. The state of Buddhahood is the fifth path, the path of no more learning, sometimes called the eleventh stage. A Buddha is endowed with a Truth Body (*dharmakāya*) and a Form Body (*rūpakāya*), with the Form Body being of two types: the Complete Enjoyment Body (*saṃbhogakāya*), which appears only to advanced Bodhisattvas, and the Emanation Body (*nirmāṇakāya*), which is the Buddha that appears in the world.[4]

With this background, the divisions of the sūtra by Kamalaśīla, Atīśa, and Śrīmahājana can be considered. Kamalaśīla simply states the correspondence and provides no explanation for dividing the sūtra as he does.

Kamalaśīla's Structure

The Paths of Accumulation and Preparation

The Bodhisattva, the Mahāsattva, the Superior Avalokiteśvara said this to the venerable Śāriputra: "Śāriputra, a son of good lineage or a daughter of good lineage who wishes to practice the profound perfection of wisdom should view [things] in this way: They should correctly view those five aggregates also as empty of inherent existence. Form is emptiness; emptiness is form. Emptiness is not other than form; form is not other than emptiness. In the same way, feeling, discrimination, compositional factors, and consciousnesses are empty.

The Path of Seeing

Śāriputra, in that way, all phenomena are empty, that is, without characteristic, unproduced, unceased, stainless, not stainless, undiminished, unfilled.

The Path of Meditation

Therefore, Śāriputra, in emptiness, there is no form, no feeling, no discrimination, no compositional factors, no consciousness, no eye, no ear, no nose, no tongue, no body, no mind, no form, no sound, no odor, no taste, no object of touch, no phenomenon. There is no eye constituent, no mental constituent, up to and including no mental consciousness constituent. There is no ignorance, no extinction of ignorance, up to and including no aging and death and no extinction of aging and death. Similarly, there are no sufferings, no origins, no cessations, no paths, no exalted wisdom, no attainment, and also no non-attainment.

The Vajra-like Samādhi

Therefore, Śāriputra, because Bodhisattvas have no attainment, they depend on and abide in the perfection of wisdom and their minds are without obstructions and without fear.

The Actual Path of No More Learning

Having completely passed beyond all error they go to the completion of nirvāṇa.

The Complete Enjoyment Body and Emanation Body

All the Buddhas who abide in the three times have been fully awakened into unsurpassed, perfect, complete enlightenment through relying on the perfection of wisdom.

Atīśa divides the sūtra into two major portions, the teaching for Bodhisattvas of dull faculties and the teaching for Bodhisattvas of sharp faculties. All the sūtra up to the mantra is the former, the mantra is the latter. Thus, Bodhisattvas of sharp faculties are able to understand everything that was taught up to that point in the sūtra simply by hearing the mantra. (Gung-thang explains specifically how the sūtra is included in the mantra on pp. 183-184.)

Atīśa discusses the five paths in terms of the four objects of observation set forth in the eighth chapter of the *Saṃdhinirmocanasūtra:* the non-conceptual reflection (*nirvikalpakabimba, rnam par mi rtog pa'i gzugs brnyan*), the conceptual reflection (*savikalpakabimba, rnam par rtog pa dang bcas pa'i gzugs brnyan*), the limit of things (*vastvanta, dngos po'i mtha'*), and the consummate purpose (*kṛtyānuṣṭhāna, dgos pa yongs su grub pa*).[5] The sūtra states that the first is calm abiding (*śamatha, zhi gnas*), the second is special insight (*vipaśyanā, lhag mthong*), and the third and fourth involve both.[6] According to Atīśa, these correspond to the path of accumulation, the path of preparation, the path of seeing, and the path of no more learning, respectively.

The observation with special insight, which is a conceptual reflection, is indicated by, "Śāriputra, a son of good lineage or a daughter of good lineage who wishes to practice the profound perfection of wisdom should view [things] in this way." According to Atīśa, this statement sets forth the conceptual wisdom of suchness that occurs on the path of accumulation. Here emptiness is conceived to exist as something real among a variety of aspects, unlike on the path of seeing where such varieties are not seen, because there all objects are realized to be equal in emptiness. This wisdom on the path of accumulation lacks samādhi and thus is said to have a nature of mere calm abiding. It is also a mere reflection of the non-conceptual wisdom that occurs on the path of seeing.

The same sentence of the sūtra also implies the path of preparation and the observation with calm abiding which is a non-conceptual reflection. This wisdom is not actually non-conceptual but is not directed outward as are the wisdoms arisen from hearing and thinking nor does it conceive of a variety of objects; it considers one object and is directed inward.

The path of seeing is the observation of the limit of things. Things are such phenomena as forms and their limit is their nature or their reality. This wisdom is indicated by the statement, "They should correctly view even those five aggregates as empty of inherent existence."[7] Atīśa's correspondence of the observation of the limit of things to the path of seeing and the thoroughly established necessity with the path of no more learning is supported by the *Saṃdhinirmocana*, which says that observations which are conceptual reflections and non-conceptual reflections occur before the path of seeing, that those two plus the observation of the limit of things occur on the paths of seeing and meditation, where signs and the assumption of bad states are destroyed, and that the observation of the consummate purpose is attained on the final Bodhisattva stage and in the state of Buddhahood.[8] From this, Atīśa's structuring of the sūtra would seem to be as follows:

The Paths of Accumulation and Preparation

The Bodhisattva, the Mahāsattva, the Superior Avalokiteśvara said this to the venerable Śāriputra: "Śāriputra, a son of good lineage or a daughter of good lineage who wishes to practice the profound perfection of wisdom should view [things] in this way:

The Path of Seeing

They should correctly view those five aggregates also as empty of inherent existence. Form is emptiness; emptiness is form. Emptiness is not other than form; form is not other than emptiness. In the same way, feeling, discrimination, compositional factors, and consciousnesses are empty.

Śāriputra, in that way, all phenomena are empty, that is, without characteristic, unproduced, unceased, stainless, not stainless, undiminished, unfilled. Therefore, Śāriputra, in emptiness, there is no form, no feeling, no discrimination, no compositional factors, no consciousness, no eye, no ear, no nose, no tongue, no body, no mind, no form, no sound, no odor, no taste, no object of touch, no phenomenon. There is no eye constituent, no mental constituent, up to and including no mental consciousness constituent. There is no ignorance, no extinction of ignorance, up to and including no aging and death and no extinction of aging and death. Similarly, there are no sufferings, no origins, no cessations, no paths, no exalted wisdom, no attainment, and also no non-attainment.

The Path of Meditation

Therefore, Śāriputra, because Bodhisattvas have no attainment, they depend on and abide in the perfection of wisdom and their minds are without obstructions and without fear. Having completely passed beyond all error they go to the completion of nirvāṇa.

The Vajra-like Samādhi and the Path of No More Learning

All the Buddhas who abide in the three times have been fully awakened into unsurpassed, perfect, complete enlightenment through relying on the perfection of wisdom.

The Tibetan commentator Gung-thang elaborates on and provides a rationale for Atīśa's structure. For example, he says that in the sentence, "A son of good lineage or a daughter of good lineage who wishes to practice the profound perfection of wisdom should view things in this way," the phrase "who wishes to practice" indicates the path of accumulation because it is on this path that the Bodhisattva sets out to become a

Buddha out of compassion for others, while "should view things in this way" indicates the path of preparation, where the Bodhisattva develops a clear image of emptiness. It is on the path of seeing that the Bodhisattva directly realizes the emptiness of all phenomena in the universe. Therefore, the long enumeration of the negations, "They should view correctly . . . and also no non-attainment." suggests the path of seeing. "It is on the path of meditation, which comprises the second through tenth stages, that the Bodhisattva abandons the afflictive obstructions and the obstructions to omniscience. This is indicated by "Therefore, Śāriputra, because Bodhisattvas have no attainment they depend on and abide in the perfection of wisdom and their minds are without obstructions and without fear. Having completely passed beyond all error they go to the completion of nirvāṇa." The sentence before the epithets of the mantra, "All the Buddhas who abide in the three times have been fully enlightened into unsurpassed, perfect, complete enlightenment through relying on the perfection of wisdom." corresponds to the vajra-like samādhi, which is the final moment of the path of meditation and also corresponds to the path of no more learning, which is Buddhahood. "All the Buddhas who abide in the three times have been fully enlightened" corresponds to the vajra-like samādhi. "Unsurpassed, perfect, complete enlightenment" corresponds to the path of no more learning. According to Atīśa, "all the Buddhas" refers to Bodhisattvas of the tenth stage who are called Buddhas at *Abhisamayālaṃkāra* I.XX. His point is that it is Bodhisattvas who become fully enlightened; Buddhas are already enlightened.[9]

The most elaborate correlation of the path to sūtra is undertaken by Śrīmahājana, who finds parallels between the fourfold profundity and the four levels of the path of preparation, the eightfold profundity and the sixteen moments of the path of seeing, and the section of the sūtra, "in emptiness, there is no form, . . . no non-attainment" and the abandonment of thirty-six misconceptions concerning subjects and objects that occurs on the path of meditation. His approach can be illustrated by the section on the path of seeing. Śrīmahājana describes the path of seeing in terms of the Sarvāstivāda categories of the sixteen moments of doctrinal forbearance (*dharmakṣānti*) and doctrinal knowledge (*dharmajñāna*). These are set forth concisely in Vasubandhu's commentary on *Abhidharmakośa* VI.26-28. According to this explanation, the path of seeing consists of fifteen moments of realization of the four truths, the sixteenth moment occurring on the path of meditation. There are four moments of realization with regard to each of the four truths. The first moment is that of doctrinal forbearance of the truth of suffering with regard to the desire realm (*kāmadhātu*). In this moment, the afflictions of the desire realm associated with the truth of suffering are abandoned. This is followed by a moment of doctrinal knowledge of the truth of suffering with regard to the desire realm, which is the state of understanding that the afflictions of that level have been abandoned. This is followed by a moment of realization called subsequent forbearance (*anvayakṣānti*) in which the afflictions associated with the truth of suffering in the upper realms, the form realm (*rūpadhātu*) and the formless realm (*ārūpyadhātu*) are abandoned. This is followed by subsequent knowledge of the truth of suffering with regard to the upper realms. This sequence of four moments, doctrinal forbearance and doctrinal knowledge (which are concerned with the desire realm) and subsequent forbearance and subsequent knowledge (which are concerned with the form and formless realm together), is repeated for the remaining truths of origin, cessation, and path. In each case, the moments of realization called forbearance are the time when afflictions are actually abandoned and are called uninterrupted paths (*anantaryamārga*) because they cannot be interrupted or impeded in their severing of the hold of the afflictions. The eight moments of knowledge are the state of realizing that the afflictions of the particular level have been abandoned. They are called the path of liberation (*vimuktimārga*). An uninterrupted path followed by a path of liberation are likened to throwing a thief out and locking the door behind him.[10]

As is evident below, Śrīmahājana's presentation of the sixteen moments bears little resemblance to that of Vasubandhu. As he does elsewhere in his commentary, Śrīmahājana uses classical Buddhist philosophic categories to gloss the words of the *Heart Sūtra* with a twofold concern for numerical correspondence and doctrinal creativity. Here he aligns the eight moments of realization of doctrinal knowledge and subsequent knowledge of the four truths with the eight profundities.

> From among the sixteen moments having the nature of forbearance and knowledge observing the four truths, the eight forbearances are concomitant with the uninterrupted path. The moments of knowledge that follow the path of liberation can be known in the extensive teaching here because the cause [the forbearances] is understood through the effect [the knowledges]. Furthermore, they do not occur in a different order; the initial knowledge is the doctrinal knowledge and that which comes at the end through the power of the doctrinal knowledge is called the subsequent knowledge.
>
> Regarding that, the complete knowledge that the truth of suffering is empty of inherent existence is the doctrinal knowledge of suffering.

The subsequent knowledge of suffering is the realization that it is without character through realizing that it is empty of inherent existence. The knowledge that the truth of origin is not inherently produced is the doctrinal knowledge of origin. The subsequent knowledge of origin is the realization that it is not ceased because it is not feasible that that which is not produced could be anything else. The complete knowledge that the truth of cessation is not inherently connected with stains is the doctrinal knowledge of cessation. The subsequent knowledge of cessation is the realization that it is not stainless because of its not being inherently mixed with stains, that is, the purity which is the lack of stains, is adventitious. Regarding the truth of the path, because the objects of abandonment are adventitious, they do not inherently exist. Therefore, its not being diminished by the discordant class due to the power of antidote is the doctrinal knowledge of the path. The subsequent knowledge of the path is [the understanding that] because there is nothing that is not included in the dharmadhātu, then just as [the objects of abandonment] do not diminish, it is not feasible that the antidotes increase.[11]

Śrīmahājana begins his division of the sūtra with the path of preparation because he says that a son or daughter of good lineage is a Bodhisattva already on the path of accumulation.

The Path of Preparation

The Bodhisattva, the Mahāsattva, the Superior Avalokiteśvara said this to the venerable Śāriputra: "Śāriputra, a son of good lineage or a daughter of good lineage who wishes to practice the profound perfection of wisdom should view [things] in this way: They should correctly view those five aggregates also as empty of inherent existence. Form is emptiness; emptiness is form. Emptiness is not other than form; form is not other than emptiness. In the same way, feeling, discrimination, compositional factors, and consciousnesses are empty.

The Path of Seeing

Śāriputra, in that way, all phenomena are empty, that is, without characteristic, unproduced, unceased, stainless, not stainless, undiminished, unfilled.

The Path of Meditation

Therefore, Śāriputra, in emptiness, there is no form, no feeling, no discrimination, no compositional factors, no consciousness, no eye, no ear, no nose, no tongue, no body, no mind, no form, no sound, no odor, no taste, no object of touch, no phenomenon. There is no eye constituent, up to and including no mental consciousness constituent. There is no ignorance, no extinction of ignorance, up to and including no aging and death and no extinction of aging and death. Similarly, there are no sufferings, no origins, no cessations, no paths, no exalted wisdom, no attainment, and also no non-attainment.

The Path of No More Learning

Therefore, Śāriputra, because Bodhisattvas have no attainment, they depend on and abide in the perfection of wisdom and their minds are without obstructions and without fear. Having completely passed beyond all error they go to the completion of nirvāṇa. All the Buddhas who abide in the three times have been fully awakened into unsurpassed, perfect, complete enlightenment through relying on the perfection of wisdom.

Part II

Tibetan Commentaries

Chapter 10

Commentary on the *Heart Sūtra*, Jewel Light Illuminating the Meaning

by bsTan-dar-lha-ram-pa

The bee of clear awareness gathers the honey of
precepts from the bKa-gdams instructions.
Contentment comes from the good taste of the doctrine.
May I be protected with excellent fortune by the supreme
spiritual friend [gLong-grol-bla-ma,
Ngag-dbang-blo-bzang, 1719-1794],
The glorious one who bears the banner of the
Subduer's teaching.

I pay homage with the crown of my head at the
lotuses at the feet of Munīndra.
The gold mountain of his Form Body is surrounded by
the light of the major and minor marks.
In the ocean of sport of his auspicious speech are
reflected the objects of knowledge.
The sun of his mind destroys the dark troubles of the world.

Goddess Sarasvatī, graced with the glory of youth
Like a goose playing in a lotus lake,
Remain happily in the clear pond of my unmuddied mind
And bestow upon me supreme courage.

I respectfully revere Nāgārjuna and Asaṅga
Whom the Conqueror himself in countless scriptures
Showered with flowers of explicit praise
Saying, "They are valid persons, unmistaken."

Although the bee of my mind cannot comprehend
The vastness of the sky of topics of the profound
perfection of wisdom,

This discourse, holding as much as can be taken
with the point of a hair,
Is made to refresh those who seek much hearing.

Here, the explanation of the meaning of the *Heart Sūtra* has two parts, the general meaning and the meaning of the parts.

The speaker of the Perfection of Wisdom sūtras is Śākyamuni. [There are a variety of assertions among the Buddhist philosophical schools] concerning the nature of his speech. The Vaibhāṣikas assert that it is a non-associated compositional factor (*viprayuktasaṃskāra*), the composite of words, terms, and letters. The Sautrāntikas assert that the nature of words, terms, and letters is external form. The Prāsaṅgikas, because they agree with the world, assert that [the word of the Buddha] is sound and matter. The Cittamātrins say that if the word [of the Buddha] and the treatises were real sound, then there would be no word [of the Buddha] or treatises in the continuum of a person who had emitted them as speech. [That is, the words of the Buddha could not exist in the Buddha's mind before he spoke them or in the minds of his audience after he had spoken them.] Consequently, [according to the Cittamātrins,] all phenomena must be established in terms of the individual's mind. Therefore, a Buddha is the wisdom directly realizing all phenomena which is constantly in meditative equipoise on the cessation that is the limit of reality. Through the combination of the fulfillment of the aspirational prayers of the Buddha and the pure actions and ripened continuua of his disciples, however, the Complete Enjoyment Body (*saṃbhogakāya*) appears as a teacher to Bodhisattvas and the Emanation Body (*nirmāṇakāya*) appears as a teacher to śrāvakas and so forth. The appearance of the doctrine spoken by those [Buddha Bodies] is asserted to be the word [of the Buddha]. The source for this is a passage in Haribhadra's *Abhisamayālaṃkārāloka* [cited in] Tsong-kha-pa's *Legs bshad gser 'phreng*. Specifically, Asvabhāva's *Mahāyānasaṃgrahopanibandhana* says:

> The appearance of prose and poetry as sound are words in the minds of the listeners that operate in accordance with [their] desired aims. If that is the case, how do Bodhisattvas set forth [sūtras if sūtras are actually in the mind of the listener]? The mind of the listener is not what they set forth. [Because the mind of the listener arises] by the power of that [i.e., the Bodhisattvas' discourse, that discourse] is called [a sūtra]. It is like discovering a treatise or a mantra during a dream due to the power of a deity, etc. [in which a deity causes one to discover something present in one's own mind].

Next, whence do the the Perfection of Wisdom sūtras arise? They arise from the mouth of the Buddha as well as from other persons due to the power of his blessing.

Where were the Perfection of Wisdom sūtras taught? On Vulture Peak. Why is it called Vulture Peak? It is obvious that there are many ways of explaining this because [the following] appear in sDe-srid Sangs-rgyas-rgya-mtsho's (1653-1705) *Bai durya g.ya' sel:* [1] the mountain is shaped like a vulture, [2] it is shaped like a pile of vultures, [3] it was given that name because [vultures] protect the mountain where many vultures ate corpses, [4] it is called a pile due to the brilliance of the birds who are beings who understand emptiness, and [5] when the Subduer was fifty-eight years old in the Fire Snake year, he went to that mountain, which was shaped like a vulture's head. A demon who had magically changed himself into a vulture took the Teacher's robe and dropped it on the mountain, where it turned to stone in four layers and is known as the "great vulture pile." Because that mountain is the place where the Buddhas teach the perfection of wisdom, it, like the Vajra Seat [in Bodhgāyā], cannot be destroyed by hardness or fire and is immovable. Therefore, it is explained that although other mountains do not impede beings of the intermediate state [*bar do*], this one does.

When were the Perfection of Wisdom sūtras taught? The scholars of astrology known as "the three oceans," rTsad-chung-chos-grags-rgya-mtsho, Phug-pa-lhun-grub-rgya-mtsho, and mKhas-grub-nor-bzang-rgya-mtsho asserted that he taught the Perfection of Wisdom sūtras on the full moon day of the third lunar month and entered nirvāṇa on the fifteenth day of the next month.

'Jam-dbyangs-bzhad-pa'i-rdo-rje refutes [the thirteenth century scholars] mChims, the translator Chag, and others in his *Phar phyin mtha' dbyod* (*Analysis of the Perfection of Wisdom*). In his system, he asserts that the Teacher set forth the Perfection of Wisdom sūtras the year after he achieved Buddhahood. Some people, however, doubt that. When the Teacher achieved enlightenment on the fifteenth day of the fourth lunar month, a son was born to Amṛtodana, and that was Ānanda. At the time when he set forth the Perfection of Wisdom in the third lunar month, twelve months after he achieved Buddhahood, it had been just slightly more than ten months since Ānanda was born. How, then, could Ānanda have been in the audience when the Perfection of Wisdom was spoken? To that, 'Jam-dbyangs-bzhad-pa responds that there is no fault because Ānanda was not in the audience when the Perfection of Wisdom sūtras were initially spoken, but he was present when they were spoken later. There are also doubts about this. The prologue to the *Aṣṭasāhasrikāprajñāpāramitāsūtra* says:

> Thus did I hear at one time. The Transcendent Victor was staying at Vulture Peak in Rājagṛha with a great assembly of monks, 1250 monks. They were all arhats who had exhausted the contaminants . . . in control of all minds, and had achieved the excellent perfection, with the exception of one person and this was the venerable Ānanda.

If this prologue is the prologue from the time when the *Aṣṭasāhasrikāprajñāpāramitāsūtra* was initially spoken, then it contradicts ['Jam-dbyangs-bzhad-pa's assertion] that Ānanda was absent. If this is the prologue from the time when the word [of the Buddha] was compiled, it contradicts the fact that Ānanda was an arhat at that time. If this is a prologue from sometime in between, it seems to contradict the [Buddha's] instruction [to Ānanda] in the *Dharmasaṃgīti* to use these words when compiling [his] word: "Monks, collect the doctrine [adding] 'Thus did I hear at one time.'"

Some say that Ānanda was even present before the Teacher demonstrated the way to become enlightened, because it is explained in Bu-ston's *Chos 'byung* as well as in the *Lalitavistara* that when the young prince Siddhārtha was tested in the [martial] arts, Ānanda shot [an arrow], the distance of two *krośa* [approximately four miles]. Some say that there was an elder and younger Subhūti, Ānanda, Udayin, and Sutiṣya, etc., with one appearing earlier and [the other] later, so that the Ānanda who appeared in the company of the young Bodhisattva was someone other than the son of Amṛtodana.

According to the *Bai durya g.ya' sel*, the Superior Subhūti must have just attained the state of an arhat at the time that the Perfection of Wisdom was spoken, and Subhūti saw the truth for the first time on the day of the [Buddha's] Descent from the Heaven [of the Thirty-Three, to which he had ascended to teach the doctrine to his mother]. The *Vinaya* also says that he attained the state of an arhat not long after that. Therefore, having provided many reasons why it is correct that the Perfection of Wisdom sūtras were spoken after the Descent from Heaven, [sDe-srid Sangs-rgyas-rgya-mtsho] explains that the Perfection of Wisdom sūtras were spoken in the Fire Snake Year when the Subduer (*muni*) was fifty-eight years old. But below, on page 402 [of the *Bai durya g.ya' sel*], he explains that [the Buddha] set forth the Perfection of Wisdom cycle in the Iron Dog year, when he was fifty-one.

There must be a reason why that many scholars disagree. This is what I think. [Consider] the example of the year of the Teacher's birth. In Chos-rjes-skya-pa's system, it is Earth Dragon [832 B.C.E.], in *mahā-*

paṇḍita Śākyaśrī's system it is Fire Snake [843], in the Kālacakrin gYung-ston's system it is Earth Mouse [836], in Atīśa's system it is Wood Ox [835], in Bu-ston's system it is Fire Horse [854], in Phug's system it is Iron Monkey [876], and, according to the system of Chinese scholars, it is Wood Tiger [1027].[1] Although all are proven with scripture and reasoning, according to common standards, the year of the Teacher's birth is beyond the purview of those scholars. Is [the year of his teaching the Perfection of Wisdom sūtras] a similar case?

The Perfection of Wisdom sūtras are renowned in Tibet by names such as the seventeen mothers and sons. The most important ones, however, are three—the vast, intermediate, and brief. The vast is the *Śatasāhasrikāprajñāpāramitā* (*100,000 Stanzas*), the intermediate is the *Pañcaviṃśatisāhasrikāprajñāpāramitā* (*25,000 Stanzas*), and the brief is the *Aṣṭasāhasrikāprajñāpāramitā* (*8000 Stanzas*). These names are given from the standpoint of the number of ślokas.

In general, there are [five texts] renowned in Tibet as "the five sets of one hundred thousand". The *Prajñāpāramitā Sūtra* is the hundred thousand of mind, the *Nirvāṇa Sūtra* is the hundred thousand of speech, the *Ratnakūṭa Sūtra* is the hundred thousand of body, the *Avataṃsaka Sūtra* is the hundred thousand of auspicious qualities, and the *Laṅkāvatāra Sūtra* is the hundred thousand of activities. These are called the five sets of one hundred thousand. The reason for designating them as one hundred thousand is that the vast *Prajñāpāramitā* has one hundred thousand ślokas. The *Nirvāṇa Sūtra* has one hundred thousand testaments made by the Buddha when he was about to pass into nirvāṇa. The *Ratnakūṭa Sūtra* has one hundred thousand different names of the Buddha. The *Avataṃsaka Sūtra* has one hundred thousand aspirational prayers (*praṇidhāna*). The *Laṅkāvatāra Sūtra* has ways of taming one hundred thousand demons.

There are also sūtras, known as "the five royal sūtras," that are condensations of the meanings of the five sūtras. The condensation of the meaning of the *Mother* is the *Heart Sūtra*. The condensation of the *Nirvāṇa Sūtra* is the *Ātajñāna*. The condensation of the meaning of the *Ratnakūṭa Sūtra* is the *Vajravidāraṇī*. The condensation of the meaning of the *Avataṃsaka Sūtra* is the *Bhadracarīpraṇidhāna*. The condensation of the meaning of the *Laṅkāvatāra Sūtra* is the *Āpattideśanā*. I believe that the reason those are called "royal sūtras" is that in the past the religious kings of Tibet recited those five sūtras in their religious services. The *Heart Sūtra* is the sūtra on view, the *Ātajñāna* is the sūtra on deeds, the *Vajravidāraṇī* is the sūtra on ablution, the *Bhadracarī* is the sūtra on prayers, and the *Āpattideśanā* is the sūtra on the confession of sins.

The three—the vast, intermediate, and brief [Perfection of Wisdom sūtras]—were spoken simultaneously because all of the requestors are the same and [the sūtras] are similar in that there is a prophecy about sister Gaṅgādevī at the point [of explaining] the practice of the pure land. [These sūtras were necessarily spoken simultaneously] because it is not feasible that the same Buddha would repeatedly prophesize the enlightenment of the same person. This point was made by the omniscient Bu-ston.

The time when the Perfection of Wisdom sūtras were recorded in books is known as the time of the third compilation of the word [of the Buddha]. It is not the case, however, that the word did not exist at all in written form prior to that. If it is asked how the Perfection of Wisdom sūtras were propagated and in which country, [it is necessary to know] who owned the Perfection of Wisdom [sūtras] after the Teacher passed into nirvāṇa. The eight groups of gods, and so forth, gathered together but because they could not agree through discussion, there was a scramble for them. The nāgas got the *Vast Mother* [the *Śatasāhasrikāprajñāpāramitā*], the gods got the *Aṣṭādaśasāhasrikāprajñāpāramitā*, the humans got the *Pañcaviṃśatisāhasrikāprajñāpāramitā*, the demigods got the *Daśasāhasrikāprajñāpāramitā*, the king of the yakṣas, Kubera, got the *Aṣṭasāhasrikāprajñāpāramitā.*

Regarding how the vast *Mother* got back to India, the king of the nāgas was ill and nothing could help him. A girl told his fortune, saying that in the land of humans was a master named Nāgārjuna who was skilled in the meaning of the two truths and who, if invited, would cure [the king]. In accordance with the prophecy, he went to the land of the nāgas; this is called the retrieval of the *Śatasāhasrikāprajñāpāramitā.* Another version explains that the master went to the land of the nāgas looking for some sandalwood to erect an image of Tārā. This is called the retrieval of the *Vast Mother.* When the *Vast Mother* was taken from the land of the nāgas in that way, four chapters from the end were left in the land of the nāgas: the *Maitreyaparipṛcchā*, the *Dharmodgata*, the *Sadāprarudita*, and the *Parīndanā.* Therefore, some say that because those are not present at the end of the present version of the *Vast Mother*, it is not complete. Others say that the present version of the *Vast Mother* has the full one hundred thousand ślokas and [the missing chapters] are combined in the *avikāradharmatva* chapter at the end. Therefore, it is, in fact, complete. Others have a way of filling in [the sūtra] from the *25,000* and the *8000* by taking the *Maitreyaparipṛcchā* and the *Dharmodgata* to be one chapter on vows, the *Sadāprarudita* to be the second chapter, and the *Parīndanā* to be the third. Adding those three chapters to the end of some [versions of] the *Mother* in effect makes the five chapters. Chos-grub of Gos says that they are also in the Chinese translation.

Regarding how [the Perfection of Wisdom sūtras] were propagated in the snowy land of Tibet, during the time of Khri-srong-sde-btsan (740-c. 798), Nyang-kham-pa, also known as rLangs-kham-pa Go-cha-bya-pa, acquired the ability to memorize without forgetting and was sent to [India] to bring back the Perfection of Wisdom. He memorized the *Vast Mother*, covered his back with a cover of gold, covered his front with a cover of turquoise, tied it with a string of pearls, and returned [to Tibet]. What he had in his mind was dictated in four volumes. It did not say *śatasāhasrikā* in Sanskrit and is called "the red draft," "the translation of the mind of rLangs," and "[the text] kept in a deer leather bag." Also, Mañjuśrī of sBas and Indravaro of Nyang translated the Indian text in four volumes. It had *sāhasrikā* in Sanskrit and was called the "hundred thousand taxes" and the blue draft. These versions were greatly condensed books, almost like notes. The red [draft] was written with vermillion mixed with blood from the nose of the Dharma king [Khri-srong-sde-btsan] himself. The blue [draft] received its name from being written with indigo mixed with singed hair from [his] head. The [text] kept in a leather bag was named for the vessel in which it was kept. The container in which it was placed was a deer skin bag. The "hundred thousand taxes" was so-called because it was translated after taxes had been gathered from the subjects.

Also, Vairocana translated it in six volumes. It had *āryaśatasāhasrikā* in Sanskrit and is called the intermediate translation of the lama. sKa-pa dPal-brtsegs and Cog-ro Klu'i-rgyal-mtshan translated it in sixteen volumes. It said, "Obeisance to all the Buddhas, Bodhisattvas, śrāvakas and pratyekabuddhas" under the title and is called the great translation of the lama. In the earlier versions of the *Mother*, there were only one hundred-nineteen samādhis. The translator rNgok bLo-ldan-shes-rab added the samādhis "lamp of wisdom" (*prajñāpradīpa*), "clear appearance" (*śuddhapratibhāsa*), and "lamp of the moon" (*candrapradīpa*) from the *Śatasāhasrikā* he received from Pham-mthing [in Nepal], making one hundred-twenty-one. [This version], without the subscribed *ya* and the extra suffix *da* [which had been dropped from many words during the reign of king Ral-pa-can] is called the translation of rNgok.

There are three well-known translations of the *Pañcaviṃśatisāhasrikā*. There are six translations of the *Aṣṭasāhasrikā*, three of which are very famous: the *Mālika*, the *Śreṇika* and the *Sainya*. The variations in terminology and differences in length among these three is said to be due either to their being [based on] different Indian editions or to differences in translation; the *Mālika* is the most extensive. Regarding the method of differentiating those three, in the sKo and

Jog translation, the Subhūti chapter comes after the mendicant Śreṇika appears, in the Vairocana translation, the Subhūti chapter comes after the mendicant Sainya appears, in the translation by rNgok, the omniscience chapter comes after that, and in that of rGyal-ba'i-'byung-gnas of 'Brom the omniscience chapter comes after the mendicant Mālika appears.

Regarding the measurement of the vast, intermediate, and brief [Perfection of Wisdom sūtras] made by the translators, it is said that the *Vast Mother* has three hundred sections, seventy-two chapters, 100,000 ślokas, 100,000 vertical strokes (*shad*), and 4,100,000 dots. The *Pañcaviṃśatisāhasrikā* has seventy-eight sections, seventy-six chapters, 20,000 ślokas,[2] 100,000 vertical strokes dots, and 1,100,000 dots. The *Aṣṭasāhasrikā* has twenty-four sections, thirty-two chapters, 8000 ślokas, and 352,000 dots. This reckoning of numbers and some translations are based on the defective edition dictated by the scholar Ko-cha. Therefore, there are doubts as to whether or not they are accurate. They are recorded as something for scholars to analyze.

Regarding what are referred to as the impressions with seven levels of seals, the seal [or imprint] of a dot [keeps] syllables from being confused, the seal of a vertical stroke [keeps] groups of words from being confused, the seal of a chapter [keeps] the meaning of words from being confused, the seal of a section (*bam po*) [keeps] ślokas from being confused, the seal of a section number [keeps] sections from being confused, the seal of the margin [keeps] the end [of the page] from being confused, and the seal of the margin title [keeps] the volume from being confused. This makes seven. Some people speak [of another set of seven]: the string of the book cover is sealed with seven [knots], the book cover is sealed [or imprinted] with carving, the golden border is sealed with *lañca* script, the ornamental mark [in the upper left corner of the page] is sealed with the page number, the section is sealed with the chapter, the margin is sealed with the margin number, and the red vertical stroke is sealed with a blue vertical stroke. The margin title in this context refers to the name of the text, which is written on either side of the page number at the edge of the volume. [Those who hold to this latter listing of the seven cite as their source] Haribhadra's *Abhisamayālaṃkārāloka*, which says, "Put it away having tied it tightly with seven sashes with knots in seven places and having put the seal of your name on it seven times." It seems that [this difference in what the seven seals refer to can be accounted for by the fact that the former] is based on the volumes of the earlier translations in Tibet, whereas what appears in [Haribhadra's] great commentary on the *Aṣṭasāhasrikā* is based on the volumes of Āryadeśa [India]. Therefore, the question is whether it is suitable. It should be analyzed by scholars.

With regard to the second, the meaning of the parts [of the *Heart Sūtra*], there are two sections, the preliminary [stanzas] and the actual [sūtra]. Regarding the first, in great monasteries such as Se-ra and 'Bras spung (Drepung), before reciting the sūtra, it is customary [to recite] these verses of praise and obeisance.

> I bow down to the mother of the Conquerors of the three times,
> The perfection of wisdom, inexpressible by words or thoughts,
> Which is unproduced and unceased [like] the entity of the sky,
> The object of the wisdom of unique knowledge.

It is said that these verses are words recited by the [Buddha's] son, Rahula, to his mother. The meaning is that the wisdom that goes and is gone beyond saṃsāra does so by means of the wisdom that directly realizes emptiness; [that wisdom] is not an object that can be expressed by speaking words or thinking thoughts. Because that wisdom is not created by way of its own entity, it is not destroyed, but, like the expanse of the sky, is the negation of being established by way of its own entity. That very thing which serves as the sphere of the unique knowledge of meditative equipoise is the mother that gives birth to all the Conquerors of the three times. It is obeisance to the wisdom that know emptiness directly.

With respect to the second, the actual explanation, there are also two parts, the meaning of the title and the meaning of the text. That which in the language of India is *Bhagavatīprajñāpāramitāhṛdaya*, when translated into Tibetan is "The Heart of the Transcendent and Victorious Perfection of Wisdom," and that is the title of the sūtra. Regarding the purpose for stating the title, if a name were not given, there would be no way of finding out which sūtra it was. Hence, the name is stated at the beginning. Regarding the word "heart," for example, [the place] where all the consciousnesses that pervade the entire body gather is called the heart. In the same way, all the meanings of the vast, intermediate, and condensed Mother sūtras are gathered here. Therefore, it is called the sūtra of sūtras or the heart of sūtras. All of the intentions of the Transcendent Victor are gathered in this sūtra. As Tsong-kha-pa says in his *Legs bshad snying po chung ba:*

> Whatever you have spoken
> Begins from dependent arising
> And is for the purpose of passing beyond sorrow.
> You have no activities that do not bring peace.

The Transcendent Victor thinks only of methods by which sentient beings may pass beyond sorrow, and the method by which they pass beyond sorrow is the wisdom realizing emptiness. Therefore, it is called the essence of wisdom. That which passes beyond sorrow is the reality of sentient beings' minds. Therefore, it is called the essence of Tathāgatas. When it is understood that everything in the sūtras and tantras only sets forth methods for purifying the taints of sentient beings' minds, it is realized that all the teachings are without contradiction. Therefore, because all the Buddhas of the three times are born from the wisdom realizing emptiness, that wisdom is referred to with the term "mother." This is the idea behind *bhagavatī*.

"One section" and Obeisance to the Transcendent and Victorious Perfection of Wisdom" are words written by the translators. In general, there is no certainty about the length of a section. Three hundred ślokas constitute a section in texts like Haribhadra's *Sphuṭārthā*. Ninety ślokas constitute one section in the *Mañjuśrīparipṛcchā*. Seventy-five ślokas make three sections in the *Tathāgathasaṃgīti Sūtra*. In accordance with [the latter], twenty-five ślokas make one section of the *Heart Sūtra*.

In general, with respect to going beyond (*pāramitā*), beyond a common being is a Superior (*ārya*), beyond the conventional is the ultimate, beyond saṃsāra is nirvāṇa, and beyond ignorance is knowledge. From among those, the last is the [referent of the] term "wisdom gone beyond" (*prajñāpāramitā*). According to the Cittamātrins, the wisdom of the non-duality of subject and object, that is, the marvelous realization of one's own purpose, refers explicitly to the Sugata. Dignāga says in the *Prajñāpāramitāpiṇḍārtha:*

> The perfection of wisdom is the non-dual wisdom;
> It is the Tathāgata.

Because they are endowed with methods for attaining the state of a Sugata, the goal, [the term] "perfection of wisdom" is used to designate texts and path. That same text says:

> That term [is used] for texts and paths
> Because they have that object [as their] goal.

The discussion of the meaning of the text is in two parts, a discussion of the prologue that produces the sūtra and a discussion of the actual sūtra produced from that. With respect to the first, the common prologue is from "This did I hear at one time" to "great assembly of Bodhisattvas." The purpose of the prologue is to have the listeners understand that the compiler listened without adding anything or subtracting anything so that they can pay careful attention to him. According to the master Haribhadra, "at one time" means that by the blessings of the Buddha, all the words of the sūtra were heard by Ānanda in one instant. He says in his *Abhisamayālaṃkārāloka*, "Because an ear consciousness to which the entire meaning of the sūtra arose in one instant." The master Bhāvaviveka asserts that because the perfection of wisdom sūtras are not within the sphere of śrāvakas, their compiler is Vajrapāṇi. Haribhadra asserts that although Ānanda was not capable of doing so himself, he [compiled the sūtras] through the blessing of the Buddha and, therefore, is the compiler of the Perfection of Wisdom sūtras. Although such things should be explained, an explanation would be too lengthy.

The reason for saying both Rājagṛha and Vulture Peak is for the sake of indicating the combination of the two places for laymen and those who have gone forth [from the world], with the former being the best among places in the afflicted class and the latter being the best of places among the pure class. With regard to Rājagṛha ["the residence of the king"], there was a famous place in the city of Kuśinagara that became uninhabitable due to being repeatedly burned down by nonhumans. The king ordered that henceforth those whose homes burned down must build their homes in the charnel ground of Sitavana and remain there. At that time, by the power of karma, the king's palace was the first to be lost in a fire. The king then went there and made his abode. That is how it got the name "Residence of the King". This is explained in the *Śālistambhasūtra*.

Regarding "monk," the actuality of monkhood can be attained by any of the ten ways of receiving ordination; in this context, it refers to an arhat. As Śāntideva says in the *Bodhicaryāvatāra* (IX.45ab):

> Monkhood is the root of the teaching
> But even monkhood is difficult.

The saṃgha is a gathering of four or more monks; the etymology is that which has the aspiration not to be separated by demons from the Teacher Buddha, the teaching of the excellent doctrine, and friends who practice purity. Candrakīrti's *Triśaraṇasaptati* (*Seventy Stanzas on Refuge*) says:

> Because they cannot be separated
> From the Buddha, Dharma, and Saṃgha
> By billions of demons,
> It is clearly called "saṃgha."

Regarding the word "great," it is explained many times in the Indian commentaries that it means a large number. "Bodhisattva" is explained many times in such texts as the *Vairocanābhisambodhi* and the *Sañcayagāthāprajñāpāramitāsūtra.* The simple etymology is that because they have purified all faults and accomplished all good qualities, they are *bodhi* and because they contemplate the welfare of all transmigrators and have annihilated demons, they are *sattva.* Or, because they have studied the two truths again and again and have arrived at the meaning of them, [they are called] *bodhi* and because they have endured hardship in contemplating the two truths again and again, [they are called] *sattva.* Regarding great, the *Sañcayagāthāprajñāpāramitāsūtra* says:

> Those who abide in the supreme Mahāyāna of the Conqueror
> [Have] great giving, great awareness, and great power.
> They wear great armor and have tamed the deceiving demons.
> Therefore, they are called Mahāsattvas.

"Together" (*sārdham*) means behavior or activity and means concordant; in brief it means that the audience was of concordant activity. Abide has four meanings: abide in physical posture, abide in teaching the doctrine, abide in samādhi, and abide in correctly residing within. This is [a case of] abiding in a physical posture.

The unique prologue is, "At that time the Transcendent Victor was absorbed in a samādhi on the categories of phenomena called 'perception of the profound.' Also at that time, the Bodhisattva, the Mahāsattva, the Superior Avalokiteśvara was contemplating the meaning of the profound perfection of wisdom and saw that those five aggregates also are empty of inherent existence." The difference between the common and the unique prologue is that the common is shared with other sūtras whereas the unique prologue is found in this sūtra and not in others. "At that time" means at the time of teaching the doctrine when the roots of virtue of the audience had ripened. Regarding the "profound" of "perception of the profound," it is that which is difficult to appear to the mind. For example, it is not difficult to perceive the reflection of sun or moon in a lake, but it is difficult for the limits of space to appear [on the surface of the lake]. In the same way, it is easy to perceive the conventional but it is difficult to perceive the ultimate. "Perception" means the wisdom that understands something so profound. The categories of phenomena are the aggregates, constituents, sources, and so forth. "Also at that time" is a term of emphasis meaning at that very time at which the disciples' continua were ripe.

Regarding "the Superior Avalokiteśvara," he who has risen far above the level of common beings has the power to free from suffering all sentient beings who can be seen by his eyes. The "practice of the profound" means the observation of emptiness. Observing it means contemplating it. The word "also" in the phrase "these five aggregates also" means that he saw not only the aggregates but also the sources and constituents to be empty of inherent existence. The *ba* prefix on *blta'o* was added by the scribe and is not correct.

With regard to the second, the meaning of the actual sūtra, there are three parts: how Śāriputra asked his question, how Avalokiteśvara answered, and how that was admired by the Teacher. The first is from, "Then by the power of the Buddha," to "who wishes to practice the profound perfection of wisdom." "Then" means after Avalokiteśvara had been empowered by the Tathāgata to fully understand the meaning of what was to be explained. "Venerable" is a term which is generally famous for addressing those junior, but if this term is a term that occurs in the context of the compilation of the word [of the Buddha], it is not correct that Śāriputra was junior in training to the compiler [Ānanda]. Therefore, it is spoken with the special meaning of one endowed with a life that has abandoned the afflictions and that is free from birth and death by actions and afflictions. Regarding "Śāriputra," a child, who was an emanation of [the Bodhisattva] Sarvanivaraṇaviṣkambhin, was born from the union of his mother Śārikā, who had eyes like a *śārika* bird that lives in the reed or *nalandra* forests, and his father Tiṣya. His name taken from his father was Upatiṣya and his name taken from his mother was Śāriputra. Because he was of the Śāradvati family, he is also called Śāradvatiputra. "Son and daughter of good lineage" means those who have the Mahāyāna lineage. The purpose of saying son and daughter is that only those who are male or female can create all the good qualities of the path and the realizations; eunuchs and impotent people cannot. Therefore, [it is said] in order to exclude them. "Whosoever" means distinctions are not made; that is, anyone who does not fear emptiness and has interest is suitable.

With respect to "How should one train who wishes to practice the profound," that which is the profound practice of the perfection of wisdom is the practice of the meaning [of the perfection of wisdom]. He asks how those who wish to act, that is, who wish to practice, should practice. The occurrence of the phrase, *spyod pa spyad par 'dod pa* in the majority of texts these days is incorrect; it should say *spyad pa spyod par 'dod* because *spyad pa* and *spyod pa* refer to the object of achievement and the means of achievement or to the object of practice and the practitioner. Vimalamitra says in his vast commentary, "In some editions it says, 'those who wish to practice.' This means that there is no difference between do and achieve." The master Praśāstrasena says in his commentary, "The practitioner is the person, the Bodhisattva. The practice is the doctrine, the perfection of wisdom."

Regarding the second, how Avalokiteśvara answered, the short answer is from "[Avalokiteśvara] said this . . . should view [things] in this way", to "They should correctly view those five aggregates also as empty of inherent existence." The extensive answer is from "Form is emptiness" up to [when the Buddha says], "Well done." Because the individual words are easy to understand, they do not need to be explained. The word "also" in "those five aggregates also" indicates that not only is the "I" empty of inherent existence, but the "mine" also is empty of inherent existence. Thus, it indicates the stages of understanding of the two selflessnesses [of persons and phenomena]. "Empty of inherent existence" means empty from its own side. Therefore, it means that [phenomena] are not established objectively or from the side of the object. For example, when a house appears in a dream, it does not appear from the side of a basis appearing toward [the subject] but rather is projected out from the side of the perceiving consciousness. Therefore, it must be understood that the conventional status of phenomena is just like that. According to the Prāsaṅgikas, inherent establishment is the object of negation of reasonings analyzing the ultimate. Hence, even though the qualification "ultimate" is not affixed explicitly to the object of negation, it is affixed implicitly. Therefore, it is of definitive meaning (*nītārtha*) and is literal. When "Form is emptiness; emptiness is form. Emptiness is not other than form; form is not other than emptiness." is understood in a coarse way, according to the Cittamātrins it means, "This appearance of form is one's own mind, which is empty of the duality of subject and object. One's own mind is the appearance of form. One's own mind is not other than the appearance of form. The appearance of form is also not other than one's own mind." According to the Prāsaṅgikas, it means, "Because something appears as form it does not exist. Because it does not exist it appears as form. This appearance as form itself does not exist but it is not to be sought apart from its non-existence. Since it appears as form while not existing, form does not exist as something separate from that."

In general, there are five kinds of emptiness. The absence of yogurt at the time of milk is the emptiness that is non-existence at a prior [time]. The absence of milk at the time of yogurt is the emptiness that is non-existence after having been destroyed. The non-existence of a pot in a place where there is no bulbous thing is the emptiness of the utterly non-existent. The non-existence of a horse in an ox is the emptiness that is the non-existence of one thing in another. The non-existence of a human at the time of mistaking a cairn for a human is the emptiness of entityness. The mode of emptiness in this case is the last mode of emptiness; this is an essential point. Therefore, with respect to that there are many terms such as empty by way of its own entity, empty of inherent existence, and empty by way of its own character, and there are many examples such as an illusion, a dream, a mirage, a moon in water, and an emanation. I do not explain this [at such length] because I have nothing else to explain. Therefore, analyze from various perspectives using the example that appears easily to your mind, and when dependent arising appears as the meaning of emptiness, it is best. Until that point, one should create what seems like a fear, worrying that the majority of phenomena, such as forms, have become the object negated by reasoning. Otherwise, even though you say things like, "A pot does not truly exist, inherently exist, or exist by way of its own character," if the way in which it does not exist is not perceived, you cannot be counted among those who have analyzed emptiness.

Thus, having explicitly applied the four modes of emptiness to the form aggregate, the purpose of merely saying, "In the same way, feeling . . ." with respect to the other four aggregates is that from among the five aggregates, form is like a basis or vessel whereas the latter four aggregates are primarily consciousness and are like the water that is supported in that vessel. Hence, just as when the supporting vessel is destroyed, the supported water is also destroyed, so when the form aggregate is understood to be empty, it is easy to understand that the consciousness aggregates that are supported by that are also empty. That is the intention.

In brief, in order to put an end to common beings becoming attached to form and falling to the extreme of saṃsāra, it teaches that form is emptiness. In order to put an end to some becoming attached to emptiness and falling to the extreme of peace, it teaches that emptiness is form. For example, if a blind person were to go down a narrow path that had thorns on the left and a cliff on the right, and if a sighted person were to say, "There are thorns," there is a danger of the person falling off the cliff. If he were to say, "There is a cliff," there is a danger of his falling into the thorns. In order that he not fall to either extreme, a middle path is taught. Those modes are the way to meditate on emptiness on the occasion of [the paths] of accumulation and preparation.

With respect to the mode of meditation on the path of seeing, it says in the instructions of Atīśa set down by Legs-pa'i-shes-rab of rNgog that, having addressed Śāriputra, "Thus, all phenomena are empty" indicates the door of liberation emptiness; "without characteristic, unproduced, unceased, stainless, not stainless" indicate the door of liberation signlessness, and "undiminished, unfilled" indicate the door of liberation wishlessness. Mahājana's commentary says that "emptiness" and "without characteristic" are, respectively, the objects of observation of the doctrinal knowledge (*dharmajñāna*) and subsequent knowledge (*anvayajñāna*) with respect to suffering. Similarly, "unproduced" and "unceased" are [the objects of observation] of the doctrinal knowledge and subsequent knowledge with respect to sources. "Stainless" and "not stainless" are [objects of observation] of the doctrinal knowledge and subsequent knowledge of the path, and "undiminished" and "unfilled" are explained to be the objects of observation of the doctrinal knowledge and subsequent knowledge of cessation.

Some editions say, "Therefore, all phenomena are empty" and "stainless and free from stain" and there are those who comment on it in that way, but in many Indian and Tibetan commentaries it says, "In that way, all phenomena," and "not stainless." It is clear that it is more meaningful if it is explained in accordance with the two negative terms appearing in succession.

With regard to the second, the mode of meditation on the path of meditation, in both the commentary of Vimalamitra and the oral tradition of Atīśa it is explained [in terms of the] resulting [translation], "Therefore, at that time, in emptiness there is no form . . . ". In some commentaries, it is explained with the resultant translation "Thus, emptiness is not form." There is not a great difference in meaning. The supreme scholar 'Jam-dbyangs-dga'-ba'i-blo-gros explains that "in emptiness there is no form", and so forth means that form and so forth do not exist in the sight of the meditative equipoise on the path of meditation. Vimalamitra has this in mind in his commentary when he says, "in the perception of emptiness, there is no perception of form." Thus, the non-appearance of the five aggregates to the sight of the meditative equipoise is, "There is no form . . . there is no consciousness". The non-appearance of the twelve sources is "no eye . . . no phenomena". The non-appearance of the eighteen elements is "no eye constituent . . . no mental consciousness constituent." The non-appearance of the thoroughly afflicted and completely pure dependent arising is "no ignorance . . . up to and including no extinction of aging and death." The non-appearance of the objects of observation is "no suffering . . . no path." The non-appearance of the observer is "no exalted wisdom." The non-appearance of any attainment or non-attainment of the fruition is "no attainment and also no non-attainment." In that way, the twelve sources and the eighteen constituents should be taken as substrata.

Regarding that, the non-Buddhist Sāṃkhyas [assert] that what is called the self, the conscious *puruṣa* abides among the aggregates. They assert that apart from forms being seen and sounds being heard through the sense powers, such as the eye, there is no need for a separate eye consciousness that sees forms and that is other than the self. mKhas-grub-rje says in his *sDe bdun yid kyi mun sel* (*Clearing Away Mental Darkness About the Seven Works [of Dharmakīrti]*) that [the section of the sūtra discussed above] is for the purpose of refuting that assertion [that the self is found in the consciousnesses].

The conception of self asserted by the non-Buddhists is an artificial conception of self. The innate is the conception of a substantially existent person in the sense of self-sufficiency asserted by the Svātantrikas and below. In that mode of conception, the self that serves as the basis of conception thinking "I" does not depend on or rely on the aggregates but appears as the controller or master of the aggregates, and the aggregates appear as the controlled or the servant of the self. [This is demonstrated by the fact that] what an individual conceives of as "my form" and "my feelings" appear to be things that an individual would certainly be willing to give in exchange for those of others if [that were possible].

The reasoning employed by the non-Buddhists to prove the existence of a substantially existent self of persons is, "The subject, the mind thinking 'I' operates correctly because it operates naturally upon seeing the aggregates without the mind being previously directed, as is the case, for example, with the apprehension of blue." [That is, the non-Buddhists argue that the self exists because the conception of it is intuitive; the mind automatically and naturally thinks "I" upon seeing the body, just as the mind thinks "blue" upon perceiving a patch of blue.] The reasoning that the Buddhists use to refute the existence of a substantially existent person is, "The subject, a self-sufficient person that is not imputed to either the collection or the continuum of the aggregates, does not inherently exist because of not being either the same as or different from the aggregates, as is the case, for example, with the horns of a rabbit."[3]

Qualm: This is not a correct reason because that which is stated as the subject does not exist.

Answer: There is no fault. If the accumulated meaning that is the opposite of the composite of the two, a basal subject (*rang rten gyi chos can*) and the predicate of the probandum, is refuted by valid cognition, the reason is not correct; but if the accumulated meaning that is the composite of the two, a mere subject (*chos can 'ba' zhig ba*) and the predicate of the probandum, is eliminated with valid cognition, the fault of an incorrect reason is not entailed because, in a syllogism that states non-affirming negatives as both the sign and the predicate of the probandum, it is suitable to have a non-existent as the subject. Thus, the subject of the syllogism, a self-sufficient person who is not imputed to the collection or continuum of the aggregates, is called a mere or stated subject. The meaning of the term "self-sufficient person," that is, the appearance of the self-sufficient person to thought is the basal subject or the imputed subject of that syllogism. The actual basis of the refutation of permanence in the proof of impermanence with respect to sound by the sign of being a product is the appearance of the opposite from non-sound to thought. At that time, sound itself is not appearing to thought directly just as it is. However, I wonder whether there is the fine point that the appearance of opposite from non-sound is not the basal subject in that proof.[4]

Furthermore, not only do the non-Buddhists just assert substantial existence in the sense of self-sufficiency; it is clear that the Sautrāntikas and Cittamātrins assert that gross form and consciousness are substantially existent (*dravyasat, rdzas yod*) in the sense of self-sufficiency because those proponents of true existence assert that if something is imputedly existent (*prajñaptisat, btags yod*), it is imputed to a basis of designation that is substantially existent in the sense of self-sufficiency. How can one know this? It is proven by what is said by Tsong-kha-pa in his *dGongs pa rab gsal,* (*Illumination of the Thought*). "The others [the non-Prāsaṇgika Buddhist schools] assert that things that are imputedly existent are imputed in dependence on a basis of designation that is substantially existent in the sense of self-sufficiency." Because this passage is very clear, it does not need to be twisted [to determine its meaning]. With regard to the subtle selflessness of persons in terms of consciousness and gross form in the systems of the proponents of true existence [the non-Prāsaṇgika schools], the non-existence of consciousness as an object of use by a person who is substantially existent in the sense of self-sufficiency is posited as the selflessness of persons of consciousness. The other can be inferred.

The mode of training on the path of no more learning is, "Therefore, Śāriputra, because Bodhisattvas have no attainment . . . through relying on the perfection of wisdom." The meaning is that the conventional does not appear to the sight of meditative equipoise. Therefore, Bodhisattvas practice the perfection of wisdom, abide in it, and go to the completion of nirvāṇa. It is teaching that all of the Buddhas of the three times have also become Buddhas in that way.

Everything up to this point is for disciples of dull faculties. The instructions for those of sharp faculties are, "Therefore, the mantra of the perfection of wisdom . . . should train in the perfection of wisdom in that way." Vimalamitra's commentary says, "It is a secret mantra because of being a consciousness and because of being a protector." As he says, the original term *mantra* means mind and protector. The mantra of the perfection of wisdom is the path of accumulation. The mantra of great knowledge is the path of preparation. The unsurpassed mantra is the path of seeing. The mantra equal to the unequalled is the path of meditation. The mantra that completely pacifies suffering is the path of no more learning. In accordance with what is seen by this profound perfection of wisdom, it should be known to be true; that is, if an individual meditates in this way, one will know that it is the cause of going to Buddhahood. *Tadyathā* means it is so; that is, it is so that saṃsāra and nirvāṇa are of one taste in being without true existence. *Gate gate* means "go, go"; the former is to the path of accumulation and the latter is to the path of preparation. *Pāragate* means go to the path of seeing. *Pārasaṃgate* means go to the path of meditation. *Bodhi svāhā* means be founded in enlightenment, that is, "attain the path of no more learning." This correlation with the five paths appears in Mahājana's commentary and is not clear in the other Indian commentaries. Tibetan lamas uphold this, but it is clear that there are other ways of asserting [the meaning of the mantra]. *Oṃ* and *svāhā* bless the mantra with power. The absence of *oṃ* here is incorrect because it says in the *Prajñāpāramitāhṛdayasādhana* written by Nāgārjuna:

> If you are tired, recite the mantra of truth
> Adding *tadyathā* and *oṃ*.

Some scholars say that this mantra is not included in the tantras, thinking that it is placed in the sūtra system basically, but because the sādhanas of Nāgārjuna and Dārikapa are clearly in the mantra system, there must be a context for including this mantra in the tantras. However, mKhas-grub-rje said that the sādhanas of Nāgārjuna and Dārikapa are spurious and some scholars say that they are authentic. Also, there is a commentary on the *Heart Sūtra* in the mantra system by "Śrīsiṃha." Therefore, it seems difficult to analyze.

The third [section is], the way the Teacher admired [Avalokiteśvara's teaching], that is, "Then, the Transcendent Victor rose from that samādhi . . . praised the words of the Tathāgata." The meaning is easy to understand for the most part. His saying "Well done" twice is words of sincerity, not of number. "It is just so. It is like that . . ." means "Avalokiteśvara, your explanation is just like the mode of being of all phenomena. What I have understood is like that." The words, "the Transcendent Victor said this" and "having said this" in the prologue and at the end of the text are words [added with] the permission [of the Buddha]. Śāriputra's question and Avalokiteśvara's answer are words [spoken] through the blessing [of the Buddha]. "Well done . . . Even the Tathāgatas admire this" are words spoken from the mouth [of the Buddha].

With regard to the way to overcome demons [through reciting the sūtra], mKhas-grub refutes this in his *rGyud sde spyi rnam* (*General Presentation of the Tantras*) saying, "Regarding the way to overcome demons, those in [prayers] such as the 'clear light' and the 'prologue' are fabrications." There are, however, statements such as "The king of gods Śakra [Indra] thought about the meaning of the profound perfection of wisdom and recited it in order to overcome sinful demons." Because those words are similar to words in the *Aṣṭasāhasrikā* and because, moreover, there are instructions that are said to have been given by Nāgārjuna [that it is permissible to recite the sūtra in order to overcome demons], it should be analyzed.

That I have not explained in detail the profound
 meaning, difficult to fathom,
Is not due to the fault of having nothing to explain;
It is only because of the fault of narrowness of
 my own intelligence
That I have simply repeated some statements of others.

If you knew that I have turned away from the thought
 of the Subduer
Through engaging in sophistry,
Then just as a loving mother does not become angry
 at the misdeeds of her unfortunate child,
You would not be scornful, but would think of me with love.

Like the barley collected by a beggar,
This is a mixture into one of a variety of texts.
It is not filled with profound statements,
But because it was done with a mind not black,
 I don't think I am to be blamed.

By this virtue may the white elephant of my mind,
Its body adorned with ornaments of the virtue
 of much hearing,
Hold in its trunk of intelligence the sword of
 emptiness of duality
And vanquish all the armies of the conception
 of true existence.

Commentary on the Heart Sūtra, Jewel Light Illuminating the Meaning was written at the request of dKon-mchog-bzod-pa, the king of proclaimers of the profound texts. It was collected from a variety of texts and set down by the Ngag-dbang-bstan-dar of A-lag-sha, who is called Lha-ldan-grva-skor. It was printed at sKu-'bum-byams-pa-gling.

Chapter 11

An Explanation of the *Heart Sūtra* Mantra, Illuminating the Hidden Meaning

by Gung-thang dKon-mchog-bstan-pa'i-sgron-me

Namo Guru Munīndrāya

The *Heart Sūtra* mantra is, *tadyathā oṃ gate gate pāragate pārasaṃgate bodhi svāhā.* In Tibetan, it is, "It is thus: Proceed, proceed, proceed beyond, proceed far beyond, be founded in enlightenment." When the meaning is explained, "it is thus" [is first]. In the beginning, when the Teacher's long cultivated capacity of the lineage of the supreme vehicle burst forth, he was moved by great compassion, the root of the practice, and he wished that transmigrators would be completely liberated. He saw that the bonds from which [they] were to be freed was the conception of self. He understood that he who had not already liberated himself could not liberate others. He became fully accustomed to selflessness—the actual antidote to that conception—together with method and thereby extinguished the obstructions that impede the vision of reality together with their predispositions. *Only this*, which he saw and actualized when his vision was completely pure, did he see to be the sole path of progress for all followers. Therefore, ["it is thus" conveys] the greatness of the Teacher, the noble source of doctrine, establishing that he is the only valid person. From his own experience he advised that the natural center, which refutes both misleading extremes, *is thus*; that is, it is the union of emptiness and dependent arising.

Furthermore, all of saṃsāra and nirvāṇa are similar in that they are made by the mind; the arising of the inferior and the superior, [their] occurring separately, are differences [due] only to minds being mistaken and non-mistaken. If the mind does not accord with fact, it is mistaken; if it accords, it is not mistaken. Hence, having understood how to establish the factual and to discard the wrong, one must proceed to the real. The path to be traversed is the middle [path] beyond the chasms of permanence and annihilation, the door to peace, the path without a second. Although it pervades all objects of observation whatsoever, it is free from the elaborations of disparate distinctions. *Only this,* which is seen non-dualistically by the wisdom of individual knowledge and which, like honey, is of a single taste, [conveys] the greatness of the teaching in comprising the profound explicit teaching of the three "Mother of the Conquerors Sūtras" [the Perfection of Wisdom sūtras of 100,000, 25,000, and 8000 stanzas].

The marvels of a Buddha and the troubles experienced by transmigrators are neither natural attributes nor are they created by some other [agent]; they result from their good and bad modes of activity. Sentient beings desire happiness, but through creating the causes of suffering, they go lower and lower. If that is reversed, they go higher, but they do not go immediately. Therefore, the mode of progressing gradually from the lower realizations to the higher, the non-mistaken complete stages of the path travelled by the earlier Buddhas is *only this,* teaching [in a way] that includes the realizations, the hidden meaning of the Mother sūtras. Therefore, these two [the teaching of the explicit and hidden meanings of the Perfection of Wisdom sūtras] indicate the greatness of the doctrine as well as the purpose, and so forth.[1]

A mantra is that which protects the mind from being completely polluted by the demon of ignorance and thereupon establishes [the mind] in unsurpassed bliss. With respect to the meaning of [the *Heart Sūtra*] mantra, there are two parts, the general meaning and the meaning of the words.

The General Meaning

Regarding "proceed", whence and where does one go? One goes from saṃsāra to nirvāṇa. When considered in detail, it should be delineated in terms of where we abide now, the cause of our abiding there, where we are going from there, and the path which goes to that [destination]; in other words, [it should be delineated] in terms of the four truths.

As soon as one takes birth in the place where we now abide, saṃsāra having the nature of the appropriated aggregates, although happiness is found in such things as abode, possessions, and friends, we do not pass beyond suffering, just as wherever one touches the point of a needle, there is no happiness, and when one stays in a pile of filth, the stench does not go away. This is the chief of true sufferings.

Although ignorance, action, and so forth impel us into that situation, it is the attachment that craves the pleasures of saṃsāra that binds us there without separation. Like the sleep of a pig that loves filth, thus is the imprudent sleep of those who do not know suffering to be suffering, but fancy it to be clean and pure and cling tightly to it. Therefore, although contaminated actions and afflictions are sources [of suffering], the main thing that actually binds us is attachment.

The place where we are going is liberation, the extinguishment of those sufferings of saṃsāra. Furthermore, the true cessation that is the mere extinguishment of saṃsāra is the enlightenment of the Hīnayāna, "the lesser nirvāṇa." The true cessation that is the extinguishment of the root of that suffering together with its predispositions, the unlocated nirvāṇa adorned with the two marvelous aims, is highest enlightenment, the final destination.

The path that goes there is the non-conceptual wisdom of meditative equipoise of Superiors of the three vehicles which directly sees the meaning of the absence of inherent existence exactly as it is. It is the chief of the true paths. Broadly speaking, the lower conceptual awarenesses that are similar to that [wisdom] in their mode of apprehension are also paths. Because they serve as branches that prepare for and benefit that [wisdom], meditation on impermanence, suffering, and so forth are included within the designation "path of liberation," just as a portion of the route is called the path. Nāgārjuna said in the *Bodhicittavivaraṇa:*

> The three, called impermanence, emptiness, and suffering
> Are purifiers of the mind.
> The doctrine that supremely purifies the mind
> Is the absence of inherent existence.[2]

Śāntideva said in the *Bodhicaryāvatāra* [IX.1]:

> All of these branches were set forth
> By the Subduer for the sake of wisdom.

To illustrate with an example the stages by which we go from our abode here in saṃsāra to nirvāṇa, there was once a fool who was blithely sleeping in prison. A compassionate wise man called to him and woke him, explaining how there would be many hardships if he remained there. He was frightened by this and said, "I wonder if there is a way to escape?" [The wise man] explained that the place to go was the king's palace and [told] him how to get there. If he did this, he would be freed.

To apply that to the meaning, the initial call, together with explanations about the disadvantages and advantages awaken one from the sleep of non-conscientiousness in which the doctrine has not even been discerned. The person who says "Proceed" is the teacher of refuge, the Subduer, the Transcendent and Victorious Buddha. He is not different from the actual lama of the present time. Even though the call resounds in your ear, if you do not get out of bed, if you do not do what has been explained, it is pointless. In the same way, even though you hear the doctrine, if you do not practice and become dissatisfied with saṃsāra, the hearing has been pointless. The contemplation of gross and subtle impermanence and suffering through the paths of beings of lesser and middling capacity and, thus, their creation of a sense of dissatisfaction with saṃsāra is like creating the wish to escape from prison, but escaping is not the actual act of entering the path; the arrival at the path to liberation occurs at the point of finding the correct view. However, the land of the enemy is not crossed over by merely entering the path; [the path] has two parts, that which has been crossed over and that which has not. The state of common beings who have realized emptiness [inferentially] but have not realized it directly is like not having crossed beyond the land of the enemy. The state of Superiors who have realized emptiness directly is like crossing beyond the land of the enemy. Furthermore, merely crossing beyond the land of the enemy is not enough; [the man] has to arrive at the royal palace itself. In the same way, one must achieve enlightenment by becoming accustomed to the direct realization of emptiness over a long time. To do this, just as one must first listen to the explanation of how to proceed, think about it well and gain certainty, and then [accumulate] what one needs to go, so one must train from the point of view of not separating the triad of hearing, thinking, and meditating. Because one must have all three—a teacher of the path, the actual path, and helpers along the path—[the necessity of] going for refuge itself is established by this.

Thus, all the stages of the common path are included: the four truths, which are the great synthesis of what to adopt and what to discard; and the divisions of those, the pair, the forward and reverse order of the dependent arising of the afflicted and the pure, making four;[3] the five paths, which are the entity of the pure class; refuge, which is the support; and hearing, thinking, and meditation, which are the mode of practice.

Because hearing is necessary at the beginning, the object to be heard—the spiritual friend—is established as the root of the path. Moreover, it is not sufficient that he be merely a teacher of hearsay who says, "The path appears to be such according to the explanation";

one must have a teacher who says, "Based on my experience, it is this." The statement, "It is thus" (*tadyathā*) indicates the qualifications of the spiritual friend. The four ways of gathering students[4] are fully present in the category of deeds for the welfare of others in accordance with one's own practice of the meaning, and because it is said that those [four] as well as the six perfections, the three trainings [in ethics, samādhi, and wisdom] and the two collections [of merit and wisdom] are included within each other, [the path implied by the mantra] has all of those. Because one is urged from within to act for the welfare of others without entrusting it to others, all of the uncommon practices of the Mahāyāna, such as the seven cause and effect precepts[5] and the exchange of self and other,[6] are implicitly established. In brief, all the essentials of the path can be known from this category of the general meaning [of the mantra].

The Meaning of the Words

"Proceed" indicates the path of accumulation. The next "proceed" indicates the path of preparation. "Proceed beyond" indicates the path of seeing. "Proceed completely beyond" indicates the path of meditation. "Be founded in enlightenment" indicates the path of no more learning.

Question: Regarding that, if this [explanation of the mantra] is to be understood in terms of all disciples, it is impossible to include [their practices] in the five paths alone because it is feasible to apply [this mantra] to [three types of going]: [1] going to a special high status [within saṃsāra]—the basis for the practice of the doctrine—via the path of beings of small capacity;[7] [2] going to the definite goodness [i.e., the nirvāṇa] of the three vehicles via the path of beings of intermediate and great capacity; and [3] all of them going finally to the nirvāṇa unlocated in any extreme. And, when [the explanation of the mantra] is understood in terms of the Mahāyāna alone, it would be good if it referred to the progress to the fruition—the Truth Body—by way of the practice of the four applications,[8] in which case is it not overly broad to take [the mantra to refer to] the five paths in general?

Answer: The meaning of this [first] "proceed" is the movement in the direction of liberation or nirvāṇa by the mind of renunciation. Therefore, "according with a portion of that [liberation]"[9] refers to anything beyond that; the achievement of high status [in saṃsāra] is not the meaning of the term "proceed." [The meaning] of passing beyond something through passing beyond sorrow and emerging from something through definite emergence and the statements "proceed" are synonymous here; emerging in this context means going elsewhere, like emerging from prison to the outside. [Therefore, "proceed" in the mantra does not refer to movement within saṃsāra.]

It also does not refer solely to the Mahāyāna. [As it says in sūtra], "One who thinks, I would be a śrāvaka of the Sugata . . . " or "Subhūti, even one who wishes to practice on the level of a śrāvaka must practice this very perfection of wisdom." Because such statements establish [that this path is] the single path of progress, although the Mahāyāna is the primary referent [of the mantra], the other two vehicles should also be included in a secondary way.

Question: The important point is, however, how do you know that [the words of the mantra] must refer only to the five paths, since there are many cases of repeatedly setting forth a single important point in many forms?

Answer: It is known through the force of the words [of the mantra] itself because the term "beyond" is not affixed to the first two and is affixed to the third and fourth. Regarding the boundary between here and the beyond, for example, just as the border between the near and far regions of a country is designated with an intermediary ridge of mountains, so there is a dividing line between common beings and Superiors. The sun of the wisdom directly realizing reality, having shone forth, extinguishes the thick darkness and the pangs of cold of the three things that entangle one in saṃsāra.[10] This, which common beings have not actualized and which exists in the state of Superiors, is called "the beyond." The place of continual abode of sentient beings oppressed by the dense shadows and the feeling of cold from the three entanglements is called "here"; the sun of such wisdom has not shone [there]. Due to the potency of action, they see only that and wander there. Therefore, they are called "nearsighted" [literally, "those who see this side"].

The far side and this side are relative, but because the Buddha taught the doctrine for the sake of specially intended disciples, the ground of Superiors is said to be "the far side" in relation to the chief among those [disciples]. In terms of the Buddha himself, however, [the ground of Superiors] is "this side." When many beings in their last lifetime [in saṃsāra] became fully ordained monks, the Buddha said, "Come here," meaning, "Having severed attachment to saṃsāra, come here to the place of liberation, the pacification of suffering," thereby producing the aspiration for nirvāṇa. Due to its great power, all of the functions of the [texts] on the bestowal [of monastic vows] for training in the practices are performed by his merely saying, "Act purely," which [is stated] at the beginning of [those texts].

Question: Since both the paths of accumulation and preparation are similar in being on this side, is not one "Proceed" sufficient? Or, should there not be individual ["proceeds"] for the three levels of the path of accumulation and the four levels of the path of preparation?

Answer: It is necessary to understand well the manner and reasons for dividing this [mantra] into the five paths. The five paths are not divided from the viewpoint of method but from the viewpoint of the wisdom realizing emptiness. It is explained that the path of accumulation is [so called] because although one has not attained a similitude of a clear perception of reality, one proceeds in such a manner as to accumulate the causes for attaining it later. The partial concordance with definite discrimination (*nirvedhabhāgīya, nges 'byed cha mthun*) or path of preparation is so called because although one does not have an actual clear appearance [of emptiness] such as that of the definite discrimination, the path of seeing; one creates a similitude of it. The path of seeing is so called because one clearly sees emptiness directly for the first time. The path of meditation is so called because one grows accustomed to what has already been seen. The path of no more learning is so called because there is no further cultivation or training to be done.

Therefore, because there is a great difference in the way in which reality is seen on the paths of accumulation and preparation, they are mentioned separately. For example, someone going along the bottom of a dark valley without ascending toward the mountain pass does not go higher and does not see more clearly. In the same way, at the time of path of accumulation, it is not said that even this or that manifest object of abandonment is abandoned nor is there even anything equivalent to differences in the increasingly clear perception of the mental image (*arthasamānya, don spyi*) [of emptiness]. On the path of preparation, the manifest [mis]conceptions of subjects and objects that are abandoned on the path of seeing are gradually suppressed. Therefore, there are differentiations in the modes of conception that are to be abandoned and, by the power of that, there are increases in the clear appearance of the mental image of reality. For example, with each step upward having begun the ascent to the pass, one goes higher and, consequently, the sunlight gradually becomes clearer. Therefore, it is said that heat is the attainment of appearance, peak is the increase of appearance, and so forth.

Regarding the etymology of "heat," [the first of the four stages of the path of preparation] because it is the presage of the fire of the non-conceptual wisdom, it is said that it becomes warm. If the example of firesticks is considered, until they are rubbed together, they do not become warm. Then they are just warm, then they are very hot, then they start to smoke, then there are sparks, and then they blaze brightly red. These great changes, which occur gradually, can actually be seen. Before the arising of heat, there are no such great distinctions. Still, if one does not rub [the sticks] together in the beginning, heat will not arise. Even though heat arises, if they are not rubbed repeatedly, fire will not arise. And without going along the breadth of the shady side of the valley, one will not arrive at the ascent to the pass and, without climbing the pass, will not go to the other side. Just so, there is no way of proceeding to the path of preparation without generating the path of accumulation and there is no way of proceeding to the path of seeing without generating the path of preparation. If this is understood well, one will understand the meaning of the refutations in the three *Bhāvanā-krama* and the statements of the Foremost One [Tsong-kha-pa] [refuting] those who propound that all conceptions are hindrances and, therefore, one must enter into the non-conceptual from the start. By not separating the three—hearing, thinking, and meditating—as well as explanation and practice, one will find certainty in the essentials of the teaching and in the complete corpus of the path.

In that way, the first "proceed" indicates the mode of progress on the path of accumulation in which one primarily hears and thinks about reality. The second indicates the mode of progress on the path of accumulation in which there is primarily [the wisdom] arisen from meditation, having a clear perception of the mental image [of emptiness]. Therefore, both the paths of accumulation and preparation are indispensible paths of liberation that must be traversed. They are not true paths or ultimate paths, however, because they are included on this side, the saṃsāra side, according to Asaṅga's *Abhidharmasamuccaya* [which says] from the point of view of their basis, they are included [under the second truth], origin. When one achieves the path of seeing, the three thorough entanglements are abandoned. As it is said [in *Abhidharmakośa* V.44a]:

> Not wishing to go, mistaking the path,
> And all doubts about the path whatsoever.[11]

Specifically, according to sūtra, "Doubt is overcome, indecision is overcome, one does not rely on others, one cannot be led away from the teaching by the teaching of others." As it says, this progressing without qualms on the sole correct path is like going to one's country after passing through the land of one's enemy, therefore, it receives the name "true path." It is also described as the ultimate place because it is the ultimate abode to proceed to. As it is said:

> Due to having progress higher and higher
> Those are asserted to be levels.

Because on the paths of accumulation and preparation one does not actually go there, except with belief, they are described as the stages of engagement through belief. Therefore, [Candrakīrti's *Madhyamakāvatāra*, I.5cd-6a says:]

> Since from that point on, they have achieved it,
> They are called by the term "Bodhisattva."
> They also are born into the lineage of Tathāgatas.

This is the boundary line of abiding on an ultimate stage, of birth into the ultimate lineage, and of becoming an ultimate Bodhisattva. Even in the lower vehicle, from this point [one abides on] a true path and becomes a Spiritual Community Jewel (*saṃgharatna*).

Therefore, since the *pāra* of *pāragate* is explained as "the beyond," it should also be explained as "ultimate"; by adding letters to it [it becomes] *paramārtha*, which is used for "ultimate." Furthermore, the Sanskrit term for the path of preparation is *prayogamārga*. When the *pra* is made into *pāra*, it is explained that this means [that the path of preparation] is a preparation for the ultimate. The reason for this is not that "this side" and "the far side" are things that are objectively established by way of their own entity, [rather] they are inauspicious or auspicious modes of imputation by the mind. Having come under the influence of signs of true establishment and not being capable of passing beyond that, the wandering in the mistaken appearances of conventionalities is the meaning of "this side." Having passed into the state of ultimate signlessness upon destroying the foci of observations apprehending signs and having crossed beyond that is the meaning of "the far side." That discrimination is "this side" was proclaimed by the Leader, who said, "Destroying and abandoning discrimination, one goes to the far side."

Question: Since [there are cases of] even common beings realizing the ultimate and [there are cases of] even Superiors apprehending signs, are they not both mixed [that is, are not common beings and Superiors both on this side and the far side]?

Answer: There is no fault. Although [there are cases of] common beings who realize reality, they have not entered into it as being of one taste. Therefore, it must appear in a manner of [reality being] different from themselves. And, because they do not have a mode of perception in which [emptiness] does not appear to them [as] objectively [existent], they do not pass beyond the discrimination of signs. The mode of perceiving reality by Superiors has passed into a state in which there is no difference between knower and known, like water poured into water. Therefore, it is called the non-dual wisdom and is explained as seeing the Truth Body within oneself. Although they have the conception of true existence, they are not under its power, just as a powerful king suppresses common enemies with his magnificence. Also, the statement in the root text of Dharmakīrti's *Pramāṇavārttika*, "The seers of the truth [do not newly accumulate karma] that impels [rebirth]" rests on this point. Therefore, because in general the meaning of "the far side" must be considered in light of the fact that it is posited in relation to the near-sighted who discern signs, all situations of Superiors must be designated as that [i.e., the far side]. If it is understood, however, in terms of the main or final [meaning] in which it must refer solely to the stage of a Buddha which is set forth by only the term "accomplished deed,"[12] [then, "the far side" means] the complete abandonment of the cause, the conception of self together with its predispositions, and the effect, subtle and gross saṃsāras. Dignāga's *Prajñāpāramitā-piṇḍārtha* says:

> The perfection of wisdom is the non-dual wisdom;
> It is the Tathāgata.
> That term [is used] for texts and paths
> Because they have that object [as their goal].

If this is taken literally, it seems as if the perfections of wisdom of those training are merely imputed [perfections of wisdom], but if one seeks the intention [of the statement], it is like what is said in Tsong-kha-pa's *Legs bshad gser phreng*. It appears that Dignāga's assertion was made with respect to the primary [the Buddha] and the secondary [those training in the perfection of wisdom]; it does not seem to mean an actual and imputed [perfection of wisdom]. It must be said that Dignāga says this thinking that [paths and texts] are not the primary meaning [of the perfection of wisdom].

Therefore, since to achieve final enlightenment, it is not sufficient to merely go beyond, upon having made effort for many aeons, one must still proceed to a higher path. Therefore, after *pāragate*, "proceed beyond," [the mantra] adds *pārasaṃgate* "proceed completely beyond."

Question: If the manner of positing the ultimate stages and paths is from the point of view of how reality is seen, then since even on the stage of Buddhahood, there is no way to perceive reality which surpasses that of the path of seeing from the point of view of there not being even subtle dualistic appearance and [the mind] abiding [in reality] as one taste, like water poured in water, what is the difference by which one posits higher and higher paths?

Answer: The *Daśabhūmikasūtra* says:

> Just as the wise cannot express or see
> The trail of any bird across the sky,
> So none of the grounds of the children of the Conqueror
> Can be expressed. Then how can one listen?
>
> However, with love, compassion, and aspirations,
> A series of levels is explained,
> But not by way of [emptiness, which is] the object
> of activity of the [Bodhisattva's] mind.

It is said that when a bird flies through the sky, its tracks cannot be distinguished in different areas of the sky, but describing [the flight] in terms of the earth, there is a way to show [that the bird flew] in this or that direction, such as that of mountains, plains, rivers, forests, and cities. In the same way, from the viewpoint of how reality is seen, [the stages] cannot be differentiated, but from the viewpoint of being qualified by factors of method, such as love, compassion, and prayers, there are different levels of fulfillment of capacity. Some excellent individuals say that it is like the fact that the sun when it has dawned over an eastern peak does not differ from the sun which arrives at the center [of the sky], but there is a difference in its capacity to warm the earth. That one's capacity increases from the viewpoint of method is designated with the term "complete purification" according to the *Abhisamayālaṃkāra* [I.48-70]. Here, if the *sam* of *pārasaṃgate* is taken as *saṃśodha*, it is used for "complete purification." When it is taken as *saṃtāna*, it means "continually," and thus comes to mean that one must grow accustomed to it over a long period of time, making it increase.

Here, when (*saṃ*) is explained as "complete" in terms of what is well-known, Asaṅga says in the *Madhyāntavibhāga* regarding "complete," "Not other, not erroneous." When [this] explanation that it means "not erroneous" is applied in this context, the discerning of signs is posited as erroneous. The path of seeing passes merely beyond that, but because it is insufficient and one must pass completely beyond that, it must be understood within connecting it to the statement earlier [in the *Heart Sūtra*] where the path of meditation is explained, "Having passed completely beyond error, they go to the completion of nirvāṇa."

This is so [because] if one primarily cultivates the wisdom realizing emptiness alone, one can achieve a mere nirvāṇa, but, as Maitreyanātha's *Uttaratantra* (I.20b) says, [it is a *mere* nirvāṇa] "Because of lacking [fear of coarse suffering] and because of having fear [of the obstructions to omniscience.]"[13] Apart from the mere non-existence of the sufferings of saṃsāra on this side, the marvelous welfare of others is not achieved and, moreover, one cannot protect other beings from all fears. Therefore, it is a partial nirvāṇa and a trifling nirvāṇa; it is not a final or complete nirvāṇa. Therefore, when one goes to final nirvāṇa, as Maitreyanātha's *Abhisamayālaṃkāra* (III.1) says:

> One does not abide in the extremes of this side or the far side
> Or even in between them.

Wisdom puts an end to the extreme of saṃsāra, "this side," and the factor of method that is conjoined with it, included in the individual complete purifications, puts an end to the extreme of peace, "the far side." An individual must attain nirvāṇa that is unlocated, the center apart from those two extremes.

Question: Does it not say that one does not abide between them?

Answer: The way of not abiding between the two extremes is conventional, because when one achieves the abandonment of the two extremes, it must be understood that one does not abide in an ultimately existent [center] rather than a conventionally existent one.

Question: If there is no difference in the way in which reality is seen on the individual stages, why does it say in Maitreyanātha's *Mahāyānasūtrālaṃkāra*, "The meaning of being omnipresent, the meaning of being supreme" [that is,] on the first [stage] one realizes the dharmadhātu as having the sense of being omnipresent, on the second [stage] one realizes it to be the meaning of the supreme, and so forth?

Answer: Through realizing during meditative equipoise that all, oneself and others, are inseparable in the dharmadhātu, in the state subsequent [to equipoise on the first stage] there arises special giving in which one gives away all of one's possessions to others without the slightest desire to keep them; and through realizing in meditative equipoise that both ethics and immorality are empty, in the state subsequent [to equipoise on the second stage] there arises a special ethics upon seeing the need to view these two, [ethics and immorality], within mere illusory appearance, undeniably as things that must be deemed with fine distinctions to be superior and inferior and to be adopted and discarded. Moreover, the root of this, from the level of beginners on, is that through the power of the unified practice of both factors of method, such as giving, and wisdom, the one develops the capacity for the other.

Then, to indicate the path of no more learning, there is *bodhi svāhā* [in the Sanskrit]. In the translation by Seng-ge-rgyal-mtshan of the master Vajrapāṇi's commentary, it is translated as "become enlightened." In many other [translations], it says "proceed to enlightenment" for consistency with the earlier explanations, apparently in consideration of its being the final destination. With respect to proceeding on this or that path, however, if this were understood in terms of a path to be attained in the future, then it should be "go to enlightenment." "Proceed by way of such and such a path that is possessed in one's continuum," however, is in terms of a simultaneous basis and that which is based, for example, like going on a ship in the sea or a bird going through the sky. Therefore, because there is no place to progress to from the perspective of enlightenment—the path of no more learning—there is no need to say "proceed" [in enlightenment] because, otherwise, is would be acceptable that "proceed beyond" be applied even to common beings.

The use of the imperative form "proceed" rather than using a term like [the present] "going" or "goes" is for the purpose of understanding that all those higher qualities must be achieved earnestly from the viewpoint of the four practices[14] and the four applications.

With respect to the word "enlightenment," the great paṇḍita says in his commentary to the *Bodhipathapradīpa*, "Enlightenment is the complete purification of the two obstructions and the complete understanding of all the modes and varieties of phenomena." It is acceptable to differentiate [*bodhi*] into the meanings of *byang* and *chub* and apply them to [the faults] to be abandoned and the [qualities] to be realized, but the primary [meaning] is:

> The knowledge of cessation of defilements and
> [The knowledge] of non-production is called enlightenment.[15]

That is, it must refer to the wisdom which is the simultaneous direct perception of all phenomena through having exhaustively abandoned the obstructions of attachment, the impedimentary obstructions, and the obstructions of inferiority without remainder.[16] [This wisdom] is indispensible for achieving all the aspects of others' welfare, this being the main goal sought. The *Pañcaviṃśatisāhasrikāprajñāpāramitā* says:

> "Transcendent Victor, what is unsurpassed, complete, perfect enlightenment like?" The Transcendent Victor said, "Subhūti, as is the reality of all phenomena, so also is unsurpassed, complete, perfect enlightenment."

Thus, the final wisdom that sees the two truths exactly as they are with respect to all phenomena is said to be enlightenment. Therefore, this primarily and explicitly indicates [that the meaning of the term "enlightenment"] occurs in the context of the earlier exposition of the stages of how to proceed on the path in terms of the wisdom realizing emptiness. Therefore, it must refer to the knower of all aspects that realizes the modes, which, when considered in terms of its isolatable factor, is a subsequent continuation of similar type of that [realization of emptiness].

In general, however, all three of the great goals must be fulfilled here [in the term *bodhi* in the mantra]:

> The great thought of supremacy among all sentient beings. It is the chief of methods [for achieving] the knowledge of the varieties. Through cherishing everyone more than oneself, one becomes the highest of all beings.
>
> The great abandonment which is the state of having abandoned all obstructions.
>
> The great realization which sees the [final] mode [of being].[17]

This is because the teaching of those three, which are indicated by the three phrases, "highest," "without obstructions," and "complete, perfect enlightenment" earlier [in the sūtra] must be included in the mantra where it says *bodhi.*

Although there are two traditions of the text, one in which the mantra has *oṃ* and one in which it does not, the one which has *oṃ* should be taken as correct, because it says in the *sādhana* written by Nāgārjuna, "adding *tadyathā* and *oṃ* . . .". With regard to this statement, Śrīmahājana also explains, "*Oṃ* and *svāhā* are words of blessing for the purpose of obtaining the effect of repetition." Regarding the manner of blessing, the *Vajraśekharatantra* says:

> Say what *oṃ* is.
> It means the supreme, it bestows wealth,
> It has the aspects of glory, happiness, and good fortune,
> It means promise and good luck,
> It is the bejewelled mantra.

Thus it is said that [it causes] the arising of many benefits and good qualities, both temporarily and in the long term. The non-Buddhist Vaidikas assert that *oṃ* has such qualities, but they say that the sound naturally has such power regardless of motivation. The position of this tantra is that if the mantra is said while being mindful of its symbolic meaning, then such benefits arise. Regarding the symbolic meaning, it says in the chapter explaining the suchness of the mantra in the *Vajramāla* explanatory tantra that *oṃ* is formed by combining three letters: The first and fifth [Sanskrit] vowels with the last [letter] of the *pa* row, and that those three symbolize the three vajras of body, speech, and mind. All the sūtras and tantras are included within the mindfulness of the meaning of the three vajras of body, speech, and mind in that all the methods of the sūtra system act to establish body and speech and all of the factors of wisdom act to establish mind, and there is nothing that is not included in those two [method and wisdom].

All the paths of Action and Performance Tantra are included in the four concentrations. The [first] three branches of repetition of the initial concentration act to establish exalted body, the last branch and concentration abiding in fire and the concentration abiding in sound act to establish exalted speech. Therefore, all paths having signs are included in those. The concentration bestowing liberation at the end of sound acts to establish exalted mind and all paths of the signless are included in that.[18] Also, with respect to the fruition, with the exception of the sādhana of the Supreme Enjoyment Body Vairocana, which includes all three lineages of Performance Tantra, Action and Performance Tantra are similar in being treated as having three lineages. Moreover, the meaning of these is the three vajras of body, speech, and mind.

The four sections of the Yoga Tantra *Tattvasaṃgraha* include all paths and fruitions in four seals. The great seal (*mahāmudrā*) acts to establish exalted body, the doctrine seal (*dharmamudrā*) acts to establish exalted speech, and the pledge seal (*samayamudrā*) acts to establish exalted mind; the action seal (*kriyāmudrā*) is the exalted activities [that act to establish] those three. Hence, there is no fault in its not being included in those three.

In Highest Yoga Tantra, that which acts to establish exalted body is the state of generation, that which acts to establish exalted speech is the conventional, the illusion stage of completion, and that which acts to establish exalted mind is the ultimate, the clear light stage of completion. The union must be posited in terms of combining them, therefore all of them are fulfilled in those three meanings.

In brief, because the final object of attainment is limited to the three bodies, that there is a limited number of all the causal paths is established from the point of view of there being a limited number of fruitions. Because there is nothing whatsoever that is not included within this, even the statement of former excellent ones that all scriptures are included solely in one syllable is made in consideration of such.

Question: Is the [mantra] to be classified in sūtra or tantra?

Answer: Vimalamitra says that it is to be classified as a secret mantra because it was taught in secret [apart] from those of dull faculties. The master Vajrapāṇi says in his commentary that from *evaṃ mayā* at the beginning, it is in part similar to the *Guhyasamāja*. He also says that this is the natural secret mantra that includes those essentials, and from among mantras for achieving the variety of activities, this is most profound. The same text says:

> Someone may have doubts concerning whether this instruction on the meaning of the heart of the perfection of wisdom is of the Definition Vehicle or the Mantra Vehicle. Although it appears to be different to the perception of sentient beings, there is no difference in the profound reality. Therefore, this mantra of the perfection of wisdom is the heart of the meaning of secret mantras . . . . It is not a mantra for pacification, increase, power, or wrath. What is it? By merely understanding the meaning of this mantra, the mind is freed. The first four syllables of the mantra [*tadyathā oṃ*] are the arising of action, the meaning of the middle four [*gate gate*] is to teach clearly, and the end summarizes the meaning of the mantra in four aspects [*pāragate pārasaṃgate bodhi svāhā*].

The sādhana written for this by Nāgārjuna accords in procedure with Highest Yoga Tantra and Ānandagarbha wrote a sādhana aligning it with Yoga Tantra. Thus, it is permissible to take the [mantra] as [Secret Mantra] in terms of certain uncommon disciples. For example, because in the past Pracandraprabha was the son of a scorpion, he could not bear even to hear the name "butter" [because scorpions are said to die if they are touched by butter]; he became angry and could not sleep until a certain doctor gave him butter mixed in medicine, and he slept. Therefore, although it was fitting to cause him to eat [butter] with skillful methods, it was not suitable to say, "Eat butter." In the same way, although it is suitable to indicate the innermost intention in conjunction with the mantra, it is not suitable to teach with the words, "Practice this according to mantra from the start."

Question: Since the path systems of sūtra and mantra are separate, is it suitable to connect [a mantric explanation] even implicitly?

Answer: Not only is it suitable to mix the two into one, they must definitely be joined. Kulikapuṇḍarīka's great commentary [on the *Kālacakratantra*], *Vimalaprabhā* (*Stainless Light*) says, "Regarding the Vajra Vehicle, it is a mixture into one of the mode of Mantra and the mode of the Perfection Vehicle, which have the nature of the effect and the cause." However, if one teaches the intended disciples of that [Perfection Vehicle], taking it [the mantra] as the Mantra system from the start, one does not distinguish the intention of the Teacher in setting forth sūtra and mantra separately and incurs the fault of confusing contexts. Tsong-kha-pa's *Rim lnga gsal sgron (Lamp Illuminating [Nāgārjuna's] "Five Stages")* says:

> The explanation in the commentary on the *Heart Sūtra* that there is meditation on vase-like [breath yoga] and the explanation of some that in some contexts in the lower tantras there is a system of concentrating on important places in the body [as is done in Highest Yoga Tantra] are made by fabricators who do not understand well the difference between sūtra and mantra and between the paths of the higher and lower tantras. Therefore, they are unreliable.

Thus, although a portion of the final object of attainment of the Effect Mantra path is taught [in the sūtra vehicle], the intended disciples of sūtra are taught and practice initially from the standpoint of it being possible to achieve that [final object of attainment] by the sūtra path alone. Then, when they have gained the realization [resulting from] the training in the common path, it is at this point that the mantra path is taught, saying, "The fruition cannot be achieved without the addition of mantra." Apart from that, the path of these additional skillful methods is not taught simultaneously [with the sūtra path] from the outset. Therefore, the *Rim lnga gsal sgron* says:

> In the Perfection Vehicle, the causal method [of achieving] the bliss of enlightenment, the fruition—the great innate bliss of the path—is not taught. Therefore, although it is allowed that great bliss is explained in the context of the fruition [in the sūtra system], there is a great difference between the two vehicles.

In the explicit and implicit meaning of the words of this statement [by Tsong-kha-pa], it is necessary to distinguish between two ways of differentiating factors [in a text]. Even Mantra has nothing additional to describe concerning the fruitional state [of Buddhahood] that exceeds the qualities described in such statements [from the sūtras] as, "In a single particle are Buddhas as numerous as the particles [of the universe]," [from the *Bhadracarīpraṇidhāna*]. Therefore, each of the individual unique points of Mantra [presentation of Buddhahood], such as those set forth in Candrakīrti's *Pradīpodyotana*, are set forth in the process of using the principle of "final explanation"[19] in [commenting on] that [statement from the *Bhadracarīpraṇidhāna*]. Because that passage, however, [as well as the *Heart Sūtra*] do not set forth [the fruition] together with the path that achieves it, it does not belong to the Mantra Vehicle. Also, in the Cittamātrin system, even though the *Bhavasaṃkrānti Sūtra* is a Hīnayāna sūtra the verse within it:

> In whatsoever phenomenon
> Expressed by whatsoever names,
> Those do not exist.
> This is the reality of phenomena.[20]

need not be a Hīnayāna sūtra. In the same way, [Tsong-kha-pa] implicitly indicated a way of differentiating factors within the words of a sūtra such that it is not contradictory that the *Heart Sūtra* be of the Definition Vehicle although this mantra within it be an actual mantra.

In general, all sūtras flow into Mantra, but among these [sūtras], the Perfection of Wisdom sūtras have ways of directly flowing into Mantra that are unlike other sūtras. One should understand the many ways in which this occurs, such as: [1] how a mantra appears within [a sūtra] as in this case [of the *Heart Sūtra*], [2] how there comes to be an explanation of a hidden meaning, unlike other sūtras, and [3] how the name "mother of Conquerors" is asserted to teach the great seal (*mahāmudrā*) of definitive meaning. Therefore, because the sādhanas of this [sūtra] are designed for the uncommon disciples who are ready to enter into Mantra, they are Mantric for them but are not necessarily Mantric in general.

When [the question] is considered from a perspective common [to Sūtra and Mantra], according to the statements of Vimalamitra and Atīśa, that which is taught secretly is designated as mantra. How is this designation arrived at? Implicit teachings and hidden meanings are different. An implicit teaching can be found in any text and can be understood through the power of reasoning that analyzes the meaning of the explicit teaching. A hidden meaning is something that cannot be understood with independent analysis without being indicated through the instructions of a lama. The fact that the convention "hidden meaning" is not used for other sūtras whereas it is used for the Perfection of Wisdom sūtras is a sign that they are intimately close to the tantras of Highest Yoga (*anuttarayoga*). When there is a way of indicating a path as the hidden meaning of a statement that explicitly has emptiness as its object, there must also be ways of indicating the wisdom of the path of seeing, the final body [of Buddhahood], and so forth. Therefore, the meaning of the four modes[21] fully appears. Thus, because this mantra indicates the stages of clear realization (*abhisamaya*), the hidden meaning of the *Heart Sūtra*, [Vimalamitra and Atīśa] call the mantra Mantra. Because the whole text has mainly taught emptiness, one might wonder how to practice it. [Avalokiteśvara] having aligned the meaning of the sūtra with the stages of the path, indicates through this [mantra how to practice emptiness] to those disciples of very sharpest faculties who are able to understand through the mere mention of headings [such as *gate gate*].

Therefore, although it is widely circulated that the explicit teaching of the Perfection of Wisdom sūtras is the stages of emptiness and the hidden meaning is the stages of clear realization, it can be explained in an easily understandable manner how the explicit teaching and hidden meanings occur, and this can be done using the *Heart Sūtra* because everyone has it in mind, whereas the [other Perfection of Wisdom] sūtras are so vast that most people do not know the words of those texts.

Those who assert that the repeated statements of the divisions of the five paths [set forth] in the earlier and later chapters of Maitreyanātha's *Abhisamayālaṃkāra* are systems of the path alone assert that [statements concerning] the [paths] of preparation and seeing and so forth in the later chapters are mere imputations. It is asserted, however, that because there are individual differences in the modes of meditation and the purposes at [different] points along the path, they are asserted to be actual paths of preparation, seeing, meditation, and so forth. Thus, such [Perfection of Wisdom sūtras as] the vast, the middling, the *Aṣṭasāhasrikāprajñāpāramitā*, and the *Sañcayagāthā* sūtra, which are to be aligned with the [categories of the] *Abhisamayālaṃkāra*, also repeatedly set forth many sets of the five paths. Because this *Heart Sūtra* is brief, the hidden meaning, the set of the five paths of clear realization, is not set forth more than once.

Moreover, although Mahājana explains the way of dividing the sections of the sūtra in a different way, Atīśa agrees with the ideas of Vimalamitra, and it will be explained according to their system. Avalokiteśvara's statement to Śāriputra, "A son of good lineage or a daughter of good lineage who wishes to practice the profound perfection of wisdom should view things in this way," indicates the paths of accumulation and preparation. Within this, the part up to, "who wishes to practice" primarily indicates the path of accumulation of a person abiding in the Mahāyāna lineage who has come under the influence of compassion and has generated the aspiration to enlightenment and who is training mainly in the vast deeds of the two collections conjoined with [aspiration]; it ancillarily indicates the path of preparation where a clear perception of reality is achieved.

"Should view things in this way" mainly indicates the path of preparation that views reality through a clearly appearing mental image. This is similar in part to the path of seeing. Ancillarily, it indicates the path of accumulation that arrives at a mere ascertainment of the meaning of the [reality] through hearing and thinking.

"They should correctly view . . . and also non-attainment" indicates the path of seeing. At that time, one must abandon the artificial conception of true existence with respect to all phenomena. Therefore, it is said that one realizes the dharmadhātu as it applies to everything and must directly realize emptiness with respect to all objects of knowledge. On the path of meditation, one becomes accustomed to that which has already been realized; there is no reality to be realized that has not been realized before. Therefore, all objects of observation are collected and explained in the context of the path of seeing; a separate set of objects of observation is not set forth for the path of meditation.

Regarding the way in which the objects of the path of seeing are set forth, the five aggregates are stated in a relatively extensive way, the twelve sources are merely enumerated, and just the beginning and end of the eighteen constituents and the twelve branches of dependent arising are stated. The aspects that are to be associated with those objects of observation are called the eight profundities. When condensed, they are subsumed in the three doors of liberation. The emptiness of true existence of all phenomena in terms of their own entity and the lack of common and uncommon characteristics that would serve as the means of positing [objects] is the door of liberation emptiness. Although the phenomena in saṃsāra are distinguished by being produced, the twelve branches of saṃsāra, and so forth, are not ultimately produced nor ultimately ceased. Although one must seek purity, ultimately, stains do not abide in the mind; therefore, [the sūtra says] "stainless." Because the natural nirvāṇa primordially lacks becoming free from stains, [the sūtra says] "not stainless." These four [unproduced, unceased, stainless, not stainless] are the door of liberation signlessness. Because, in that case, there is no wish that faults be ultimately diminished or exhausted and that one be [ultimately] filled or expanded with good qualities, these [undiminished, unfilled] are the door of liberation wishlessness. Furthermore, because the last two liberations can be included in the first, it is the sole door of peace.

The true cessations that are the complete abandonment of all sufferings and sources are achieved by the true paths that are meditations on the emptiness of all the aggregates, constituents, and sources from the viewpoint of those eight aspects. However, the wisdom that is the method for actualizing that and the attainment of cessation through that do not ultimately exist at all, but rather are mere designations, like an illusory lion killing an illusory elephant. Therefore, the way to practice the union of appearance and emptiness is indicated by "There are no sufferings . . . and also no non-attainment." Some Indian texts at the point of "no wisdom" add "no non-wisdom", but if the meaning is analyzed, it seems unnecessary.

The path of meditation is indicated by, "Therefore, because Bodhisattvas have no attainment they depend on and abide in the perfection of wisdom and their minds are without obstructions and without fear. Having completely passed beyond all error, they go to the completion of nirvāṇa." It is said that one must progress to nirvāṇa by abiding and remaining for a long time, relating the meaning realized on the occasion of the path of seeing with the purifications that occur on the individual stages.[22] Progressing by stages higher and higher, they gradually thoroughly *pass beyond* the types of mistaken objects of abandonment to be abandoned on the path of meditation, such as the subtle and gross afflictive obstructions and obstructions to omniscience, etc. Because [the true cessation which is] the great final abandoning spoken of in this context is the path of meditation, the actual abandoning antidote, the fault of confusing the context in teaching through associating the antidotes to it with the objects of abandonment does not occur.

Some excellent ones do not accept the statement in ['Jam-dbyangs-bzhad-pa's] *dbU ma'i mtha' dpyod* (*Analysis of the Middle Way*) concerning the manner in which the twenty-two thorough obscurations and the eleven assumptions of bad states [by arhats who have entered the Mahāyāna] are abandoned on the individual stages, but Vimalamitra speaks about this in this context and Atīśa also accepts [Vimalamitra's treatment] without tampering with it.

The special vajra-like period of the special path [the path of meditation] together with the path of no more learning is indicated by, "All the Buddhas who abide in the three times have been fully awakened into unsurpassed, perfect, complete enlightenment through relying on the perfection of wisdom." The Buddhas [referred to are the tenth stage Bodhisattvas alluded to in *Abhisamayālaṃkāra* I.70]:

> Having passed beyond the ninth stage, the wisdom
> By which one abides on the stage of a Buddha
> [Is to be known as the tenth
> Stage of a Bodhisattva.]

Because the wisdom at the end of the continuum [as a sentient being] serves as the direct cause of both the great realization and the great mind, it is indicated at this point. The three greatnesses of the path of no more learning are like what has already been explained earlier.

Objection: Although this way of associating the sūtra with the five paths accords with the commentary of Atīśa, why is it not explained like this by Vimalamitra?

Answer: This is a case of not having carefully analyzed [Vimalamitra's position]. One must understand how Vimalamitra divided the sūtra, associating the parts of the sūtra with the four objects of observation [set forth] in the *Saṃdhinirmocana*. Since on the path of accumulation, one mainly analyzes reality through hearing and thinking, [its object] is an analytical reflection. On the path of preparation, although one achieves [the wisdom] arisen from meditation, one has not achieved the wisdom of individual analysis like that of the path of seeing. Therefore, in relation to that [path of seeing] it is mainly calm abiding, due to which it [its object] is a non-analytical reflection. Since both of these involve mental images, [the objects] are described as "reflections." On the path of seeing one directly realizes the reality of all things which are the objects [of the path of seeing]; [its object] is called the "limit of things."

Regarding the path of meditation, the statement [from the *Abhidharmakośa*, VI.lcd]:

> The path of meditation has two aspects
> [Whereas the path of] seeing is [just] uncontaminated.

cannot be taken literally [because the path of seeing has both contaminated and uncontaminated aspects]. Because it is drawn from sūtra, however, it is something partially [true] that has become renowned as a statement of what is generally [true]. Also, regarding the object observed on the [path of meditation], all three, that is, the two reflections and the limit of things occur and do not need to be set forth separately. Because the great purpose of progressing higher and higher in realization and abandonment as one's familiarity increases is to be accomplished [on the path of meditation], from the viewpoint of its imprint, [the path of meditation] is explained as having an object of observation which is the thorough accomplishment of the purpose. Through those explanations, [the way to align Vimalamitra's way of dividing the sūtra in terms of the four objects of observation] with the five paths can be understood.

All the meanings of the sūtra up to this point [of the mantra] are contained in this mantra. The fact that the Transcendent Victor was absorbed in the samādhi "perception of the profound" and that Avalokiteśvara also spoke within equipoise on emptiness [denotes] the quintessential instruction of how one must teach from within the wisdom realizing the inner meaning, possessing the unbroken continuum from the Buddha to the spiritual friend. [These things] contained in the prologue are indicated by *tadyathā*. The final meaning of *evaṃ*, which appeared in the prologue, this being the nature of the body, speech, and mind [of the Buddha], is indicated by *oṃ*. "Śāriputra, a son of good lineage or a daughter of good lineage who wishes to practice the profound perfection of wisdom should view [things] in this way," the hidden meaning of which is the path of accumulation and preparation is indicated by *gate gate*. "They should correctly view . . . and also no non-attainment", the hidden meaning of which is the path of seeing is indicated by *pāragate*. "Therefore, Śāriputra, because Bodhisattvas have no attainment, they depend on and abide in the perfection of wisdom and their minds are without obstructions and without fear. Having completely passed beyond all error they go to the completion of nirvāṇa," the hidden meaning of which is the path of meditation, indicated by *pārasaṃgate*. The path of no more learning, which is [the hidden meaning of] "All the Buddhas who abide in the three times have been fully awakened into unsurpassed, perfect, complete enlightenment through relying on the perfection of wisdom" is indicated by *bodhi.*

Svāhā is "may it be so" and means "establish a foundation." One achieves the meaning symbolized by the *oṃ* at the beginning [of the mantra] through the practice of the five paths. From the perspective common [to sūtra and tantra], one must establish a foundation which has an essence of emptiness and compassion, as is said [in Maitreya's *Uttaratantra*], "Abiding in emptiness and not forsaking sentient beings." When applied to the lower tantras, one must establish the foundation which is the union of the profound emptiness and the manifestations of a divine maṇḍala. According to Highest Yoga Tantra, one must establish a foundation which is the indivisibility of the innate great bliss and emptiness.

Some [scholars say that] the statement, "The mantra of the perfection of wisdom, the mantra of great knowledge, the unsurpassed mantra, the mantra equal to the unequalled, the mantra that thoroughly pacifies all suffering" refers to the five paths individually. According to some, it refers to illusoriness and the three doors of liberation. These are praises, however, of one thing [i.e., the mantra] from many perspectives, such as that which brings about realization of the ultimate, the abandonment of ignorance, the way of seeing of which there is none higher, that which causes one to be equal to the unequalled (the Buddha or space), and that which protects from all suffering.

Because all the meanings of the sūtras are included in this text [the *Heart Sūtra*], when the former and later sections are taken apart, all of the eight subjects and seventy topics that are set forth in the *Abhisamayālaṃkāra* should be present. Because the complete path is not set forth more than once [in the sūtra], however, there is no way to apply [the sūtra] to the [topics of the] *Abhisamayālaṃkāra* in the order [in which they appear in Maitreyanātha's text]. However, I will illustrate just one way in which one could begin to analyze the manner of applying the sūtra to the *Abhisamayālaṃkāra* (I.5-6):

> Creation of the aspiration, precept,
> Four limbs of discrimination,
> The nature of the dharmadhātu,
> Which is the basis of achievement,
> Object of observation, intent,
> Armor, activity of entry,
> Collections, and emergence

[Characterize] a Subduer's exalted knowledge of all
aspects.

Creation of the aspiration, which is designated with the name of the wish for enlightenment, the first of the ten qualities stated to characterize the knowledge of all aspects, is indicated by "who wish to practice the profound." Precept is indicated by Śāriputra's humble request of Avalokiteśvara for precepts on the profound and [Avalokiteśvara's] answer. The path of preparation [called] "limb of discrimination" is indicated by "should view." The natural lineage, which is the dharmadhātu, the basis of achievement, is indicated by "a son of good lineage or a daughter of good lineage." The object of observation of Mahāyāna practices is indicated by "the five aggregates . . .". The goal, which has the nature of the three greatnesses, is indicated by "without obstruction, they go to the completion of nirvāṇa. All the Buddhas who abide in the three times have been fully awakened into unsurpassed, perfect, complete enlightenment." The four, the achievement through armor, the achievement through entry, the achievement through the collections, and the emergent achievement are indicated by, "the perfection of wisdom," "the practice of the profound," "depend on and abide," and "having passed beyond error." The order is not the same, but the meanings are complete. Thus, the quintessence of the 84,000 collections of doctrine is the Perfection of Wisdom sūtras, and the quintessence of the *Aṣṭasāhasrikāprajñāpāramitā* and so forth is the *Heart Sūtra*, and the concentrated meaning of that is this mantra. Therefore, it is established by reasoning that it [the mantra] is the pith of all doctrines and it should also be inferred that it contains the beneficial qualities of all of those.

By virtue of this advice [which was written]
In order to refresh my memory
And to increase the great awareness and lifespan of
those who seek the essence of the practice of the sūtras
May [all beings] realize the meaning of the mother.

Regarding this explanation of the *Heart Sūtra* mantra, [I], the venerable dKon-mchog-bstan-pa'i-sgron-me thought that there must be vast meaning in this [mantra] and beseeched the honorable 'Jigs-med-dbang-po, the sole father endowed with the wisdom body of all the Subduers, [to teach me], and I began writing down what I came to understand. At that time, fearing fabrication, I began to read the original commentaries and [found that] they accorded with what I had understood. Therefore, I added a little from them as well. [The work] was dictated during the noon break in a winter retreat of the Fire Rat year [1816]. The scribe was sNgag-ram-pa dKon-mchog-kun-dga'o.

May virtue and goodness increase!

Notes

Introduction

1. This admittedly bold claim should not be made without some justification. The *Lotus Sūtra* exercised greater influence over the development of Buddhist thought, especially in East Asia, but the *Heart Sūtra*, due to both its content and its length, assumed a wider popularity. Evidence that could be cited as support for deeming it "the most famous Buddhist sūtra" includes the presence of seven extant Indian commentaries; scores of commentaries in Chinese, Japanese, Korean, and Tibetan; the common recitation of the sūtra in Zen monasteries and temples, both in Japan and the West; the common recitation of the sūtra in Tibetan Buddhist ceremonies throughout Inner Asia; and the numerous translations of the sūtra (again, due in large part to its brevity!) into European languages. It is, to my knowledge, the only Buddhist sūtra that has been printed on neckties, as can be purchased in Japan.

2. Edward Conze, "Praśāstrasena's *Ārya-Prajñāpāramitā-Hṛdaya-Ṭīkā*," in L. Cousins, A. Kunst, and K. R. Norman, eds., *Buddhist Studies in Honour of I. B. Horner* (Dordrecht: D. Reidel Publishing, 1974), p. 51.

3. Alex Wayman offers a dissenting view. It is his view that the authors of the Indian commentaries, "seemed to be experiencing some difficulty in exposition, as though they were not writing through having inherited a tradition about this scripture going back to its original composition, but rather were simply applying their particular learning in Buddhism to the terminology of the sūtra." This deficiency caused Wayman to compose his own commentary. See Alex Wayman, "Secret of the Heart Sūtra" in Lewis Lancaster, ed., *Prajñāpāramitā and Related Systems: Studies in Honor of Edward Conze* (Berkeley: Berkeley Buddhist Studies Series, 1977), pp. 135-152.

4. Jacques Derrida, *Of Grammatology*, trans. by Gayatri Chakravorty Spivak (Baltimore: Johns Hopkins University Press, 1976), p. 102.

5. Adapted from Lama Chimpa and Alaka Chattopadhyaya, trans., *Tāranātha's History of Buddhism in India* (Simla: Indian Institute of Advanced Study, 1970), pp. 274-275.

6. Edward Conze, *The Prajñāpāramitā Literature* (The Hague: Mouton,

1960), p. 9. Conze outlines nine stages in the evolution of Prajñāpāramitā thought in another essay. See "The Development of Prajñāpāramitā Thought" in his *Thirty Years of Buddhist Studies* (Columbia, S.C.: University of South Carolina Press, 1968), pp. 123-147.

7. See Hajime Nakamura, *Indian Buddhism: A Survey with Bibliographical Notes* (Osaka, Japan: KUFS Publication, 1980), p. 160.

8. On the development of the *Aṣṭasāhasrikā*, see Edward Conze, "The Composition of the Aṣṭasāhasrikā Prajñāpāramitā" in *Thirty Years of Buddhist Studies*, pp. 168-184; Lewis Lancaster, *An Analysis of the "Aṣṭasāhasrikāprajñāpāramitāsūtra" from the Chinese Translations* (Ann Arbor: University Microfilms, 1968); and Andrew Rawlinson, "The Position of the *Aṣṭasāhasrikā Prajñāpāramitā* in the Development of Early Mahāyāna" in Lewis Lancaster, ed., *Prajñāpāramitā and Related Systems* (Berkeley: Berkeley Buddhist Studies Series, 1977), pp. 3-34.

9. This passage occurs on page 203 of R. Mitra's edition (Calcutta, 1888) of the Sanskrit text. For an English translation, see Edward Conze, *The Perfection of Wisdom in Eight Thousand Lines and Its Verse Summary* (Bolinas, California: Four Seasons Foundation, 1973), p. 150.

10. See Étienne Lamotte, ed. and trans., *Saṃdhinirmocana Sūtra: L'Explication des Mystères* (Paris: Adrien Maisonneuve, 1935), pp. 85, 206-207.

11. See E. Obermiller, trans., *History of Buddhism by Bu-ston.* Part II (Heidelberg, 1932), pp. 49-50.

12. For this and another prophecy concerning Nāgārjuna, see E. Obermiller, *History of Buddhism by Bu-ston*, Part II, pp. 110-111.

13. See his "The Prajñāpāramitā-Hṛdaya Sūtra" in *Thirty Years of Buddhist Studies*, pp. 148-167.

14. Avalokiteśvara also appears in the tantric Prajñāpāramitā text, the *Svalpākṣarā prajñāpāramitāsūtra.*

15. P 5222, Vol. 96, 297.3.7-297.4.2. See also E. Obermiller, trans., *History of Buddhism by Bu-ston*, p. 49.

16. This work is described by Tucci in his *First Bhāvanākrama of Kamalaśīla: Sanskrit and Tibetan Texts with Introduction and English Summary*, Minor Buddhist Texts, Part II: Série Orientale Roma IX.2 (Rome: Is.M.E.O., 1958), pp. 115-121.

17. For a traditional biography of Vimalamitra, see Tarthang Tulku, *Crystal Mirror*, Vol. V (Berkeley: Dharma Publishing, 1977), pp. 191-195. See also Eva M. Dargyay, *The Rise of Esoteric Buddhism in Tibet* (Delhi: Motilal Banarsidass, 1977), Chapter 2.

18. Conze did not hold Vimalamitra's commentary in high regard. He found

it "none too helpful. Laboured, over-elaborate and unsystematic, it does not always represent the main stream of Buddhist thinking. A lay Tantric, with often strange views, Vimalamitra could not maintain himself in Tibet against the orthodoxy of Kamalaśīla and had to leave for China." See his "Praśāstrasena's *Ārya-Prajñāpāramitā-Hṛdaya-Ṭīkā*", in L. Cousins, A. Kunst, and K. R. Norman, eds., *Buddhist Studies in Honour of I. B. Horner* (Dordrecht: D. Reidel Publishing, 1974), p. 51.

19. See George N. Roerich, trans., *The Blue Annals* (Delhi: Motilal Banarsidass, 1979), pp. 858-859. For other information on Vajrapāṇi, see pp. 855-860.

20. The *Blue Annals*, however, credits him with two other commentaries on Perfection of Wisdom sūtras. See George N. Roerich, trans., *The Blue Annals* (Delhi: Motilal Banarsidass, 1979) p. 859.

21. P 5519, Vol. 94, 291.5.8-292.1.3.

22. Conze, "Praśāstrasena's *Ārya-Prajñāpāramitā-Hṛdaya-Ṭīkā*", in L. Cousins, A. Kunst, and K. R. Norman, eds., *Buddhist Studies in Honour of I. B. Horner* (Dordrecht: D. Reidel Publishing, 1974), p. 51.

23. For studies of the Council and its antecedents, see Paul Demieville, *Le Concile de Lhasa*, Bibliothèque de l'Institut des Hautes Études Chinoises, Vol. VIII (Paris: Presses Universitaires de France, 1952), Giuseppe Tucci, ed., *First Bhāvanākrama of Kamalaśīla: Sanskrit and Tibetan Texts with Introduction and English Summary*, Minor Buddhist Texts, Part II: Série Orientale Roma IX.2 (Rome: Is.M.E.O., 1968), G. W. Houston, *Sources for a History of the bSam yas Debate* (Sankt Augustin: VGH Wissenschaftsverlag, 1980), Luis O. Gómez, "Indian Materials on the Doctrine of Sudden Enlightenment" in Whalen Lai and Lewis Lancaster, eds., *Early Ch'an in China and Tibet* (Berkeley: Berkeley Buddhist Studies Series, 1983), pp. 393-434, Luis O. Gómez, "The Direct and Gradual Approaches of the Zen Master Mo-ho-yen" in Robert Gimello and Peter Gregory, eds., *Studies in Ch'an and Hua-yen* (Honolulu: University of Hawaii Press, 1983), pp. 69-167, and Jeffrey Broughton, "Early Ch'an Schools in Tibet", also in Gimello and Gregory, eds., pp. 1-68. Luis Gómez is currently completing a major study of the Council of Lhasa that will include translations of all three *Bhāvanākrama*.

24. Both the root text and autocommentary have been translated by Richard Sherburne as *The Lamp for the Path and Commentary* (London: Allen and Unwin, 1983).

25. This can be surmised from the fact that, according to the colophon of his commentary, he aided in the translation of the text with Seng-ge-rgyal-mtshan. A translator known as Seng-ge-rgyal-mtshan studied under bLo-ldan-shes-rab of Ngog (1059-1109). See George N. Roerich, trans., *The Blue Annals* (Delhi: Motilal Banarsidass, 1979), p. 220.

26. The story appears in Samuel Beal, trans., *Buddhist Records of the*

Western World, Vol. II (London: Kegan Paul, Trench, Trübner, and Co., 1884), p. 224.

27. For a contemporary lament on the state of Tibetan Buddhism prior to the arrival of Atīśa, see S. Karmay, "The Ordinance of the lHa Bla-ma Ye-shes-'od" in Michael Aris and Aung San Suu Kyi, *Tibetan Studies in Honour of Hugh Richardson* (Warminster, England: Aris and Phillips, Ltd., 1980), pp. 150-162.

28. Edward Conze, *Memoirs of a Modern Gnostic*, part 1 (Sherborne: Samizdat Publishing Co., 1971), p. 143.

29. The edition used here is found in bsTan-dar-lha-ram-pa, *Collected gsung 'bum of Bstan-dar lha-ram of A-lag-sha*, Vol. 1 (New Delhi: Lama Guru Deva, 1971), pp. 291-322.

30. The edition used is found in Gung-thang dKon-mchog-bstan-pa'i sgron-me, *The Collected Works of Gung-thang Dkon-mchog-bstan-pa'i sgron-me*, Vol. 1 (New Delhi: Ngawang Gelek Demo, 1972), pp. 682-715.

Chapter 1: The Sūtra

1. The edition of the sūtra translated here is that appearing in the Peking edition of the Tibetan Tripiṭaka (P 160, Vol. 6, 166.1.7-166.4.5.) This Tibetan translation is used here because it was translated by the *Heart Sūtra* commentator Vimalamitra and a team of Tibetan translators at bSam-yas, probably in the late eighth century. At present, the fullest study of the text of the sūtra in English is that of Conze, "The Prajñāpāramitā-hṛdaya Sūtra" in his *Thirty Years of Buddhist Studies* (Columbia, South Carolina: University of South Carolina Press, 1968), pp. 148-167. A Sanskrit edition of the sūtra is also available in P. L. Vaidya, ed., *Mahāyānasūtrasaṃgraha* (Darbhanga, India: The Mithila Institute, 1961), Part 1, pp. 98-99. For a brief survey of Japanese scholarship on the text of the sūtra, see Hajime Nakamura, *Indian Buddhism: A Survey with Bibliographical Notes* (Osaka: KUFS Publication, 1980), p. 164, note 47.

Chapter 2: The Title

1. These four mistaken beliefs are known as the four inverted views (*viparyāsa*).

2. P 5220, Vol. 94, 292.2.4-8.

3. See R. Pandeya, ed., *Madhyānta-Vibhāga-Śāstra* (Delhi: Motilal Banarsidass, 1971), p. 151. For a discussion of the six excellences and the six perfections, see É. Lamotte, *La Somme du Grand Véhicule d'Asaṅga* (*Mahāyānasaṃgraha*) (Louvain: Institut Orientaliste, 1973), Tome 1, pp. 59-60, Tome 2, pp. 184-187.

4. P 5217, Vol. 94, 279.5.5-6. He goes on to cite the *Aṣṭasāhasrikāprajñā-pāramitā* for support.

5. According to Candrakīrti, it is *pāram* rather than *pāra* because in this

instance the accusative singular ending is not elided before the second member of the compound. See Louis de la Vallée Poussin, ed., *Madhyamakāvatāra par Candrakīrti*, Bibliotheca Buddhica IX (Osnabruck: Biblio Verlag, 1970), p. 30. For a discussion of Jayānanda's commentary on this point, see Tsong-kha-pa, *dbU ma dgongs pa rab gsal* (Sarnath: Pleasure of Elegant Sayings Press, 1973, pp. 79-80.

6. See Lamotte, *La Somme du Grand Véhicule d'Asaṅga* (*Mahāyāna-saṃgraha*), (Louvain: Institut Orientaliste, 1973), Tome 1, p. 60, Tome 2, p. 186.

7. See P. Pradhan, ed., *Abhidharmakośabhāṣyam of Vasubandhu*, (Patna: K. P. Jayaswal Research Institute, 1975), p. 267.

8. Louis de la Vallée Poussin, *Madhyamakāvatāra par Candrakīrti*, pp. 30-1.

9. See U. Wogihara, ed., *Abhisamayālaṃkāra Prajñāpāramitāvyākhyā* (Tokyo: Toyo bunko, 1973), p. 23.2-6.

10. P 5219, Vol. 94, 288.3.5.

11. On the meaning of *pāramita*, see also Franklin Edgerton, *Buddhist Hybrid Sanskrit Dictionary* (Delhi: Motilal Banarsidass, 1970), s.v. *pārami, pāramita*; Étienne Lamotte, *Le Traité de la Grande Vertu de Sagesse de Nāgārjuna* (*Mahāprajñāpāramitāśāstra*), Tome II (Louvain: Institut Orientaliste, 1967), p. 1058; and 'Jam-dbyangs-bzhad-pa, *Phar phyin skabs dang po'i mtha' dpyod* (Varanasi: Mongolian Lama Guru Deva, 1963), pp. 220-226.

12. Oral commentary of Yeshe Thupten. At a number of points in the study, I provide information from "an oral commentary." In most cases, the source of this commentary is Yeshe Thupten, abbot emeritus of bLo-gsal-gling College of 'Bras-spung Monastery. He is among a handful of distinguished dGe-lugs scholars who received their training in Tibet prior to 1959. In 1982, I read with Yeshe Thupten the first of the two Tibetan commentaries translated at the end of this work, that of bsTan-dar-lha-ram-pa. I did not read the Pāla commentaries with him. dGe-lugs scholars are most useful as informants on the texts which form the basis of their curriculum: Maitreyanātha's *Abhisamayā-laṃkāra*, Candrakīrti's *Madhyamakāvatāra*, Dharmakīrti's *Pramāṇavārttika*, Vasubandhu's *Abhidharmakośa*, and Guṇaprabha's *Vinayasūtra*. Yeshe Thupten's knowledge of the constellation of topics surrounding the perfection of wisdom derive from his extensive study of the works of Maitreyanātha and Candrakīrti. His comments are occasionally given here to provide an additional perspective on a key term or doctrine. I do not propose that his interpretation is definitive or that it represents the views of the Pāla commentators. Nonetheless, the oral commentary of a Tibetan polymath on a difficult point is almost always illuminating, despite the fact that it is often synthetic, such that its historical origin is not always easily traceable. Yeshe Thupten's comments are cited from time to time for the insight they provide on the topic in question.

13. P 5220 Vol. 94, 292.2.7-292.3.2.

14. For Sanskrit and Tibetan editions of the text, see Giuseppe Tucci, "Minor Sanskrit Texts on the Prajñāpāramitā. I. The Prajñāpāramitā-piṇḍārtha of Diṅnāga", *Journal of the Royal Asiatic Society*, April 1947, pp. 53-75. It is also cited by Haribhadra in the *Abhisamayālaṃkārāloka.* See U. Wogihara, ed., *Abhisamayālaṃkāra Prajñāpāramitāvyākhyā* (Tokyo: Toyo bunko, 1973), p. 23.10-11. Haribhadra glosses the line at 23.7-9. The Sanskrit is: *prajñāpāramitā jñānam advayaṃ sā tathāgataḥ | sādhyā tādarthyayogena tācchabdyaṃ grantha-mārgayoḥ.*

15. See 'Jam-dbyangs-bzhad-pa, *Don bdun cu'i yig cha* in *bLo rig dang sa lam dang don bdun cu bcas* (Mundgod, India: Loseling Press, no date), p. 132.

16. See Pan-chen bSod-nams-grags-pa, *Phar phyin spyi'i don* (Buxadour: modern blockprint), 46b6-47a2.

17. See P. 5208, Vol. 94, 2.4.3-6 and 'Jam-dbyangs-bzhad-pa, *sKabs dang po'i mtha' dpyod* (Sarnath: Mongolia Lama Guru Deva, 1963), p. 222.

18. Pan-chen bSod-nams-grags-pa, *Phar phyin spyi'i don*, 47a3-6.

19. See 'Jam-dbyangs-bzhad-pa, *sKabs tang po'i mtha' dpyod* (Mongolian Lama Guru Deva, 1963), p. 220.

20. Ibid., p. 223.

21. See Étienne Lamotte, ed. and trans., *Saṃdhinirmocana Sūtra: L'Explication des Mystères* (Paris: Adrien Maisonneuve, 1935), p. 145.

22. See R. Pandeya, ed., *Madhyānta-Vibhāga-Śāstra* (Delhi: Motilal Banarsidass, 1971), pp. 151ff.

23. For a summary of how the term was understood in Pali Buddhism, see Buddhaghosa's *Visuddhimagga*, VII 53-64. The two interpretations contained in the Indian commentaries to the *Heart Sūtra* of *bhagavat* implying both the destruction of demons and the possession of fortune is contained in the Pali, *akāsi bhaggan ti garū ti bhāgyavā* (he has caused destruction and is fortunate) at *Visuddhimagga*, VII 56. An English translation of this section is available in Bhadantācariya Buddhaghosa, *The Path of Purification* (*Visuddhimagga*), trans. by Bhikku Ñyānamoli (Colombo, Ceylon: A. Semage, 1964), pp. 224-229. For a Mahāyāna discussion of the term, deriving probably from northwestern India in the fourth century see Étienne Lamotte's translation of the *Mahāprajñāpāramitāśāstra, Le Traité de la Grande Vertu de Sagesse*, Tome I (Louvain: Institut Orientaliste, 1949) pp. 115-126.

24. In the *Abhisamayālaṃkārāloka*, Haribhadra cites a verse to support an etymology, apparently deriving from Vedic Sanskrit, that *bhagavan* is a person who destroyed (*bhagnāvan*), the afflictive obstructions and the obstructions to omniscience. See U. Wogihara, ed., p. 7.25-27. Haribhadra then goes on to discuss the more common etymology of *bhagavan* as one endowed with fortune.

25. For a study of the nature of the two obstructions as delineated by

Bhāvaviveka and Candrakīrti, see Donald S. Lopez, Jr., "Do *Śrāvakas* Understand Emptiness?" *Journal of Indian Philosophy*, Fall, 1987.

26. According to later Tibetan doxographers of the dGe-lugs-pa school, the Prāsaṅgikas assert that the conception that persons and phenomena are inherently established (*svabhāvasiddha*) constitutes the chief of the afflictive obstructions and that the subtle predispositions that cause persons and phenomena to appear to the senses to inherently exist constitute the obstructions to omniscience. The Sautrāntika-Svātantrikas hold that the conception of a self of persons, that persons substantially exist, is the basic afflictive obstruction and the conception of a self of phenomena, that phenomena truly exist, is the basic obstruction to omniscience. Based primarily on statements made by Haribhadra in his commentaries on the *Abhisamayālaṃkāra*, the Tibetan doxographers describe the Yogācāra-Svātantrika position to agree essentially with the Sautrāntika-Svātantrikas on the nature of the afflictive obstructions although asserting that the obstructions to omniscience have two forms. The coarse obstruction to omniscience is the conception of the existence of external objects whereas the subtle obstruction to omniscience is the conception that phenomena truly exist. For a brief exposition of this topic, see the Mādhyamika chapter of dKon-mchog-'jigs-med-dbang-po's *Grub pa'i mtha'i rnam par bzhag pa rin po che'i phreng ba* (Dharamsala, India: Shes rig par khang, 1969).

27. For modern studies of the four Māras, see Alex Wayman, "Studies in Yama and Māra", *Indo-Iranian Journal* III: (1959), pp. 44-73, 112-131. The specific discussion of the four Māras occurs at pp. 112-125. For a more general study, see James W. Boyd, "Symbols of Evil in Buddhism", *Journal of Asian Sutdies*, Vol. 31, No. 1 (1971), pp. 63-75. For an analysis of the role of Māra in Theravāda Buddhism, see Trevor O. Ling, *Buddhism and the Mythology of Evil* (London: Allen and Unwin, 1962).

28. See Lamotte, *Le Traité de la Grande Vertu de Sagesse*, pp. 339-340, which states that the *kleśamāra* is destroyed upon becoming a Bodhisattva, the *skandhamāra* is destroyed upon attaining the *dharmakāya*, the *mṛtyumāra* is destroyed upon attaining the path and the *dharmakāya*, and the *devaputramāra* of the Heaven of Controlling Others' Emanations (*paranirmitavaśavartin*) is destroyed when Bodhisattvas are of a single mind (*ekacitta*), are not attached to any realm, and enter into the unshakeable samādhis (*acalasamādhi*).

29. In commenting on *Kośa* II.10, Vasubandhu discusses various positions on the relationship between the life faculty factor (*jīvitā-saṃskāraḥ*) and longevity factor (*āyus-saṃskāraḥ*). In this context, he reported that the Vaibhāṣikas asserted that the Bodhisattva defeated the *devaputramāra* under the Bodhi tree during the first watch of the night, that he defeated the *kleśamāra* during the third watch of the night, that in Vaiśāli, three months before his passage into nirvāṇa, he rejected the longevity factor that would prolong his life, thereby defeating the *maraṇamāra* (for studies of this incident and its meaning, see André Bareau, *Récherches sur la Biographie du Buddha dans les Sūtrapiṭaka et les Vinayapiṭaka Anciens*, Tome 1 (Paris: École Française D'Extrême Orient,

1971), pp. 156-172 and P. S. Jaini, "Buddha's Prolongation of Life", *Bulletin of the School of Oriental and African Studies*, Vol. XXI (London: 1958), pp. 546-552) and that at Malla [Kuśinagara], he passed into the remainderless final nirvāṇa, thereby defeating the *skandhamāra*. See P. Pradhan, ed., *Abhidharmakośabhāśyam of Vasubandhu* (Patna: Jayaswal Research Institute, 1975), p. 44. See also the first Dalai Lama, dGe-'dun-grub, *mDzod tik thar lam gsal byed* (Sarnath: Pleasure of Elegant Sayings Press), 1973, pp. 85-86.

30. The *skandhamāra* is mentioned in the commentary on MK I.1. See Louis de la Vallée Poussin, ed., *Mūlamadhyamakakārikās (Mādhyamikasūtras) de Nāgārjuna avec la Prasannapadā Commentaire de Candrakīrti*, Bibliotheca Buddhica IV (Osnabruck: Biblio Verlag, 1970), p. 49, line 10.

31. *Uttaratantra* II.66b says, "Having attained the state of deathlessness and peace, he is unmoved by the Māra of death." (*samāmṛtapadaprāpti mṛtyumārāvabhaṅga*). For an English translation, see Jikido Takasaki, *A Study on the Ratnagotravibhāga*, Série Orientale Roma XXXIII (Rome: Istituto Italiano per il Medio ed Estremo Oriente, 1966), p. 333.

32. Prajñākaramati says in commenting on IX.36 that the Bhagavan is a conqueror (*jina*) because of his conquest of the four Māras. See P. L. Vaidya, ed., *Bodhicaryāvatāra of Śāntideva with the Commentary Pañjikā of Prajñākaramati*, Buddhist Sanskrit Texts No. 12 (Darbhanga, India: Mithila Institute, 1960), p. 199.14.

33. For the Sanskrit with translation, see Wayman, "Studies in Yama and Māra", pp. 112-113.

34. For Sanskrit and Tibetan editions of the *Abhisamayālaṃkāra*, see Th. Stcherbatsky and E. Obermiller, eds., *Abhisamayālaṅkāra-Prajñāpāramitā-Upadeśa-Śāstra*, Bibliotheca Buddhica XXIII (Osnabruck: Biblio Verlag, 1970).

35. The Sanskrit is: *pañcopādānaskandhāḥ* | *skandhamāraḥ* | *traidhātukāvacarāḥ kleśaḥ kleśamāraḥ* | *teṣāṃ teṣāṃ satvānāṃ* | *tasmāt tasmāt satvanikāyāḥ yan maraṇaṃ kālakriyā maraṇamāraḥ* | *yo 'sya kuśalapakṣaprayuktasya skandhakleśamṛtyuṃ samatikramāya kāmadhātūpapanno devaputraḥ aiśvaryaprāptaḥ* | *antarāyam upasaṃharati* | *vyākṣepakaraṇe* | *ayam ucyate devaputramāraḥ* ||. See Wayman, "Studies in Yama and Māra," p. 112.

36. For a list of discussions of the root and secondary afflictions, see Jeffrey Hopkins, *Meditation on Emptiness* (London: Wisdom Publications, 1983), pp. 255-266.

37. Se-ra rJe-btsun-pa, *sKabs bzhi pa'i spyi don* (Bylakuppe, India: Serjey Dratsang, modern blockprint, no date) 144b2-145a6. This statement is based on Asaṅga, who says in the *Śrāvakabhūmi, tatra yatra ca mriyate* | *yena ca mriyate* | *yaś cāsau mṛtyur yena ca mṛtyuṃ na samatikrāmaty antarāyikena vastunā*. See Wayman, "Studies in Yama and Māra," p. 112.

38. Tsong-kha-pa, *Kham gsum chos kyi rgyal po shar rgyal ba tsong kha pa*

chen po'i gsung 'bum, Vol. Tsha (New Delhi: Mongolian Lama Guru Deva, 1978), 145a1-3.

39. This is seventh of the seven kinds of Superiors (*ārya, 'phags pa*) discussed by Vasubandhu in commenting on *Abhidharmakośa* VI.62-64ab. This arhat is called one "liberated from both factors" (*ubhayatobhagavimukta, gnyis ka'i cha las rnam grol*) because he has freed himself from the afflictive obstructions through wisdom and has freed himself from the obstructions to the attainment of the eight freedoms (*vimokṣa, rnam par thar pa*) (listed in the commentary on *Abhidharmakośa*, VIII.32a.) through the meditative absorption of cessation (*nirodhasamāpatti, 'gog pa'i snyoms 'jug*).

40. rGyal-tshab-dar-ma-rin-chen, *mNgon rtogs pa'i rgyan gyi rtsa ba 'grel pa dang bcas pa'i rnam bshad snying po'i rgyan* (modern blockprint), 145b1-146a4. See also Pan-chen-bSod-rnams-grags-pa, *Phar phyin spyi don* (Buxadour: modern blockprint, 303a3-304b6 and 'Jam-dbyangs-bzhad-pa, *sKabs bzhi pa'i mtha' dpyod* (Sarnath: Mongolian Lama Guru Deva, 1964), pp. 202-203.

41. The Sanskrit, with the variant of substituting "of being fully formed" (*samagrasya rūpasya*) for "of qualities" (*guṇasya*) is cited by Haribhadra in the *Abhisamayālaṃkārāloka: aiśvaryasya samagrasya rūpasya yaśasaḥ śriyaḥ | jñānasya atha prayatnasya ṣaṇṇām bhaga iti 'śrutiḥ.* See U. Wogihara, ed., p. 7.28-29. The verse occurs in the *Buddhabhūmivyākhāna*, which provides this and five other etymologies of *bhagavān*.

42. The ten powers are: (1) knowledge of sources and non-sources, (2) knowledge of actions and their fruitions, (3) knowledge of the varieties of inclinations, (4) knowledge of the divisions of the eighteen constituents and so forth, (5) knowledge of superior and non-superior faculties, (6) knowledge of the paths leading to all forms of cyclic existence and solitary peace, (7) knowledge of the concentrations, meditative liberations, and absorptions, (8) knowledge remembering former states [of rebirth], (9) knowledge of death, transmigration, and birth, and (10) knowledge of contaminations and their extinction. Among many other places, the ten powers are listed by Candrakīrti in his *Madhyamakāvatāra* IX.19-21. See Poussin, ed., p. 369. For an extensive treatment, see Lamotte, *Le Traité*, Tome III, pp. 1505-1566.

43. See U. Wogihara, ed., *Abhisamayālaṃkāra Prajñāpāramitāvyākhyā*, p. 914.

44. P 5223, Vol. 94 300.3.4-7. Both Haribhadra, in his *Abhisamayālaṃkārāloka*, and Ratnākaraśānti, in his *Hevajratantrapañjikā*, identify "fully formed" (*samagrarūpa*) rather than "quality" as the second of the six fortunes. Śrīmahājana notes that some say this and comments that "fully formed" would then refer to the mirror-like wisdom and "glory" would mean earnest action because of being the nature of teaching the doctrine. See P 5223, Vol. 94 300.3.7-8. For a brief treatment of the six fortunes by Tsong-kha-pa, see his *Legs bshad gser 'phreng* (Sarnath, India: Pleasure of Elegant Sayings Press, 1970), pp. 33-34.

On the four wisdoms (all except the *dharmadhātujñāna*), see the *Mahāyāna-sūtrālaṃkāra* IX.67-76. The Sanskrit appears in S. Bagchi, ed., *Mahāyāna-Sūtrālaṃkāra of Asaṅga* (Darbhanga: Mithila Institute, 1970), pp. 48-49. A much more detailed exposition is provided in the *Buddhabhūmivyākhāna*, which has been translated by John Keenan. See his doctoral dissertation, "A Study of the *Buddhabhūmyupadeśa*", (University of Wisconsin, 1980), pp. 541-781. For Tibetan expositions, see Pan-chen bSod-nams-grags-pa, *Phar phyin spyi don* (Buxadour: no date), 368a1-368b3 and Jam-dbyangs-bzhad-pa, *sKabs rgyad pa'i mtha' dpyod* (Varanasi: Mongolian Lama Guru Deva, 1968), pp. 10-14.

45. P 5218 Vol. 94, 285.2.7-8.

46. Throughout this work, I have translated *bhagavan* as "transcendent victor" and *bhagavatī* as "transcendent and victorious." This translation does not derive from some preference for a Tibetan reading of the term over the Indian, but from the fact that the Pāla commentators seem to express a preference for reading the term as connoting destruction rather than fortune. Of the five commentators who provide etymologies of the word, all five evoke the Buddha's destruction of the Māras or the obstructions. Only two mention his possession of the six fortunes, and they also mention destruction. Because at least Vimalamitra and Mahājana (and possibly Vajrapāṇi) were involved in the translation of their commentaries into Tibetan, it is safe to assume that they did not find the Tibetan rendering *bcom ldan 'das* objectionable or misleading. Further, it is useful to note that Vimalamitra was the Indian paṇḍita who oversaw the translation of the *Heart Sūtra* into Tibetan, and he apparently approved the translation of *bhagavatī* as *bcom ldan 'das ma*, rather than *legs ldan ma* or some such rendering of the idea of fortune. It is certainly the case that the rich etymologies provided by the Indian commentators caused the Tibetans to construct translations that encompass more than one sense of the Sanskrit term. This makes the term difficult to render into English. In this case of Indian commentaries on the *Heart Sūtra*, Transcendent Victor (or something like it) appears to express the primary sense in which *bhagavan* was understood. "Fortunate One" would evoke the other sense of the term. As for the more common translations of bhagavan, "Blessed One" raises the question of by whom the Buddha is blessed, whereas "Lord" evokes too many Judeo-Christian connotations. There is the further problem of finding a feminine equivalent: translating *bhagavatīprajñāpāramitā* as "lady-like perfection of wisdom" does not seem quite right.

47. Oral commentary by Yeshe Thupten. See note 12.

48. See Jñānamitra, P 5218 Vol. 94 285.2.8-285.3.2. On the feminine nature of the perfection of wisdom, Conze writes, "Like a woman the *Perfection of Wisdom* deserves to be courted and wooed. Meditation on her as a Goddess has the purpose of getting inside her, identifying oneself with her, becoming her, as a man wishes to merge his body with that of a woman." See his *Thirty Years of Buddhist Studies* (Columbia, S. C.: University of South Carolina Press,

1968), p. 188. The implications of such a view in light of recent feminist literary criticism, where the notion of text as woman and interpretation as penetration has been brought to light, have yet to be explored in Buddhist Studies.

49. See Tsong-ka-pa, *Tantra in Tibet*, trans. by Jeffrey Hopkins (London: Allen and Unwin, 1977), p. 99.

50. The six mother sūtras are the *Śatasāhasrikā*, the *Pañcaviṃśatisāhasrikā*, the *Aṣṭādaśasāhasrikā*, the *Daśasāhasrikā*, the *Aṣṭasāhasrikā*, and the *Sañcaya-gāthā*. They are called "mothers" because they set forth in full the eight clear realizations (*abhisamaya*). Eleven sūtras that do not teach the eight in full are called sons. They are the *Suvikrāntavikramiparipṛcchā*, the *Saptaśatikā*, the *Pañcaśatikāprajñāpāramitā*, the *Nayaśatapañcāśatkā*, the *Prajñāpāramitā-pañcāśatkā*, the *Vajracchedikā*, the *Prajñāpāramitāhṛdaya*, the *Kauśika*, the *Subāhuparipṛcchā*, the *Svalpākṣaraprajñāpāramitā*, and the *Ekākṣarīmātā*. This list occurs in mKhas-grub-rje's *rGyud sde spyi rnam*, translated by F. Lessing and A. Wayman as *Introduction to the Buddhist Tantrica Systems* (Delhi: Motilal Banarsidass, 1978), p. 46.

51. See Obermiller, trans., *History of Buddhism by Bu-ston*, Part II, (Heidelberg, 1932) pp. 49-50.

52. bsTan-dar-lha-ram-pa, *Collected gsung 'bum of Bstan-dar lha-ram of A-lag-sha*, Vol. 1 (New Delhi: Lama Guru Deva, 1971), pp. 4b3-5a2.

53. bsTan-dar-lha-ram-pa, 6b4-5.

54. bsTan-dar-lha-ram-pa, 7b4-5. According to the T'ang dynasty translator of the *Heart Sūtra*, Hsuan Tsang, it is called the *Heart Sūtra* because it dispels wrong notions from the heart (*hsin*). See Leon Hurvitz, "Hsuan-tsang (602-664) and the *Heart Scripture*" in Lewis Lancaster, ed., *Prajñāpāramitā and Related Systems* (Berkeley: Berkeley Buddhist Studies Series, 1977), p. 106.

55. P 5218 Vol. 94, 285.2.6-285.3.4.

Chapter 3: The Prologue

1. For a study of this phrase and how it is to be read, see John Bough, "Thus Have I Heard . . .", *Bulletin of the School of Oriental and African Studies*, Vol. XIII, Part 2, (1950). An extensive commentary on the meaning of the individual words of the phrase and of the meaning of the phrase as a whole occurs in the *Mahāprajñāpāramitāśāstra*. See Lamotte, *Le Traité de la Grande Vertu de Sagesse*, Tome I (Louvain: Institut Orientaliste, 1967), pp. 56-114.

2. P 5222, Vol. 96, 297.4.8-294.5.2. For Sanskrit and Tibetan editions of the text, see Giuseppe Tucci, "Minor Sanskrit Texts on the Prajñāpāramitā," pp. 56, 68. For Triratnadāsa's commentary, see P 5208, Vol. 94, 3.1.3-3.2.2.

3. P 5219, Vol. 94, 288.1.4-5.

4. P 5256, Vol. 96, 74.2.2-3.

5. P 5218, Vol. 94, 285.4.3-4.

6. See U. Wogihara, ed., p. 6.14-15.

7. P 5220, Vol. 94, 292.3.5.

8. See P 5256, Vol. 96, 69.5.7-70.1.5.

9. P 5256, Vol. 96, 74.2.4-5. Bhāvaviveka's prolix proof that the Mahāyāna is the word of the Buddha occurs at P 5256, Vol. 96, 74.1.6-84.4.1.

10. See U. Wogihara, ed., *Abhisamayālaṃkārāloka*, p. 6.14-15.

11. See U. Wogihara, ed., *Abhisamayālaṃkārāloka*, p. 7.1-4. (This is the third of Haribhadra's three glosses of "at one time.") For a discussion of this phenomenon, see 'Jam-dbyangs-bzhad-pa, *sKabs dang po'i mtha' dpyod*, pp. 136-138.

12. P 760, Vol. 50, 63.4.6-63.5.5 and 66.2.5-6.

13. P 760, Vol. 50, 62.5.4-6. A similar statement is cited by Candrakīrti in the *Prasannapadā*. See Louis de la Vallée Poussin, ed., *Mūlamadhyamaka-kārikās (Mādhyamikasūtras) de Nāgārjuna avec la Prasannapadā Commentaire de Candrakīrti* (Osnabruck: Biblio Verlag, 1970), p. 366. Yet another version occurs in Prajñākaramati's commentary on the *Bodhicaryāvatāra*. See P. L. Vaidya, ed., *Bodhicaryāvatāra of Śāntideva*, p. 199. These statements are obvious plays on the statement found at *Digha Nikāya* III.135 and elsewhere that the Buddha taught the doctrine from the night of his enlightenment until his passage into nirvāṇa. On the Buddha's teaching powers, see Lamotte's typically masterful footnotes in his *L'Enseignement de Vimalakīrti* (Louvain: Publications Universitaires, 1962), pp. 109-110.

14. Some of these positions are reported and evaluated in bsTan-dar-lha-ram-pa's commentary. See pp. 141-143. See also E. Obermiller, trans., *History of Buddhism by Bu-ston*, Part II (Heidelberg, 1932), pp. 48-51.

15. P 5220, Vol. 94, 292.3.7-8.

16. P 5218, Vol. 94 285.5.1-2. bsTan-dar-lha-ram-pa cites five etymologies drawn from the *Bai durya g.ya sel*. See p. 141. Two of these etymologies also appear in the *Mahāprajñāpāramitāśāstra*. See Lamotte, trans., *Le Traité de la Grande Vertu de Sagesse*, pp. 168-9.

17. P 5217, Vol. 94, 278.6-7.

18. The intermediate state is discussed by Vasubandhu in the *Abhidharma-kośabhāṣya* III.12-15. See P. Pradhan, ed. *Abhidharmakośabhāṣyaṃ of Vasu-bandhu*, pp. 121-127. For a Tibetan exposition of the intermediate state, see Lati Rinbochay and Jeffrey Hopkins, *Death, Intermediate State, and Rebirth in Tibetan Buddhism* (Ithaca, New York: Snow Lion Publications, 1979),

pp. 49-57. For a brief study of the question of the existence of an intermediate state in Indian Buddhist thought see Alex Wayman, "The Intermediate-State Dispute in Buddhism," L. Cousins, et al., ed., *Buddhist Studies in Honour of I. B. Horner* (Dordrecht: D. Reidel Publishing, 1974), pp. 227-239.

19. This legend is cited by bsTan-dar-lha-ram-pa from the *Śālistambha Sūtra* and also appears in the *Mahāprajñāpāramitāśāstra*. See Lamotte, trans., *Le Traité de la Grande Vertu de Sagesse*, p. 164.

20. bsTan-dar-lha-ram-pa, p. 149.

21. P 5223, Vol. 94, 300.5.1.

22. Oral commentary by Yeshe Thupten.

23. P 5217, Vol. 94, 279.1.6. A similar etymology also appears in the Pali canon where *bhikku* is explained to mean *bhinna-kilesa*, "one who has shattered the afflictions." See VbhA 328; VvA 29, 114, 310; PvA 51.

24. P 5478, Vol. 103, 281.4.1-2.

25. Oral commentary by Yeshe Thupten. See Chapter 2, note 12.

26. The saṃgha is discussed at length in the dGe-lugs-pa commentaries to *Abhisamayālaṃkāra* I.21, specifically the phrase, "the Three Jewels, the Buddha, etc.," (*buddharatnādiṣu triṣu*). The twenty divisions of the *saṃgha* are listed in *Abhisamayālaṃkāra* I.23-24.

27. P 5217, Vol. 94, 279.1.6-7.

28. Har Dayal, *The Bodhisattva Doctrine in Buddhist Sanskrit Literature* (Delhi: Motilal Banarsidass, 1970), pp. 4-9. For other discussions of the term, see *Encyclopedia of Buddhism*, s.v. *Bodhisattva, Hobogirin*, s.v. *Bosatsu*, and especially Yuichi Kajiyama, "On the Meanings of the Words *Bodhisattva* and *Mahāsattva* in Prajñāpāramitā Literature", in L. A. Hercus, et al., ed., *Indological and Buddhist Studies*, (Canberra: Faculty of Asian Studies, 1982), pp. 253-270.

29. See bsTan-dar-lha-ram-pa, p. 150.

30. The Sanskrit is: *cittotpādaḥ parārthāya samyaksambodhikāmatā*. See Stcherbatsky and Obermiller, trans., *Abhisamayālaṅkāra-Prajñāpāramitā-Upadeśa-Śāstra*, p. 4.

31. See Haribhadra, *Abhisamayālaṃkāravṛtti Sphuṭārthā* (Sarnath: Biblioteca Indo-Tibetica, 1977), pp. 15-16. The twenty-two similes also appear in the *Mahāyānasūtrālaṃkāra* IV.15-20.

32. For the Sanskrit, see P. L. Vaidya, ed., *Bodhicaryāvatāra of Śāntideva with the Commentary Pañjikā of Prajñākaramati*, Buddhist Sanskrit Texts 12 (Darbhanga, India: Mithila Institute, 1960), p. 43.

33. The two forms of the aspiration are mentioned in the *Gaṇḍavyūhasūtra* as cited by Kamalaśīla, *Bhāvanākrama* I, Derge edition, Tibetan Tripitaka

(Tokyo, 1978), Toh. 3915, folio 25a2-3 and by Śāntideva, *Bodhicaryāvatāra*, I. 15-19. See Vaidya, ed., pp. 11-13.

34. P. L. Vaidya, ed., *Aṣṭasāhasrikā-Prajñāpāramitā*, Buddhist Sanskrit Texts, No. 4 (Darbhanga, India: Mithila Institute, 1960), p. 283.

35. Kamalaśīla, *Bhāvanākrama* I, folio 25a4. Atīśa devotes the fourth chapter of his *Bodhipathapradīpa* to a discussion of the person from whom the Bodhisattva vow should be taken.

36. Kamalaśīla, *Bhāvanākrama* I, Folio 27a6-7.

37. See Stcherbatsky and Obermiller, ed., p. 7.

38. P 5217, Vol. 94, 279.1.7-8.

39. P 5217, Vol. 94, 279.2.5.

40. See Edward Conze, trans., *The Large Sūtra on Perfect Wisdom* (Berkeley, California: University of California Press, 1975), p. 59.

41. P 5217, Vol. 94, 279.3.1.

42. See Tsong-kha-pa, *Byang chub lam rim chen mo* (Dharamsala, India: Tibetan Cultural Printing Press, modern blockprint), folio 328a3.

43. P 5223, Vol. 94, 301.2.4.

44. bsTan-dar-lha-ram-pa, p. 150.

45. P 5223, Vol. 94, 301.2.4-5.

46. Oral commentary of Yeshe Thupten.

47. P 5217, Vol. 94, 279.3.7-279.4.1.

48. P 5223, Vol. 94, 300.2.7-8.

49. P 5220, Vol. 94, 292.4.5-292.5.1.

50. For studies of Avalokiteśvara, see Marie-Thérèse de Mallmann, *Introduction a l'Étude d'Avalokiteśvara*, Annales du Musée Guimet, 57 (Paris, 1948), Giuseppe Tucci, "Buddhist Notes I: à propos Avalokiteśvara", *Mélanges Chinois et Bouddhique*, 9 (1948-1951), pp. 173-219, the *Encyclopedia of Religion and Ethics*, and the *Encyclopedia of Buddhism*, s.v. "Avalokiteśvara."

51. See Kajiyama, "On the Meanings of the Words *Bodhisattva* and *Mahāsattva* in Prajñāpāramitā Literature", pp. 261-265, Lamotte, *Le Traité*, Tome 1, pp. 309-315.

52. P 735, Vol. 21, 187.2.7-8. For a Sanskrit edition, see A. Yuyama, *Prajñāpāramitāratnaguṇasaṃcayagāthā* (Cambridge, 1976).

53. See U. Wogihara, ed., *Abhisamayālaṃkārāloka*, p. 80.

54. Ibid., p. 22.

55. P 5220, Vol. 94, 292.4.1.

56. P 5217, Vol. 94, 279.5.1.

57. P 5223, Vol. 96, 300.5.7.

58. Oral commentary by Yeshe Thupten.

59. The text reads *rnam par rtog pa* rather than *rnam par lta ba.*

60. P 5220, Vol. 94, 292.5.2-293.2.1.

61. The delineation of the three types of compassion occurs in Candrakīrti's commentary to *Madhyamakāvatāra* I.3-4abc. See Louis de la Vallée Poussin, ed., *Madhyamakāvatāra par Candrakīrti,* pp. 9-11. For an English translation of Tsong-kha-pa's commentary on this section from his *dGongs pa rab gsal,* see Tsong-ka-pa, *Compassion in Tibetan Buddhism* (Ithaca, New York: Snow Lion Press, 1980), pp. 116-125. For a translation of a detailed later dGe-lugs-pa exegesis of the three types of compassion, see Guy Newland, trans., *Compassion: A Tibetan Analysis* (London: Wisdom Publications, 1984.).

Chapter 4: The Question and the Answer.

1. P 5478, Vol. 103, 281.1.2-3.

2. E. Obermiller, trans., *History of Buddhism by Bu-ston,* vol. 1, p. 40-41.

3. See Lamotte, *Le Traité de la Grande Vertu de Sagesse,* Tome 2 (Louvain: Institut Orientaliste, 1949), pp. 630-636.

4. P 5223, Vol. 94, 304.2.7-8.

5. *Abhidharmakośa* I.2a: *prajñāmalā sānucarā abhidharmaḥ.*

6. bsTan-dar-lha-ram-pa, 10b2-3.

7. P 5223, Vol. 94, 301.3.8-301.4.5.

8. P 5219, Vol. 94, 288.3.8-288.4.2.

9. P 5218, Vol. 94, 286.1.7.

10. P 5219, Vol. 94, 288.3.3.

11. P 5219, Vol. 94, 288.4.2-4.

12. P 5223, Vol. 94, 301.4.6-7.

13. P 5223, Vol. 94, 301.4.7-301.5.3.

14. P 5223, Vol. 96, 301.5.5.6. For the Sanskrit, see Ramachandra Pandeya, ed., *Madhyānta-Vibhāga-Śāstra* (Delhi: Motilal Banarsidass, 1971), p. 157.

15. P 5223, Vol. 96, 301.5.6-7.

16. P 5220, Vol. 94, 293.2.7-293.3.1.

17. P 5220, Vol. 94 293.3.2-3.

18. The neologism "entityness" is an attempt to translate the Tibetan *ngo bo nyid*, which is a translation of the Sanskrit *rūpatvā*. Entityness is meant to suggest something that is capable of independent existence, to subsist independently of what is the case. It seems akin to what Heidegger calls "the thingness of the thing." See Martin Heidegger, *Poetry, Language, Thought* (New York: Harper and Row, 1971), pp. 22-23.

19. P 5220, Vol. 94 293.4.1-3.

20. bsTan-dar-lha-ram-pa, 11b6-12a2.

21. Ibid.

22. Ibid.

23. P 5266, Vol. 98, 270.3.6.

24. Cited by Candrakīrti in the *Prasannapadā*. See Poussin, ed., *Mūlamadhyamakakārikās*, p. 191.

25. For the edited Tibetan text, see Christian Lindtner, *Nagarjuniana: Studies in the Writings and Philosophy of Nāgārjuna* (Copenhagen: Akademisk Forlag, 1982), p. 112.

26. P 5266, Vol. 98, 229.5.6.

27. See Tsong-kha-pa, *dbU ma dgongs pa rab gsal* (Sarnath: Pleasure of Elegant Sayings Press, 1973), p. 138.

Chapter 5: Form Is Emptiness; Emptiness Is Form

1. P 5220, Vol. 94, 294.3.7-294.4.1.

2. P 5218, Vol. 94, 286.2.7-286.3.4.

3. This same point is made by the Bodhisattva Priyadarśana in the eighth chapter of the *Vimalakīrtinirdeśa*. See Lamotte, trans., *L'Enseignement de Vimalakīrti (Vimalakīrtinirdeśa)* (Louvain: Museon, 1962) pp. 308-309.

4. P 5223, Vol. 94, 302.2.1-5.

5. This discussion of the *trisvabhāva* is drawn from lCang-skya-rol-pa'i-rdo-rje, *Grub pa'i mtha'i rnam par bzhag pa gsal bshad pa thub bstan lhun po'i mdzes rgyan* (Sarnath: Pleasure of Elegant Sayings Press, 1970), pp. 175-178.

6. On the two kinds of negatives, see Yuichi Kajiyama, "Three Kinds of Affirmation and Two Kinds of Negation in Buddhist Philosophy," *Wiener Zeitschrift für die Kunde Südasiens und Archiv für Indische Philosophie*, 1973 and Anne Klein, *Knowledge and Liberation: The Sautrāntika Tenet System in Tibet* (Ithaca, New York: Snow Lion Publications, 1986), chapters 6 and 7, and B. K. Matilal, *Epistemology, Logic, and Grammar in Indian Philosophical*

Analysis (The Hague: Mouton, 1971), pp. 63-64.

7. P 5223, Vol. 94, 302.2.6-8.

8. P 5223, Vol. 94, 302.3.3-7.

9. P 5220, Vol. 94, 293.4.4-293.5.3.

10. P 5220 Vol. 94, 293.5.4-8.

11. A Sanskrit version of the chapter has been edited by Conze and Iida in *Mélanges d'Indianisme a la Mémoire de Louis Renou* (Paris: Éditions E. de Boccard, 1968), pp. 229-242. This edition has been translated into English by Conze in his *Large Sūtra on Perfect Wisdom* (Berkeley: University of California Press, 1975), pp. 644-652. For a Tibetan study of the three types of form, see Tsong-kha-pa, *Legs bshad snying po* (Sarnath: Pleasure of Elegant Sayings Press, 1973), pp. 215-225. For a translation of Tsong-kha-pa's text, see Robert A. F. Thurman, *Tsong-khapa's Speech of Gold in the Essence of True Eloquence* (Princeton: Princeton University Press, 1984). The section under discussion occurs at pp. 355-363.

12. For the Sanskrit, see Conze and Iida, eds., p. 238.

13. See Conze and Iida, eds., p. 238; Tsong-kha-pa, pp. 220-221.

14. See Conze and Iida, eds., p. 238; Tsong-kha-pa, p. 221.

15. See Conze and Iida, eds., p. 238; Tsong-kha-pa, p. 222.

16. P 5220, Vol. 94, 293.5.8-294.3.1.

17. See Ye-shes-rgyal-mtshan, *Sems dang sems byung gi tshul gsal bar ston pa blo gsal mgul rgyan* in *Collected Works of Tshe-mchog-gliṅ yoṅ-'dzin ye-ses-rgyal-mtshan* 16 (New Delhi: Tibet House, 1974), 14.5.

18. These points are made by Vasubandhu at *Abhidharmakośa* I. 21 and its autocommentary. See P. Pradhan, ed., *Abhidharmakośabhāṣyaṃ of Vasubandhu*, p. 14.

19. Oral commentary of Yeshe Thupten. See Chapter 2, note 12.

20. P 5220, Vol. 94, 294.3.1-294.4.5. The comparison of the five aggregates with the ball of foam and so forth appears in the *Saṃyutta Nikāya* III, 141-2 and a Sanskrit version appears in the *Prasannapadā*. See Louis de la Vallée Poussin, ed., *Mūlamadhyamakakārikās (Mādhyamika sūtras) de Nāgārjuna avec la Prasannapadā Commentaire de Candrakīrti*, Bibliotheca Buddhica IV (Osnabruck: Biblio Verlag, 1970), p. 41. The verse is also quoted in the *Bodhicittavivaraṇa* (12-13). The similes cited here differ from these other versions in that here compositional factors are compared to the stalk of a lotus whereas elsewhere they are compared to a plantain tree. For a discussion of various Mādhyamika interpretations of this line, see Donald S. Lopez, Jr., "Do Śrāvakas Understand Emptiness?", *Journal of Indian Philosophy*, Fall, 1987.

21. P 5219, Vol. 94, 288.5.4-289.1.1.

22. P 5217, Vol. 94, 281.1.8-281.3.5.

23. Cited by Vimalamitra at P 5217, Vol. 94, 281.1.4-5.

24. For the Sanskrit, see P. L. Vaidya, ed. *Madhyamakaśāstra of Nāgārjuna*, Buddhist Sanskrit Texts 10 (Darbhanga, India: Mithila Institute, 1960), p. 300.

25. P 5217, Vol. 94, 280.5.7-282.1.7.

26. For the edited Tibetan text, see Étienne Lamotte, ed. and trans., *Saṃdhinirmocana Sūtra: L'Explication des Mystères* (Paris: Adrien Maisonneuve, 1935), pp. 43-45.

27. lCang-skya-rol-pa'i-rdo-rje, pp. 352-353.

28. For the Tibetan, see Lamotte, ed. and trans., pp. 43-45.

29. lCang-skya-rol-ba'i rdo-rje, p. 353.

30. For the Tibetan, see Lamotte, ed. and trans., p. 47.

31. Prajñāmokṣa, in his commentary on Atīśa's *Madhyamakopadeśa*, provides a similar list of three consequences of the two truths being different and three consequences of their being the same. See P 5327.

32. *Bodhicittavivaraṇa*, 67-68. For an edition of the Tibetan text, and an English translation, see Christian Lindtner, *Nāgārjuniana: Studies in the Writings and Philosophy of Nāgārjuna* (Copenhagen: Akademisk Forlag, 1982), pp. 204-5.

33. The Sanskrit is: *na rūpaṃ śūnyatā yuktā parasparavirodhataḥ* | *nīrūpā śūnyatā nāmarūpam ākārasaṅgataṃ* || *ity ekatvavikalpasya bāddhā nānātvakalpanaṃ* | *ruṇaddhi nānyat tad rūpaṃ śūnyatāyāḥ kathaṃcana* || For Sanskrit and Tibetan editions of the *Prajñāpāramitāpiṇḍārtha* and an English translation, see Giuseppe Tucci, "Minor Sanskrit Texts of the Prajñāpāramitā. I. The Prajñā-pāramitā-piṇḍārtha of Diṅnāga", *Journal of the Royal Asiatic Society*, April 1947, pp. 53-75.

34. P 5208, Vol. 94, 9.2.3-9.3.6.

35. The most detailed discussions of the relationship of the two truths in dGe-lugs-pa literature appear to be 'Jam-dbyangs-bzhad-pa's *dbU ma 'jug pa'i mtha' dpyod lung rigs gter mdzod zab don kun gsal skal bzang 'jug ngogs* (Buxadour: Gomang, 1967), 288b3-291b6 and Ngag-dbang-dpal-ldan's *Grub mtha' bzhi'i lugs kun rdzob dang don dam pa'i don rnam par bshad pa legs bshad dpyid kyi dpal mo'i glu dbyangs* (New Delhi: Guru Deva, 1972), 49a6 ff.

36. *phan tshun mi mthun par gnas pa.* See 'Jam-dbyangs-phyogs-lha-'od-zer, *Rwa stod bsdus grwa* (Dharamsala, India: Library of Tibetan Works and Archives, 1980), 46b5-6.

37. Ibid., 46b6.

38. Ibid., 46b6-47a2.

39. Ibid., 47a2-3.

40. These examples are provided in a later *bsdus grwa* text, that of Phur-bu-lcog Byams-pa-rgya-mtsho, a tutor of the thirteenth Dalai Lama. See his *Rigs lam 'bring* in *Tshad ma'i gzhung don 'byed pa'i bsdus grwa'i rnam bzhag rigs lam 'phrul gyi sde mig* (Buxa, India: 1965), 5b1.

41. Phur-bu-lcog Byam-pa-rgya-mtsho, p. 5b1-5.

42. According to 'Jam-dbyangs-bzhad-pa, both *gcig bkag pa'i tha dad* and *ngo po gcig ldog pa tha dad* can be traced back to bLo-ldan-shes-rab (1059-1109) and his followers. See *dbU ma 'jug pa'i mtha' dpyod*, 288b3.

43. 'Jam-dbyang-phyogs-lha-'od-zer cites *Pramāṇavārttika* I.40-41 as his source.

44. If one were hypothetically to read this discussion of the relationship of form and emptiness back into the sūtra, it would seem that the *Heart Sūtra*, by opting for "form is emptiness" rather than "form is not emptiness" (neither of which is literally acceptable according to the *Saṃdhinirmocana*), expresses a preference for the experience of direct perception of a Buddha in which form and emptiness do not appear differently or the experience of meditation in which form disappears in the vision of emptiness, a preference over ratiocination in which the logical problems of the identity of the two are perhaps more evident.

45. The Sanskrit says *sarvadharmāḥ śūnyatālakṣaṇā*, which can either be read as "all phenomena are endowed with the characteristic of emptiness, reading the long *ā* as a case of simple *saṃdhi* or as "all phenomena are empty, without characteristic." The former reading is reflected in the Chinese translation. All of the Indian commentators, however, adopt the latter reading, with Vimalamitra speaking of eight aspects. If the Chinese reading were followed, there would be only seven. See Tshul-'khrims-skal-bzang, *Sher snying tshig don la cung zad dpyad pa'i gdam* (New Delhi: Western Tibetan Cultural Association, 1980), pp. 48-49.

46. Tshul-'khrims-skal-bzang, p. 40.

47. P 5218, Vol. 94 286.3.5-286.4.3.

48. The one hundred phenomena are listed and briefly described in Jeffrey Hopkins, *Meditation on Emptiness* (London: Wisdom Publications, 1983), pp. 201-212. For a detailed exposition of a somewhat different list of phenomena of the pure class, see Lamotte, *Le Traité de la Grande Vertu de Sagesse*, Tome III (Louvain: Institut Orientaliste, 1949).

49. P 5220, Vol. 94 294.4.8-295.1.2.

50. The definitive studies of the *tathāgatagarbha* doctrine in Indian and

Tibetan Buddhism are David Seyfort Ruegg's, *La Théorie du Tathāgatagarbha et du Gotra* (Paris: École Française d'Extrême-Orient, 1969) and his *Le Traité du Tathāgatagarbha de Bu ston Rin chen grub* (Paris: École Française d'Extrême-Orient, 1973). See also D. Seyfort Ruegg, "The *gotra, ekayāna,* and *tathāgatagarbha* theories of the *Prajñāpāramitā* according to Dharmamitra and Abhayākaragupta" in Lewis Lancaster, ed., *Prajñāpāramitā and Related Systems* (Berkeley: Berkeley Buddhist Studies Series, 1977), pp. 283-312. For English translations of the *Uttaratantra* with Asaṅga's commentary, see Jikido Takasaki, *A Study of the Ratnagotravibhāga* (Rome: Istituto Italiano per il Medio ed Estremo Oriente, 1966) and E. Obermiller, *The Sublime Science of the Great Vehicle to Salvation, Acta Orientalia,* Vol. IX, parts ii, iii, and iv, 1931. For a survey of Japanese scholarship on the *tathāgatagarbha*, see Nakamura, *Indian Buddhism: A Survey with Bibliographical Notes* (Osaka, Japan: KUFS Publication, 1980) pp. 229-233.

51. P 5525, Vol. 108, 27.1.6-7. The first stanza also appears in *Abhisamayālaṃkāra*, V. 21.

52. See p. 35.

53. P 760 (48), Vol. 24, 260.5.4-8. For an English translation, see Alex Wayman and Hideko Wayman, trans., *The Lion's Roar of Queen Śrīmālā* (New York: Columbia University Press, 1974).

54. P 787, Vol. 30, 181.3.1-181.4.7.

55. P 787, Vol. 31, 41.1.5-7. For a French translation, see Ruegg, *Le Traité du Tathāgatagarbha de Bu ston Rin chen grub*, pp. 113-114.

56. P, 787, Vol. 30, 184.4.8-184.5.3 and 185.3. For a French translation, see Ruegg, *Le Traité du Tathāgatagarbha de Bu ston Rin chen grub*, p. 177.

57. P 5525, Vol. 108, 27.2.2-4.

58. P 5526, Vol. 108, 39.3.3-39.4.1.

59. P 5226, Vol. 108, 39.5.2-6.

60. Cited by Candrakīrti in the sixth chapter of the *Madhyamakāvatāra.* See Louis de la Vallée Poussin, ed. *Madhyamakāvatāra par Candrakīrti*, Biblioteca Buddica IX (Osnabruck: Biblio Verlag, 1970), p. 197.

61. The Tibetan reads *"dri ma dang bral ba"* but it is clear from Vimalamitra's discussion that it should be *"dri ma med pa dang bral ba."*

62. See Kamalaśīla, *Bhāvanākrama I* Derge edition of Tibetan tripiṭaka, (Tokyo, 1978), Toh. 3915, folio 41a2-3.

63. P 5217, Vol. 94, 282.1.8-282.4.1.

64. See P. Pradhan, ed., *Abhidharmakośabhāṣyaṃ of Vasubandhu*, pp. 449-451.

65. Ibid., p. 449.

66. Cited by Gung-thang dKon-mchog-bstan-pa'i-sgron-me in his *rNam thar sgo gsum gyi rnam par bzhag pa legs bshad rgya mtsho rba rlabs* (Sarnath: Pleasure of Elegant Sayings Press, 1964), p. 2.

67. Ibid., p. 1.

68. Ibid., pp. 1, 2.

69. P 5521, Vol. 108, 16.2.8.

70. See Gung-thang dKon-mchog-bstan-pa'i-sgron-me, p. 5.

71. P 5521, Vol. 108, 16.3.1-2.

72. Gung-thang dKon-mchog-bstan-pa'i-sgron-me, p. 6.

73. Haribhadra, *Abhisamayālaṃkāravṛttiḥ Sphuṭārthā*, p. 82.

74. Gung-thang dKon-mchog-bstan-pa'i-sgron-me, p. 5.

75. Cited by Poussin, *L'Abhidharmakośa de Vasubandhu*, Tome 5, p. 184, note 1. In this note, Poussin also provides references to the three doors of liberation in the Pali canon.

76. P 5222, Vol. 94, 299.1.1-4.

Chapter 6: The Negations and Enlightenment

1. Pali sources for the doctrine of dependent arising include the *Saṃyutta Nikāya* II, 1-132 and the *Mahānidāna Suttānta*. Among the Mahāyāna sūtras, perhaps the most extensive treatment is found in the *Śālistambhasūtra*. For scholastic presentations of the process of dependent arising, see the third chapter of Vasubandhu's *Abhidharmakośabhāśya*, Buddhaghosa's *Visuddhimagga*, VII.7-22 and XVII 288-344, the first chapter of Asaṅga's *Abhidharmasamuccaya*, and the *Pratītyasamutpādahṛdayakārikā*, attributed to Nāgārjuna. In *dGe-lugs-pa* literature, the topic of the twelvefold dependent arising is treated in Tsong-kha-pa's *Byang chub lam rim chen mo*, monastic textbooks on the fifth chapter of Maitreya's *Abhisamayālaṃkāra*, Se-ra rJe-btsun-pa's *rTen 'brel spyi don* and sGo-mang Ngag-dbang-bkra-shis's *Zab mo rten jing 'brel bar 'byung ba'i mtha' dpyod*.

2. Oral commentary of Yeshe Thupten. See Chapter 2, note 12.

3. See U. Wogihara, ed., *Abhisamayālaṃkārāloka*, pp. 381-382.

4. This appears in the commentary on *Abhidharmakośa*, VI.2. See P. Pradhan, ed., *The Abhidharmakośabhāṣyam of Vasubandhu*, p. 328. See also Louis de la Vallée Poussin, "Vyādhisūtra on the Four Āryasatyas," *Journal of the Royal Asiatic Society* (1903), pp. 578-580.

5. 'Jam-dbyangs-dga'-ba'i-blo-gros, *Shes rab snying po'i tikka* (modern

blockprint), 4a6-4b3.

6. P 5217, Vol. 94, 282.4.2-3.

7. 'Jam-dbyangs-dga'-ba'i-blo-gros, 5b3-6.

8. P 5218, Vol. 94, 286.4.3-287.1.4.

9. P 5220, Vol. 94, 295.1.2-6.

10. P 5220, Vol. 94, 295.1.6-295.2.3.

11. See Poussin, ed., *Mūlamadhyamikakārikās*, p. 505.

12. See lCang-skya-rol-pa'i-rdo-rje, pp. 318-19.

13. P 5220, Vol. 94, 295.2.3-295.3.1.

14. P 5220, Vol. 94, 295.3.1-295.4.3.

15. P 5220, Vol. 94, 295.4.3-8.

16. P 5220, Vol. 94, 295.5.1-4.

17. P 5220, Vol. 94, 295.5.4-6.

18. The twenty-two and the eleven are listed by Vimalamitra at P 5217, Vol. 94, 283.2.5-283.3.8. They also appear in the *Saṃdhinirmocana*. See Lamotte, ed., pp. 127-129.

19. P 5219, Vol. 94, 290.2.8-290.5.1.

Chapter 7: The Mantra

1. D. T. Suzuki sees the inclusion of the mantra as a sign of the relative lateness of the text. In his somewhat desultory essay on the *Heart Sūtra*, Suzuki reveals a certain contempt for mantras in general when he writes of the longer Perfection of Wisdom sūtras. "The Prajñāpāramitā literature is singularly free from the intrusion of magical formulas known as Vidyā, Mantram, or Dhāraṇī." See D. T. Suzuki, *Essays in Zen Buddhism*, Third Series (London: Rider, 1985), p. 227. Nonetheless, he is able to account for the mantra of the *Heart Sūtra* as a kind of koan: "Utterly exhausted intellectually and emotionally, he [Avalokiteśvara] made a final leap. The last tie which held him to the world of relativity and 'self-power' completely snapped. He found himself on the other shore. Overwhelmed with his feelings, he could only keep uttering the *'Gate!'"* (pp. 235-236).

Conze argues that the mantra is not an interpolation. He has discovered a parallel between the passage in the *Heart Sūtra*, "The mantra of the perfection of wisdom is the mantra of great knowledge, the unsurpassed mantra, the mantra equal to the unequaled" and a passage in the *Śatasāhasrikā* which refers to the perfection of wisdom as "this great knowledge, this unsurpassed knowledge, this knowledge equal to the unequalled." (*mahāvidyeyaṃ bhagavan yad uta prajñāpāramitā. anuttareyaṃ vidyā bhagavan yad uta prajñāpāramitā. asamasameyaṃ vidyā bhagavan yad uta prajñāpāramitā.*) He does not explain how the presence of this parallel suggests that the mantra itself is not an interpolation. See Edward Conze, *Thirty Years of Buddhist Studies* (Columbia, S. C.: University of South Carolina Press, 1968), pp. 164-165.

2. The text reads *phyi* rather than *spyi.*

3. P 5220, Vol. 94, 296.2.1-296.3.1. The order of Praśāstrasena's statement has been adjusted to accord with the order of the sūtra.

4. P 5218, Vol. 94, 287.5.2-6.

5. P 5223, Vol. 94, 303.5.4-7.

6. This reading of the mantra appears to be derived from Kamalaśīla. See P 5221, Vol. 96, 297.3.1. This interpretation of the mantra is provided by both bsTan-dar-lha-ram-pa and Gung-thang in the commentaries translated in Part II.

7. For the Sanskrit, see S. Bagchi, ed., *Guhyasamāja Tantra*, Buddhist Sanskrit texts No. 9 (Darbhanga, India: Mithila Institute, 1965), p. 126.

8. P 5217, Vol. 94, 284.4.1-3.

9. P 5222, Vol. 96, 298.2.6-298.3.3.

10. The text reads *bstan* rather than *brten.*

11. P 5219, Vol. 94, 290.5.7-291.1.3.

12. P 5219, Vol. 94, 291.3.6-292.4.3.

13. P 4530, Vol. 81, 115.2.5-115.2.6. It should be noted that Tripiṭakamāla's view is rejected by Tsong-kha-pa in his *sNgags rim chen mo.* For an English translation, see Tsong-ka-pa, *Tantra in Tibet,* trans. by Jeffrey Hopkins (London: Allen and Unwin, 1977), pp. 145-150.

14. See Tsong-ka-pa, *Tantra in Tibet*, pp. 114-116.

15. The former is the *Prajñāpāramitāhṛdayasādhana* (P 3464, Vol. 77, 29.5.1-30.4.8.), the author of which is given as *kLu-sgrub-snying-po* (Nāgārjunagarbha). The latter is the *Prajñāpāramitāhṛdayasādhananāma* (P 3465, Vol. 77, 30.4.8-31.2.4.), ascribed to Dārikapa. In his *rGyud sde spyi'i ram*, mKhas-grub-rje declares both of these texts to be spurious. See F. D. Lessing and A. Wayman, *Introduction to the Buddhist Tantric Systems* (Delhi: Motilal Banarsidass, 1978), p. 108. In his commentary on the *Heart Sūtra* mantra (folio 704.4-5), Gung-thang mentions a *sādhana* written by Ānandagarbha, the title of which he does not provide, that aligns the *Heart Sūtra* with Yoga Tantra. His referent is unclear since Ānandagarbha's *Prajñāpāramitāmaṇḍalopāyika* (P 3468) makes no explicit reference to the *Heart Sūtra* or its mantra. bsTan-dar-hla-ram-pa, in his commentary on the *Heart Sūtra* (320.4), refers

to a tantric commentary on the sūtra by Śrīsiṃha, presumably Toh. 4353.

16. P 3464, Vol. 77, 30.4.1-2.

17. According to mKhas-grub-rje, these four syllables mean "Be summoned, enter, become fused with, be pleased." See Tenzin Gyatso, *The Kālachakra Tantra*, trans. and ed. by Jeffrey Hopkins (London: Wisdom Press, 1985), p. 448. According to the *Sādhanamālā*, this mantra is a condensation of a longer mantra by which the wisdom beings are forcibly drawn in and bound to the maṇḍala. See Alex Wayman, *Yoga of the Guhyasamājatantra* (Delhi: Motilal Banarsidass, 1977), p. 133.

18. The meaning of the text is not clear here. Ananta (Limitless) is certainly Amitābha (Boundless Light). Jinatva (*rgyal ba nyid*) then becomes Amoghasiddhi by a process of elimination, supported also by a statement in the *sādhana* ascribed to Nāgārjuna that when the residents of the *Heart Sūtra* maṇḍala receive initiation, Śāriputra has Jinatva on the crown of his head. See P 3464, Vol. 77, 30.3.7. It is also unclear whether the term *mtshan*, which I have translated as "with the names . . ." may instead mean "mark," perhaps referring to the residents of the maṇḍala each being marked on the top of the head with the seal of one of the five Buddha families.

19. See Tsong-ka-pa, *Yoga of Tibet*, trans. by Jeffrey Hopkins (London: Allen and Unwin, 1981), pp. 185-186.

20. See, for example, the comments of the current Dalai Lama in Tsong-ka-pa, *Yoga of Tibet*, pp. 26-27.

21. The more common listing is of sixteen emptinesses, which appear in the *Madhyāntavibhāga* (see Pandeya, ed., p. 41), Dignāga's *Prajñāpāramitāpiṇḍārtha* 8-18 (see Tucci, ed., pp. 56-57, 60-61), and Candrakīrti's *Madhyamakāvatāra* VI.180-218 (See Poussin, ed., pp. 302-338). Candrakīrti also adds a second list of four emptinesses (VI.219-223), two of which, the emptiness of things and the emptiness of non-things, are added to make a list of eighteen emptinesses. A list of eighteen emptinesses occurs in the *Saṃdhinirmocana*, VIII.109 (See Étienne Lamotte, ed. and trans., pp. 108-110). For a list in English of the eighteen emptinesses, see Jeffrey Hopkins, *Meditation on Emptiness*, pp. 204-205. The most complete exposition of the eighteen emptinesses occurs in Lamotte, *Le Traité*, Tome IV, pp. 2027-2151.

22. Gung-thang, 704.4-705.2.

Chapter 8: The Epilogue

1. P 5218, Vol. 94, 287.5.1-2.

2. P 5220, Vol. 94, 296.3.1-3.

3. P 5219, Vol. 94, 291.5.1-2.

4. P 5218, Vol. 94, 285.1.1-2.

5. P 5217, Vol. 94, 285.1.3-7.

Chapter 9: The Structure of the Sūtra and The Structure of the Path

1. For an explanation of the term *gleng bslang* see P 5220, Vol. 94, 292.5.1-2.

2. For a list of the commentaries, see E. Obermiller, "The Doctrine of Prajñā-pāramitā as exposed in the *Abhisamayālaṃkāra* of Maitreya," pp. 9-11.

3. P 5222, Vol. 94, 297.3-6-297.4.2.

4. This summary of the path is drawn from the eighteenth century Tibetan scholar dKon-mchog-'jigs-med-dbang-po's *Sa lam gyi rnam bzhag theg gsum mdzes rgyan* (Buxadour, India: sGo-mang College, 1965). This work is, in turn, based on Indian texts such as Candrakīrti's *Madhyamakāvatāra*, Haribhadra's commentaries on the *Abhisamayālaṃkāra*, and Kamalaśīla's *Bhāvanākrama*.

5. See Étienne Lamotte, ed. and trans., *Saṃdhinirmocana Sūtra, L'Explication des Mystères* (Paris: Adrien Maisonneuve, 1935), pp. 88, 115.

6. Ibid., p. 88.

7. The preceding discussion is a paraphrase of P 5222, Vol. 94, 298.3.6-298.5.6.

8. *Saṃdhinirmocana*, p. 115. See also Vimalamitra's gloss, P 5217, Vol. 94, 280.4.5-280.5.6.

9. P 5222, Vol. 96, 299.2.7-8. See also Gung-thang, 708.4-711.4.

10. This description is drawn from the *Abhidharmakośabhāṣya*. See P. Pradhan, ed., *Abhidharmakośabhāṣyam of Vasubandhu*, pp. 350-353.

11. P 5223, Vol. 94, 302.4.5-302.5.5.

Chapter 10: Commentary on the *Heart Sūtra*, Jewel Light, Illuminating the Meaning

1. These tentative conversions from the Tibetan sexegenary lunar calendar to Western dates are derived from a chart provided by the modern Tibetan historian Khetsun Sangpo in his *Biographical Dictionary of Tibet and Tibetan Buddhism*, Vol. 1 (Dharamsala, India: Library of Tibetan Works and Archives, 1973). The Chinese date of 1027 is provided by Roerich in his translation of the *Blue Annals* (Delhi: Motilal Banarsidass, 1979) p. 18. Whether my conversion of the dates is correct, they at least suffice in illustrating the author's point that there is little agreement among Tibetan scholars concerning the date of the Buddha's birth.

2. The abbreviated title of the *Pañcaviṃśatisāhasrikā* in Tibetan is *nyi khri* (20,000), leading some to think that the sūtra has 20,000 rather than 25,000 stanzas.

3. For a discussion of this reasoning, see Jeffrey Hopkins, *Meditation on*

Emptiness (London: Wisdom Publications, 1983), pp. 175-196.

4. For a discussion of the use of basal subjects and mere subjects in syllogisms, see Donald S. Lopez, Jr., *A Study of Svātantrika* (Ithaca, New York: Snow Lion Publications, 1987), pp. 174-179.

Chapter 11: An Explanation of the *Heart Sūtra* Mantra, Illuminating the Hidden Meaning

1. The "purpose, etc." refer to four factors that must be determined for any sūtra or *śāstra*. The *purpose* (*dgos pa*) is the immediate *raison d'etre* of the text, in the case of the Perfection of Wisdom sūtras, to set forth the doctrine of emptiness. The *subject matter* (*brjod bya*) is topic of the text. The *essential purpose* (*nying dgos*) is the final goal to which the text is directed, in the case of the Perfection of Wisdom, the achievement of Buddhahood. The *relationship* (*'brel ba*) is the connections among the purpose, subject matter, and the essential purpose. See 'Jam-dbyangs-bzhad-pa, *sKabs dang po'i mtha' dbyod* (Sarnath: Mongolian Lama Guru Deva, 1965), p. 10. See also Th. Stcherbatsky, *Buddhist Logic*, Vol. 2 (New York: Dover Publications, 1962), p. 1, notes 2 and 3.

2. This stanza does not appear in Christian Lindtner's edition of the *Bodhicittavivaraṇa*, which appears in his *Nagarjuniana*.

3. The forward order of the dependent arising of the afflicted is the most common delineation of the twelve links: ignorance produces action, action produces consciousness, and so forth. The reverse order of the afflicted begins with the twelfth link and proceeds backwards: aging and death are produced from birth, birth is produced from existence, and so forth. The forward order of the dependent arising of the pure is that through the cessation of ignorance, action ceases, through the cessation of action, consciousness ceases, and so forth. The reverse order of the pure is that aging and death cease through the cessation of birth, birth ceases through the cessation of existence, and so forth.

4. See page 40.

5. The seven cause and effect precepts are (1) recognizing all sentient beings as having been one's mother, (2) being aware of their kindness, (3) having the wish to repay that kindness, (4) love, (5) compassion, (6) the determination to free all beings from suffering, and (7) the aspiration to become a Buddha. These seven were derived by Tsong-kha-pa in his *Lam rim chen mo* from a statement by Atīśa in the *Bodhimārgapradīpapañjikā*, in commentary on the tenth stanza of his *Bodhipathapradīpa*.

6. This technique for developing aspiration to enlightenment is set forth in Śāntideva's *Bodhicaryāvatāra* VIII.89-186.

7. Beings of small capacity, according to Atīśa in the third stanza of the *Bodhipathapradīpa*, are those who merely seek happiness within *saṃsāra* and are concerned only for themselves. Beings of intermediate capacity seek

liberation from rebirth, whereas those of superior capacity seek to become Buddhas out of compassion for others.

8. The four applications are four of the eight major categories set forth in Maitreya's *Abhisamayālaṃkāra.* They are complete application (*sarvakaprayoga*), peak application (*mūrdhaprayoga*), serial application (*anupurvikaprayoga*), and momentary application (*ekakṣaṇaprayoga*). Together they encompass all the practices of Bodhisattvas. The most complete discussions of the four applications in English are found in E. Obermiller's "Doctrine of Prajñāpāramitā as Exposed in the *Abhisamayālaṃkāra* of Maitreya," *Acta Orientalia,* 11 (1932), pp. 1-133, 334-354 and Obermiller's *Analysis of the Abhisamayālaṃkāra* (London: Luzac and Co., 1933).

9. "According with a portion of liberation" (*mokṣabhāgīya*) is a synonym of the path of accumulation (*saṃbhāramārga*), the first of the five paths to enlightenment.

10. The three entanglements (*prayojana*) are the view of the transitory collection (*satkāyadṛṣṭi*) as real "I" and "mine," holding [bad] ethics and modes of behavior to be supreme (*śīlavrataparāmarśa*), and doubt (*vicikitsā*). These are described in *Abhidharmakośa* V.44 and the autocommentary. See P. Pradhan, *Abhidharmakośabhāṣyam of Vasubandhu* (Patna; Jayaswal Research Institute, 1975), pp. 310-311.

11. For the Sanskrit, see P. Pradhan, *Abhidharmakośabhāṣyam of Vasubandhu* (Patna: Jayaswal Research Institute, 1975), p. 310.

12. According to 'Jam-dbyangs-bzhad-pa, a perfection of wisdom which is the accomplished deed (*las sgrub kyi phar phyin*) is a wisdom that has gone beyond the coarse and subtle saṃsāras. It is synonymous with a fruition perfection of wisdom, which is the omniscience of a Buddha. See his *sKabs dang poi' mtha' dpyod* (Sarnath: Mongolian Lama Guru Deva, 1965), p. 226.

13. See 'Jam-dbyangs-bzhad-pa, *sKabs dang bo'i mtha' dpyod*, pp. 323-324.

14. The four practices are achievement through armor (*sannāhapratipatti*), which is the practice of the thirty-six combinations of the six perfections (the giving of giving, the giving of ethics, and so forth); achievement through entry (*prasthānapratipatti*) involves Mahāyāna practices that often involve entry into meditative states; achievement through the collections (*saṃbhārapratipatti*) involves the Bodhisattva's collection of various practices for the sake of achieving Buddhahood; and emergent achievement (*niryāṇapratipatti*), the practices of Bodhisattvas on the seventh, eighth, and ninth stages which cause him or her to emerge into Buddhahood. The four practices are set forth in the *Abhisamayālaṃkāra*, I. 43-47, 73.

15. *Abhidharmakośa*, VI.67ab.

16. I have not been able to find textual reference for these three terms. According to Lati Rimpoche, the obstructions of attachment (*chags sgrib*) are

the afflictive obstructions (*kleśāvaraṇa*), the impedimentary obstructions (*thogs sgrib*) are the obstructions to omniscience (*jñeyāvaraṇa*), and the obstructions of inferiority are those attitudes that prevent an individual from resolving to undertake the Bodhisattva path.

17. The three greatnesses (*mahāttva*) are mentioned at *Abhisamayālaṃkāra*, I.42.

18. For a detailed exposition of these concentrations, see Tsong-ka-pa, *Yoga of Tibet*, trans. by Jeffrey Hopkins (London: Allen and Unwin, 1981), pp. 103-171.

19. "Final explanation" or "final meaning" (*kolikārtha*) is the fourth of the four modes of explanation, which together constitute the fourth of the seven ornaments set forth by Candrakīrti in his *Pradīpodyotana*. The first three modes of explanation are (1) the meaning of the letters (*akṣarārtha*), (2) the general meaning (*samastaṅgārtha*), the (3) the hidden meaning (*garbhyārtha*). According to Tsong-kha-pa, the "final meaning" is the meaning derived through interpretation in terms of the final two stages of the stage of completion (*sampannakrama*) of Highest Yoga Tantra. The four modes of explanation are discussed by Tsong-kha-pa in his *sGron gsal mchan 'grel.* See Tsong-kha-pa, *rGyud thams cad kyi rgyal po dpal gsang ba 'dus pa'i rgya cher bshad pa sgron ma gsal ba'i tshig don ji bzhin 'byed pa'i mchan gyi yan 'grel* in *The Collected Works of the Incomparable Lord Tsong-kha-pa bLo-bzang-grags-pa*, Vol. 4 (nga) (New Delhi: Mongolian Lama Guru Deva, 1978), 10b5ff. See also E. Steinkellner, "Remarks on Tantristic Hermeneutics," in L. Ligeti, ed., *Proceedings of the Csoma de Koros Symposium* (Budapest, 1978), pp. 445-458 and M. Broido, "*bshad thabs:* Some Tibetan Methods of Explaining the Tantras," in E. Steinkellner and H. Tauscher, eds., *Contribution on Tibetan and Buddhist Religion and Philosophy*, Proceedings of the Csoma de Koros Symposium, Vienna, 1981, Vol. 2 (Vienna, 1983), pp. 15-45.

20. Cited by Tsong-kha-pa in his *Legs bshad snying po* (Sarnath: Pleasure of Elegant Sayings Press), p. 70. For the Sanskrit, see N. Dutt, *Bodhisattvabhūmi* (Patna: Jayaswal Institute, 1966), p. 33.

21. See Chapter 11, note 19.

22. See *Abhisamayālaṃkāra* I.48-70.

Selected Bibliography

Abbreviations

P: *Tibetan Tripiṭaka* (Tokyo-Kyoto: Tibetan Tripitaka Research Foundation, 1956).

Toh: *A Complete Catalogue of the Tohoku University Collection of Tibetan Works on Buddhism*, ed. by Yensho Kanakura (Sendai, Japan, 1934 and 1953).

Indian Works

Sūtras are listed alphabetically by title, with the prefixes *ārya* and *śrī* removed. *Śāstras* are listed alphabetically by the name of the traditionally ascribed author.

Asaṅga. *Mahāyānasaṃgraha*; P 5549. Tibetan edition by É. Lamotte, *La Somme du Grand Véhicûle d'Asaṅga* (*Mahāyānasaṃgraha*), vol. 2. Louvain: Institut Orientaliste, 1973.

Asaṅga. *Mahāyānottaratantraśāstravyākhyā*; P 5526.

Aṣṭasāhasrikāprajñāpāramitāsūtra; P 734. Sanskrit edition by P. Vaidya, *Aṣṭasāhasrikā-Prajñāpāramitā*. Darbhanga: Mithila Institute, 1960.

Atīśa. *Bodhimārgapradīpapañjikā*; P 5345. Translation by R. Sherburne, *A Lamp for the Path and Commentary*. London: Allen and Unwin, 1983.

———. *Prajñāhṛdayaṭīkā*; P 5222.

Bhagavatīprajñāpāramitāhṛdayasūtra; P 160. Sanskrit edition by Edward Conze in *Thirty Years of Buddhist Studies*. Columbia: University of South Carolina Press, 1968, pp. 149-154. Translation by Edward Conze in *Buddhist Wisdom Books*. New York: Harper and Row, 1972.

Bhāvaviveka. *Madhyamakahṛdayavṛttitarkajvālā*; P 5256.

Candrakīrti. *Madhyamakāvatāra*; P 5261, P 5262. Tibetan edition by Louis de la Vallée Poussin, *Madhyamakāvatāra par Candrakīrti*. Osnabruck: Biblio Verlag, 1970. Partial translations by J. Hopkins in *Compassion in Tibetan Buddhism*. Valois, NY: Snow Lion, 1980; Geshe Rabten, *Echoes of Voidness*. London: Wisdom Publications, 1983.

———. *Madhyamakāvatārabhāṣya*; P 5263. Partial translation by Louis de la Vallée Poussin, *Muséon* 8 (1907) pp. 249-317; 11 (1910) pp. 271-358; and 12 (1911) pp. 235-238.

———. *Mūlamadhyamakavṛttiprasannapadā*; P 5260. Sanskrit edition by Louis de la Vallée Poussin, *Mūlamadhyamakakārikās (Mādhyamikasūtras) de Nāgārjuna avec la Prasannapadā Commentaire de Candrakīrti*. Osnabruck: Biblio Verlag, 1970. Partial translations by J. May, *Candrakīrti Prasannapadā Madhyamakavṛtti*. Paris: Adrien Maisonneuve, 1959; also J. W. De Jong, *Cinq Chapitres de la Prasannapadā*. Paris: Paul Geuthner, 1949; M. Sprung, *Lucid Exposition of the Middle Way*. London: Routledge, 1979.

———. *Triśaraṇasaptati*; P 5478.

Dārikapa, *Prajñāpāramitāhṛdayasādhananāma*; P 3465.

Dignāga. *Prajñāpāramitāsaṃgrahakārikā*, also known as *Prajñāpāramitāpiṇḍārtha*; P 5207. Sanskrit and Tibetan editions and English translation by G. Tucci, "Minor Sanskrit Texts on the Prajñāpāramitā: The Prajñāpāramitā-piṇḍārtha of Diṅnāga." *Journal of the Royal Asiatic Society* (1947), pp. 53-75.

Guhyasamāja Tantra; P 81. Sanskrit edition by S. Bagchi, Darbhanga India: Mithila Institute, 1965.

Haribhadra. *Abhisamayālaṃkāranāmaprajñāpāramitopadeśaśāstra-vṛtti*, also known as *Abhisamayālaṃkāravṛtti-Sphuṭārtha*; P 5191. Tibetan and reconstructed Sanskrit edition by R. S. Tripathi, *Abhisamayālaṃkāravṛtti-Sphuṭārtha*. Biblioteca Indo-Tibetica 2. Varanasi: 1977.

———. *Aṣṭasāhasrikāprajñāpāramitāvyākhyānābhisamayālaṃkārāloka*; P 5192. Sanskrit edition by U. Wogihara, *Abhisamayālaṃkarāloka Prajñāpāramitāvyākhyā*. Tokyo: The Toyo Bunko, 1973.

Jñānamitra. *Prajñāpāramitāhṛdayavyākhyā*; P 5218.

Kamalaśīla. *Bhāvanākrama*; Toh. 3915.

———. *Prajñāpāramitāhṛdayanāmaṭīkā*; P 5221.

Laṅkāvatārasūtra; P 775. Translation by D. T. Suzuki, *The Laṅkāvatāra Sūtra*. London: Routledge and Kegan Paul, 1932.

Mahāparinirvāṇasūtra; P 787.

Maitreyanātha. *Abhisamayālaṃkāra*; P 5184. Sanskrit and Tibetan editions by Th. Stcherbatsky and E. Obermiller, *Abhisamayālaṃkāra-Prajñāpāramitā-Upadeśa-Śāstra*. Osnabruck: Biblio Verlag, 1970. Translation by E. Conze, *Abhisamayālaṃkāra*. Serie Orientale Roma VI. Rome: Is.M.E.O., July 1954.

———. *Madhyāntavibhāga*; P 5522. Sanskrit edition by R. Pandeya, *Madhyānta-Vibhāga-Śāstra*. Delhi: Motilal Banarsidass, 1971.

———. *Mahāyānasūtrālaṃkārakārikā*; P 5521. Sanskrit edition by S. Bagchi, *Mahāyāna-Sūtrālaṃkāra of Asaṅga*. Darbhanga: Mithila Institute, 1970. Sanskrit edition and French translation by S. Levi, *Mahāyāna-Sūtrālaṃkāra*. Paris, 1907.

———. *Mahāyānottaratantraśāstra*, also known as *Ratnagotravibhāga*, also known as *Uttaratantra*; P 5525. Sanskrit edition by E. H. Johnston, *Ratnagotravibhāga-Mahāyānottaratantraśāstra*. Patna: Jayaswal Institute, 1950. Translation by J. Takasaki, *A Study of the Ratnagotra-vibhāga*. Rome: Istituto Italiano per il Medio Estremo Oriente, 1966. Translation by E. Obermiller, *Uttaratantra or Ratnagotravibhāga*. Heidelberg: *Acta Orientalia*, 1931.

Maitreyaparipṛcchā. Sanskrit edition by E. Conze and S. Iida in *Mélanges d'Indianisme a là Mémoire de Louis Renou*, pp. 229-242. Paris: Editions E. de Boccard, 1968.

Nāgārjuna. *Bodhicittavivaraṇa*; P 2665, P 2666. Tibetan edition and translation by C. Lindtner in *Nagarjuniana*. Copenhagen: Akademisk Forlag, 1982.

———. *Madhyamakaśāstra*, also known as *Prajñānāmamūlamadhyamaka-kārikā*; P 5224. Sanskrit edition by Louis de la Vallée Poussin, *Mūla-madhyamakakārikās (Mādhyamikasūtras) de Nāgārjuna avec la Prasannapadā Commentaire de Candrakīrti*. Osnabruck: Biblio Verlag, 1970. Translations by F. J. Streng in *Emptiness: A Study in Religious Meaning* (Nashville and New York: Abingdon Press, 1967). Sanskrit edition and translation by Kenneth Inada, *Mūlamadhyamakakārikā*. Tokyo: Hokuseido Press, 1970. Sanskrit edition and translation by D. Kalupahana, *Nāgārjuna: Philosophy of the Middle Way*. Albany: State University of New York Press, 1986.

———. *Rājaparikathāratnāvalī*; P 5658. Partial Sanskrit edition by P. L. Vaidya in *Madhyamakaśāstra of Nāgārjuna*. Darbhanga: Mithila Institute, 1960, pp. 296-310. Translation by J. Hopkins and Lati Rimpoche in *The Precious Garland and the Song of the Four Mindfulnesses*. London: Allen and Unwin, 1975.

———. *Yuktiṣaṣṭikākārikā*; P 5225. Tibetan edition, partial Sanskrit edition, and translation by C. Lindtner in *Nagarjuniana*. Copenhagen: Akademisk Forlag, 1982.

Nāgārjunagarbha / Nāgārjuna. *Prajñāpāramitāhṛdayasādhana*; P 3464.

Prajñāmokṣa. *Madhyamakopadeśavṛtti*; P 5327.

Praśāstrasena. *Prajñāpāramitāhṛdayaṭīkā*; P 5220. Partial translation by E. Conze, "Praśāstrasena's *Ārya-Prajñāpāramitā-Hṛdaya-Ṭīkā*." In *Buddhist Studies in Honour of I. B. Horner*, pp. 51-62. Edited by

L. Cousins, et al. Dordrecht: D. Reidel, 1974.

Saṃdhinirmocanasūtra; P 774. Tibetan edition and translation by Étienne Lamotte, *Saṃdhinirmocana-sūtra: L'Explication des Mystères.* Paris: Adrien Maissoneuve, 1935.

Sañcayagāthāprajñāpāramitāsūtra; P 735. Sanskrit edition by A. Yuyama, *Prajñāpāramitāratnaguṇasaṃcayagāthā.* Cambridge, 1976.

Śāntideva. *Śikṣāsamuccayakārikā* P 5336; Sanskrit edition by Cecil Bendall, *Çikshāsamuccaya*, Indo-Iranian Reprints 1. The Hague: Mouton and Co., 1957.

———. *Bodhicaryāvatāra*, P 5272; Sanskrit edition by P. L. Vaidya. Darbhanga: Mithila Institute, 1960. Translation from the Tibetan by Stephen Batchelor, *A Guide to the Bodhisattva's Way of Life.* Dharmsala: Library of Tibetan Works and Archives, 1979.

Śrīmahājana. *Prajñāpāramitāhṛdayārthaparijñāna*; P 5223.

Śrīmālādevīsiṃhanādasūtra; P 760.48. Translation by A. Wayman and H. Wayman. *The Lion's Roar of Queen Śrīmālā.* New York: Columbia University Press, 1974.

Tathāgatācintyaguhyanirdeśasūtra; P 760.3.

Tripiṭakamāla. *Nayatrayapradīpa*; P 4530.

Triratnadāsa. *Prajñāpāramitāsaṃgrahakārikāvivaraṇa*; P 5208.

Vajrapāṇi. *Bhagavatīprajñāpāramitāhṛdayaṭīkārthapradīpa*; P 5219.

Vasubandhu. *Abhidharmakośabhāṣya*; P 5591; Sanskrit edition by P. Pradhan, *Abhidharmakośabhāṣyam of Vasubandhu.* Patna: Jayaswal Research Institute, 1975. Translation by Louis de La Vallée Poussin, *L'Abhidharmakośa de Vasubandhu.* Bruxelles: Institut Belge des Hautes Études Chinoises, 1971.

Vimalamitra. *Prajñāpāramitāhṛdayaṭīkā*; P 5217.

Tibetan Works

Works are listed in English alphabetical order by the root letter of the first word of the author's name.

lCang-skya-rol-pa'i-rdo-rje. *Grub pa'i mtha'i rnam par bshag pa gsal bar bshad pa thub bstan lhun po'i mdzes rgyan.* Sarnath, India: Pleasure of Elegant Sayings Press, 1970.

dGe-'dun-grub. *mDzod tik thar lam gsal byed.* Sarnath: Pleasure of Elegant Sayings Press, 1973.

Gung-thang dKon-mchog-bstan-pa'i-sgron-me. *rNam thar sgo gsum gyi rnam* par bzhag pa legs bshad rgya mtsho'i rba rlabs. Varanasi: Guru Deva, 1964.

———. *Shes rab snying po'i sngags kyi rnam bshad sbas don gsal ba sgron me.* In *The Collected Works of Guṅ-thaṅ dKon-mchog-bstan-pa'i sgron-me*, Vol. 1, pp. 682-715. New Delhi: Ngawang Gelek Demo, 1971.

rGyal-tshab. *mNgon rtogs pa'i rgyan gyi rtsa ba 'grel pa dang bcas pa'i rnam bshad snying po'i rgyan.* Toh. 5433.

'Jam-dbyangs-bzhad-pa, *sKabs dang po'i mtha' dpyod.* Sarnath, India: Mongolian Lama Guru Deva, 1965.

———. *sKabs gsum pa'i mtha' dpyod.* Sarnath, India: Mongolian Lama Guru Deva, 1965.

———. *sKabs rgyad pa'i mtha' dpyod.* Sarnath, India: Mongolian Lama Guru Deva, 1966.

———. *bLo rig dang sa lam dang don bdun cu bcas.* Mundgod, India: Drepung Loseling Press, 1985.

———. *dbU ma 'jug pa'i mtha' dpyod lung rigs gter mdzod zab don kun gsal skal bzang 'jug ngogs.* Buxadour: Gomang, 1967.

'Jam-dbyang-dka'-ba'i-blo-gros. *Shes rab snying po'i tikka.* Modern block-print, no place, no date.

'Jam-dbyangs-phyogs-hla-od-zer. *Rva stod bsdus grva.* Dharamsala, India: Damchoe Sangpo, Library of Tibetan Works and Archives, 1980.

rJe-btsun-pa, *bsTan bcos mngon par rtogs pa'i rgyan 'grel pa dang bcas pa'i rnam bshad rnam pa gnyis kyi dka' ba'i gnas gsal bar byed pa legs bshad skal bzang klu dpang gi rol mtsho.* Bylakuppe, India: Serjey Dratsang, no date.

mKhas-grub-rje. *rGyud sde spyi rnam.* Edition by Lessing and Wayman in *Introduction to the Buddhist Tantrica Systems.* Delhi: Motilal Banarsidass, 1978.

Khetsun Sangpo. *Biographical Dictionary of Tibetan Buddhism*, Vol. 1. Dharmsala: Library of Tibetan Works and Archives, 1973.

dKon-mchog-'jigs-med-dbang-po. *Grub pa'i mtha'i rnam par bzhag pa rin po che'i phreng ba.* Dharmsala, India: Shes rig par khang, 1969. Translation by Geshe Sopa and J. Hopkins, *Practice and Theory of Tibetan Buddhism.* New York: Grove Press, 1976.

———. *Sa lam gyi rnam bzhag theg gsum mdzes rgyan* in *The Collected Works of dkon-mchog-'jigs-med-dbang-po*, Vol. 7. New Delhi: Ngawang Gelek Demo, 1972.

Ngag-dbang-dpal-ldan. *Grub mtha' bzhi'i lugs kyi kun rdzob dang don dam pa'i don rnam par bshad pa legs bshad dpyid kyi dpal mo'i glu dbyangs.*

New Delhi: Guru Deva, 1972.

Pan-chen bSod-nams-grags-pa. *Phar phyin spyi don/Shes rab kyi pha rol tu phyin pa'i man ngag gi bstan bcos mngon par rtogs pa'i rgyan 'grel pa dang bcas pa'i rnam bshad snying po rgyan gyi don legs par bshad pa yum don gsal ba'i sgron me.* Buxadour, India: Nang bstan shes rig 'dzin skyong slob gnyer khang, 1963.

Phur-bu-lcog Byams-pa-rgya-mtsho. *Tshad ma'i gzhung don 'byed pa'i bsdus grva'i rnam bzhag rigs lam 'phrul gyi sde mig.* Buxadour, India: n. p., 1965.

bsTan-dar-lha-ram-pa. *Shes rab snying po'i grel pa don gsal nor bu'i 'od.* In *Collected gzung 'bum of Bstan-dar Lha-ram or A-lag-sha*, Vol. 1, pp. 291-322. New Delhi: Lama Guru Deva, 1971.

Tshul-khrims-skal-bzang. *Sher snying tshig don la cung zad dbyad pa.* New Delhi: Western Tibetan Cultural Association, 1980.

Tsong-kha-pa. *Legs bshad snying po*; P 6142. Also: Sarnath, India: Pleasure of Elegant Sayings Press, 1973. Translation by R. Thurman, *Tsong-khapa's Speech of Gold in the "Essence of True Eloquence."* Princeton: Princeton University Press, 1984.

———. *Legs bshad gser gyi phreng ba*; P 6150. Also: Sarnath, India: Pleasure of Elegant Sayings Press, 1970.

———. *Lam rim chen mo*; P 6001. Also: Dharmsala, India: Shes rig par khang, 1964.

———. *dbU ma la 'jug pa'i rgya cher bshad pa dgongs pa rab gsal*; P 6143. Also: Sarnath, India: Pleasure of Elegant Sayings Press, 1973. Partial translation by J. Hopkins in *Compassion in Tibetan Buddhism.* Valois, NY: Snow Lion, 1980.

———. *rTen 'brel bstod pa*, also known as *Legs bshad snying po chung ba*; P 6016.

Ye-shes-rgyal-mtshan, *Sems dang sems byung gi tshul gsal bar ston pa blo gsal mgul rgyan* in *The Collected Works of Tsha-mchog-gliṅ-yoṅs-'dzin ye-ses-rgyal-mtshan*, Vol. 16. New Delhi: Tibet House, 1974. Translation by H. Guenther and L. Kawamura, *Mind in Buddhist Psychology.* Emeryville: Dharma Press, 1975.

Works in English and French

Atīśa. *A Lamp for the Path and Commentary.* Translated by Richard Sherburne. London: Allen and Unwin, 1983.

Bareau, A. *Récherches sur la Biographie du Buddha dans les Sūtrapiṭaka et les Vinayapiṭaka Anciens*, 3 vol. Paris: École Française d'Extrême-Orient, 1970.

Beautrix, Pierre. *Bibliographie de la Littérature Prajñāpāramitā.* Brussels: Institut Belge des Hautes Études Bouddhiques, 1971.

Bough, John. "Thus Have I Heard . . ." *Bulletin of the School of Oriental and African Studies*, Vol. XIII, Part 2 (1950).

Boyd, James W. "Symbols of Evil in Buddhism." *Journal of Asian Studies* (November 1971), pp. 63-76.

Broido, Michael. *"bshad thabs:* Some Tibetan Methods of Explaining the Tantras." In *Contributions on Tibetan and Buddhist Religion and Philosophy*, Vol. 2, pp. 15-46. Edited by Ernst Steinkellner and Helmut Tauscher. Vienna: Arbeitskreis für Tibetische und Buddhistische Studien Universität Wien, 1983.

Broughton, Jeffrey. "Early Ch'an Schools in Tibet." In *Studies in Ch'an and Hua-Yen*, pp. 1-68. Edited by Robert M. Gimello and Peter N. Gregory. Honolulu: University of Hawaii Press, 1983.

Buddhaghosa. *The Path of Purification (Visuddhimagga).* Translated by Bhikku Ñyānamoli. 2nd edition. (Colombo, Ceylon: A. Semage, 1964).

Bugault, G. *La notion de "prajñā" ou de sapience selon les perspectives du "Mahāyāna".* Paris: E. de Baccard, 1968.

Chandra, Lokesh. *Materials for a History of Tibetan Literature.* New Delhi: International Academy of Indian Culture, 1963.

Chattopadhyaya, Alaka. *Atiśa and Tibet.* Delhi: Motilal Banarsidass, 1981.

Conze, Edward. *Abhisamayālaṃkāra.* Serie Orientale Roma VI. Rome: Is.M.E.O., July 1954.

———. *Buddhist Thought in India.* Ann Arbor: University of Michigan Press, 1973.

———. *Buddhist Wisdom Books.* New York: Harper and Row, 1972.

———. *Memoirs of a Modern Gnostic, Part I.* Sherborne: Samizdat Publishing, 1971.

———. "Praśāstrasena's *Ārya-Prajñāpāramitā-Hṛdaya-Ṭīkā.* In *Buddhist Studies in Honour of I. B. Horner*, pp. 51-62. Edited by L. Cousins, et al. Dordrecht: D. Reidel, 1974.

———. *The Large Sūtra on Perfect Wisdom.* Berkeley: University of California Press, 1975.

———. *The Perfection of Wisdom in Eight Thousand Lines.* Bolinas: Four Seasons, 1973.

———. *The Prajñāpāramitā Literature.* The Hague: Mouton and Co., 1960.

———. *Thirty Years of Buddhist Studies.* Columbia, S.C.: University of

South Carolina Press, 1968.

Cook, Francis. "Fa-tsang's Brief Commentary on the *Prajñāpāramitā-hṛdaya-sūtra.*" In *Mahāyāna Buddhist Meditation: Theory and Practice*, pp. 167-206. Edited by Minoru Kiyota. Honolulu: University of Hawaii Press, 1978.

Dayal, Har. *The Bodhisattva in Buddhist Sanskrit Literature.* Delhi: Motilal Banarsidass, 1975.

de Jong, Jan W. *Cinq Chapitres de la Prasannapadā.* Paris: Geuthner, 1949.

Demieville, Paul. *Le Concile de Lhasa.* Paris: Impr. Nationale de France, 1952.

Derrida, Jacques. *Of Grammatology.* Baltimore: Johns Hopkins University Press, 1974.

Dhargyey, Eva. *The Rise of Esoteric Buddhism.* Delhi: Motilal Banarsidass, 1977.

Eckel, M. David. *Jñānagarbha's Commentary on the Distinction Between the Two Truths.* Albany: State University of New York Press, 1986.

Fox, Douglas A. *The Heart of Buddhist Wisdom.* Lewiston, New York: Edwin Mellen Press, 1985.

Gómez, Luis O. "Indian Materials on the Doctrine of Sudden Enlightenment." In *Early Ch'an in China and Tibet*, pp. 393-434. Edited by Lewis Lancaster and Whalen Lai. Berkeley: Berkeley Buddhist Studies Series, 1983.

———. "The Direct and Gradual Approaches of Zen Master Mahāyāna: Fragments of the Teachings of Mo-ho-yen." In *Studies in Ch'an and Hua Yen*, pp. 69-167. Edited by Robert M. Gimello and Peter N. Gregory. Honolulu: University of Hawaii Press, 1983.

Gyatso, Geshe Kelsang. *Heart of Wisdom.* London: Tharpa Publications, 1986.

Hakeda, Yoshito. *Kukai: Major Works.* New York: Columbia University Press, 1972.

Heidegger, Martin. *Poetry, Language, Thought.* New York: Harper and Row, 1971.

Hopkins, Jeffrey. Translator. *Compassion in Tibetan Buddhism.* Valois, New York: Snow Lion, 1980.

———. *Meditation on Emptiness.* London: Wisdom Publications, 1983.

Houston, G. W. *Sources for the History of the bSam yas Debate.* Sankt Augustion: VGH-Wissenschaftsverlag, 1980.

Hua, Tripitaka Master. *The Heart of Prajñāpāramitā Sūtra.* San Francisco: Buddhist Texts Translation Society, 1980.

Hurvitz, Leon. "Hsuan-tsang (602-644) and the *Heart Scripture*." In *Prajñāpāramitā and Related Systems*, pp. 103-122. Edited by Lewis Lancaster and Luis Gómez. Berkeley: Berkeley Buddhist Studies Series, 1977.

———, trans. *Scripture of the Lotus Blossom of the Fine Dharma*. New York: Columbia University Press, 1976.

Inada, Kenneth. *The Mūlamadhyamakakārikā of Nāgārjuna*. Tokyo: Hokuseido, 1970.

Jaini, P. S. "Buddha's Prolongation of Life." *Bulletin of the School of Oriental and African Studies, 21* (1958), pp. 546-552.

———. "Origin and Development of the Theory of *viprayukta-saṃskāras*." *Bulletin of the School of Oriental and African Studies, 22* (1959).

Joshi, Lalmani. *Studies in the Buddhistic Culture of India*. 2d edition. Delhi: Motilal Banarsidass, 1977.

Kajiyama, Yuichi. *An Introduction to Buddhist Philosophy*. Kyoto: Kyoto University, 1966.

———. "On the Meanings of the Words *Bodhisattva* and *Mahāsattva* in Prajñāpāramitā Literature." In *Indological and Buddhist Studies*, pp. 253-270. Edited by L. A. Hercus, et al. Canberra: Faculty of Asian Studies, 1982.

———. "Three Kinds of Affirmation and Two Kinds of Negation in Buddhist Philosophy." *Wiener Zeitschrift für die Kunde Südasiens und Archiv für Indische Philosophie*, 1973.

Kalupahana, D. *Nāgārjuna: Philosophy of the Middle Way*. Albany: State University of New York Press, 1986.

Klein, Anne C. *Knowledge and Liberation: The Sautrāntika Tenet System in Tibet*. Ithaca: Snow Lion Publications, 1986.

La Vallée Poussin, Louis de. *L'Abhidharmakośa de Vasubandhu*. Bruxelles: Institut Belge des Hautes Études Chinoises, 1971.

———. Madhyamakāvatāra. *Muséon* 8 (1907), pp. 249-317; 11 (1910), pp. 271-358; 12 (1911), pp. 235-328.

———. "Vyādhisūtra on the Four Āryasatyas." *Journal of the Royal Asiatic Society* (1903), pp. 578-580.

Lamotte, Étienne. *Histoire du Bouddhisme Indien*. Louvain: Institut Orientaliste, 1958.

———. *La Somme du Grand Véhicûle d'Asaṅga* (*Mahāyānasaṃgraha*). 2 vol. Louvain: Institut Orientaliste, 1973.

———. *L'Enseignement de Vimalakīrti* (*Vimalakīrtinirdeśa*). Louvain:

Muséon, 1962.

———. *Le Traité de la Grande Vertu de Sagesse de Nāgārjuna*, Tome 1-5. Louvain: Institut Orientaliste, 1966-1980.

———. *Saṃdhinirmocana-sūtra: L'Explication des Mystères.* Paris: Adrien Maisonneuve, 1935.

Lancaster, Lewis and Gómez, Luis, ed. *Prajñāpāramitā and Related Systems: Studies in Honor of Edward Conze.* Berkeley: Berkeley Buddhist Studies Series, 1977.

Lati Rinbochay and Hopkins, Jeffrey. *Death, Intermediate State and Rebirth in Tibetan Buddhism.* Ithaca: Snow Lion Publications, 1979.

Lessing, Ferdinand and Wayman, Alex. *Introduction to the Buddhist Tantrica Systems.* Delhi: Motilal Banarsidass, 1978.

Lethcoe, Nancy. "The Bodhisattva Ideal in the *Aṣṭa* and *Pañca Prajñāpāramitā Sūtras.*" In *Prajñāpāramitā and Related Systems*, pp. 263-282. Edited by Lewis Lancaster and Luis Gómez. Berkeley: Berkeley Buddhist Studies Series, 1977.

Lindtner, Christian. *Nagarjuniana: Studies in the Writings and Philosophy of Nāgārjuna.* Copenhagen: Akademisk Forlag, 1982.

Ling, Trevor. *Buddhism and the Mythology of Evil.* London: Allen and Unwin, 1962.

Lopez, Jr., Donald S. *A Study of Svātantrika.* Ithaca: Snow Lion Publications, 1987.

Lu K'uan Yu (Charles Luk). *Ch'an and Zen Teachings, First Series.* Boulder: Shambala, 1970.

Mallmann, Marie-Thérèse de. *Introduction a l'Étude d'Avalokiteçvara.* Paris: Annales du Musée Guimet, 1948.

Matilal, Bimal K. *Epistemology, Logic and Grammar in Indian Philosophical Analysis.* The Hague: Mouton, 1971.

May, Jacques. *Prasannapadā Madhyamakavṛtti, douze chapitres traduits du sanscrit et du tibetain.* Paris: Adrien Maisonneuve, 1959.

Nāgārjuna and the Seventh Dalai Lama. *The Precious Garland and the Song of the Four Mindfulnesses.* Translated by Jeffrey Hopkins and Lati Rimpoche. New York: Harper and Row, 1975.

Nakamura, Hajime. *Indian Buddhism: A Survey with Bibliographical Notes.* Osaka: KUFS Publication, 1980.

Nishimura, Eshin, trans. "Perfection of Wisdom." In *Secrets of the Lotus*, pp. 190-211. Edited by Donald K. Swearer. New York: Macmillan, 1971.

Obaro, (Abbot). "On the Heart Sūtra." In *The Tiger's Cave*, pp. 15-125. Edited by Trevor Leggett. London: Routledge and Kegan Paul, 1964.

Obermiller, E. *Analysis of the Abhisamayālaṃkāra.* London: Luzac, 1933.

———. *Doctrine of Prajñāpāramitā as Exposed in the Abhisamayālaṃkāra of Maitreya.* Heidelberg: *Acta Orientalia*, 1932.

———. *History of Buddhism by Bu-ston.* Heidelberg: Heft, 1932.

———, trans. *Uttaratantra or Ratnagotravibhāga.* Heidelberg: *Acta Orientalia*, 1931.

Rabten, Geshe. *Echoes of Voidness.* London: Wisdom Publications, 1983.

Rawlinson, Andrew. "The Position of the *Aṣṭasāhasrikā-Prajñāpāramitā* in the Development of Early Mahāyāna." In *Prajñāpāramitā and Related Systems*, pp. 3-34. Edited by Lewis Lancaster and Luis Gómez. Berkeley: Berkeley Buddhist Studies Series, 1977.

Roerich, George N. *The Blue Annals.* Delhi: Motilal Banarsidass, 1976.

Ruegg, David Seyfort. *La Théorie du tathāgatagarbha et du gotra.* Paris: École Française du Extrême-Orient, 1969.

———. *The Literature of the Madhyamaka School of Philosophy in India.* Wiesbaden: Otto Harrassowitz, 1981.

———. *L'Traité du Tathāgatagarbha de Bu Ston Rin Chen Grub.* Paris: École Française d'Extrême-Orient: 1973.

———. "The *gotra, ekayāna,* and *tathāgatagarbha* theories of the *Prajñāpāramitā* according to Dharmamitra and Abhayākaragupta." In *Prajñāpāramitā and Related Systems*, pp. 283-312. Edited by Lewis Lancaster and Luis Gómez. Berkeley: Berkeley Buddhist Studies Series, 1977.

Shantideva. *A Guide to the Bodhisattva's Way of Life.* Translated by Stephen Batchelor. Dharmsala: LTWA, 1979.

Sopa, Geshe Lhundup and Hopkins, Jeffrey. *Practice and Theory of Tibetan Buddhism.* New York: Grove Press, 1976.

Sprung, Mervyn. *Lucid Exposition of the Middle Way.* Boulder: Prajna Press, 1979.

Stcherbatsky, Theodore. *Buddhist Logic*, 2 Vol. New York: Dover, 1962.

Steinkellner, Ernst. "Remarks on Tantristic Hermeneutics." In *Proceedings of the Csoma de Koros Memorial Symposium*, pp. 445-458. Edited by L. Ligeti. Budapest: 1978.

Steinkellner, Ernst and Tauscher, Helmut, ed. *Contributions of Tibetan and Buddhist Religion and Philosophy: Proceedings of the Csoma de Koros Symposium Held at Velm-Vienna, Austria, 13-19 September 1981,*

Vol. 1. Vienna: Arbeitskreis für Tibetische und Buddhistische Studien Universität Wien, 1983.

Streng, Frederick, J. *Emptiness: A Study in Religious Meaning*. Nashville: Abingdon Press, 1967.

Suzuki, Daisetz Teitaro. *Essays in Zen Buddhism: Third Series*. London: Rider and Company, 1958.

———. *The Laṅkāvatāra Sūtra*. London: Routledge Kegan Paul, 1932.

Takasaki, J. *A Study of the Ratnagotravibhāga*. Rome: Istituto Italiano per il Medio Estremo Oriente, 1966.

Tāranātha. *Tāranātha's History of Buddhism in India*. Translated by Lama Chimpa and Alaka Chattopadhyaya. Simla: Indian Institute of Advanced Study, 1970.

Thurman, Robert A. F. *Tsong Khapa's Speech of Gold in the "Essence of True Eloquence"*. Princeton: Princeton University Press, 1984.

Tsong-ka-pa. *Tantra in Tibet*. Edited and translated by Jeffrey Hopkins. London: Allen and Unwin, 1977.

———. *Yoga of Tibet*. London: Allen and Unwin, 1981.

Tucci, Giuseppe. *Minor Buddhist Texts, Part II: First Bhāvanākrama of Kamalaśīla*. Serie Orientale Roma, IX.2. Rome: Is.M.E.O., 1958.

———. "Minor Texts on the Prajñāpāramitā: Diṅnāga's Prajñā-pāramitā-Piṇḍārtha." *Journal of the Royal Asiatic Society* (1947), pp. 53-75.

Warder, A. K. *Indian Buddhism*. 2nd revised edition. Delhi: Motilal Banarsidass, 1980.

Wayman, Alex. "Secret of the *Heart Sūtra*." In *Prajñāpāramitā and Related Systems*, pp. 135-152. Edited by Lewis Lancaster and Luis Gómez. Berkeley: Berkeley Buddhist Studies Series, 1977.

———. "Studies in Yama and Māra." *Indo-Iranian Journal* (1959), pp. 44-73 and 112-131.

———. *Yoga of the Guhyasamājatantra*. Delhi: Motilal Banarsidass, 1980.

Wayman, Alex and Wayman, Hideko. *The Lion's Roar of Queen Śrīmālā*. New York: Columbia University Press, 1974.

Wylie, Turrell. "A Standard System of Tibetan Transcription." *Harvard Journal of Asian Studies*, Vol. 22, 1959.

Index